Outstanding Dissertations in
LINGUISTICS

edited by
LAURENCE HORN
Yale University

ON ECONOMIZING THE THEORY OF A-BAR DEPENDENCIES

WEI-TIEN DYLAN TSAI

LONDON AND NEW YORK

First published 1999 by Garland Publishing Inc.

Published 2013 by Routledge
2 Park Square, Milton Park, Abingdon, Oxfordshire OX14 4RN
711 Third Avenue, New York, NY 10017

First issued in paperback 2014

Routledge is an imprint of the Taylor and Francis Group,
an informa business

Copyright © 1999 Wei-Tien Dylan Tsai
All rights reserved

Library of Congress Cataloging-in-Publication Data

Tsai, Wei-Tien Dylan, 1964–
  On economizing the theory of a-bar dependencies / Wei-Tien Dylan Tsai.
    p.   cm. — (Outstanding dissertations in linguistics)
  Includes bibliographical references and index.
  1. Grammar, Comparative and geneal—Syntax. 2. Semantics. 3. Minimalist theory (Linguistics) I. Title. II. Series.
P291/T78 1999
415—dc21
                                                98-51530

ISBN 13: 978-1-138-86553-2 (pbk)
ISBN 13: 978-0-8153-3299-2 (hbk)

To my parents

Tsai Jen-hou & Yang De-ying

Table of Contents

Preface ix
Acknowledgements xi
List of abbreviations xv

CHAPTER ONE
FROM LEXICON TO LF

    0. To Move or Not to Move -- That is the Question 3
    1. Toward a Minimalist Design of *Wh*-Dependencies 5
    2. Merger vs. Chain Formation 7
        2.1. Disintegrate Lexical Integrity 7
        2.2. *Dou*, *Dou*, *Dou*, and *Dou* 12
        2.3. Interrogative Construals in Chinese Bare
            Conditionals 15
        2.4. Japanese *Mo*-Quantification and Chinese
            Dou-Quantification 23
        2.5. A Conceptual Problem and an Empirical Solution ... 31
    3. Nouns vs. Adverbs 36
    4. Strong vs. Weak Operator Features 43
    5. An Overview 48

CHAPTER TWO
SOME ASYMMETRIES BETWEEN CHAIN FORMATION AND UNSELECTIVE BINDING

    1. Long-Distance Construals of Amount *Wh's* 53
    2. Interrogative Construals in *Dou*- and *Mo*-Quantification 67
    3. A'-Bound Pro or Pure Variable? 73
    4. *Wh*-Extraction from Drived Nominals 78
    5. Reflection on a Syntax-LF Asymmetry 81
    6. Aftermath 91

CHAPTER THREE
TOWARD LF INTERFACE

0. ∃-Closure Extensions 93
1. Mapping as a Cyclic Operation 97
   1.1. The Cyclic Hypothesis 97
   1.2. The Mapping Geometry of Topics 102
   1.3. Summary 107
2. ∃-closure as a Last Resort Operation 107
   2.1. The Nature of ∃-closure 107
   2.2. Non-restrictive Relative Clauses 112
   2.3. Existential Constructions and Predication Licensing 122
      2.3.1. Existential Predicates and (In)definiteness Restrictions 122
      2.3.2. Weak Existential Predicates and Secondary Predication 126
      2.3.3. A Dilemma 133
      2.3.4. Bare Indefinites 138
   2.4. A Refinement 140
   2.5. Not Unlikely Extensions 149
      2.5.1. Small Clauses 149
      2.5.2. Secondary Temporal Predicates 151
      2.5.3. Resultative Complements 158
      2.5.4. A Preverbal-Postverbal Asymmetry of Temporal Adjuncts 161
3. Chain-formation as a Copying Operation 162
   3.1. A Few Good Questions 162
   3.2. Lowering or Copying? 165
   3.3. An Individual Variable Account of Stage-Individual Asymmetries 168
   3.4. Disagree Chinese Agreement 173
4. Concluding Remarks 180
Notes 181
Bibliography 193
Index 203

Preface

This book is divided into two parts. The first part is essentially a response to a minimalist question: how perfect is language? Well, as perfect as it can be. To show that a particular language stems from a perfect design is a daunting task, if not impossible. There are so many factors involved in hiding the true nature of a language from casual observers. On the other hand, it is a lot easier to put a few languages side by side and show that the apparent "imperfection" actually comes from the diversity of their lexicons. By comparing *wh*-construals in Chinese, Japanese, English and Hindi, it becomes clear that these languages follow an optimal design of operator-variable dependencies as best as they could. As best as their individual morphologies allow, for that matter.

The second part of this book addresses the issue how syntax interacts with semantics in a minimalist way. Evidence from (in)definiteness effects suggests that it is necessary to adopt a dynamic view of syntax-semantics mapping, which is envisioned as cyclic and derivational. This line of research has produced some interesting results as to how quantification interacts with predication on the LF interface, and how notions such as Last Resort play a role in semantics.

Also I would like to take this opportunity to thank Larry Horn and Jim Huang, without whose help and encouragement this book may never come out in print.

Acknowledgements

Being an outlander, I often feel awkward in expressing either regret or gratitude, sometimes too little, sometimes too much, sometimes untimely, sometimes timely but ungracefully. Since here I need to deal with only one of them (and the easier one, too), I hope I can do a better job.

Above all, I am in great debt to the members of my dissertation committee: Noam Chomsky, Ken Hale, James Huang, and Howard Lasnik. From the first time I picked up a linguistics textbook to the end of my thesis defence, Noam has always been the inspiration to me. It's a long, long journey, but I never regret it. I would like to thank him for sharing his visions with us, and for putting up with my gibberish and ignorance for the past four years. From Ken, I learned the self-devotion of a humanist, the sage of a hermit, and the chivalry of a lone ranger. More than once, he drew me back from the brink of being devoured by technicality and shortsightedness, and I often suspect that he is the only person who actually has the UG. Since the early years of my career, Jim Huang has led me to appreciate the art of argumentation and the beauty of the generative architecture. He gives me a sense of direction in this intellectual maelstrom, making me proud of being one of the Chinese linguists. Most importantly, he has helped me to find out who I am, and where my root is planted in. Howard, on the other hand, gives me a sense of history and tradition, alarming me of the everlasting arrogance residing in intellectual minds. He also shows me in person the definition of open-mindedness, and the power of logical reasoning.

I would also like to thank the members of my generals committee: Morris Halle, Wayne O'Neil, and David Pesetsky. Morris used to exclaim to me in his vigorous voice "We want to educate you!", which he did. He rid me of self-pity, and kept me going through those darkest hours of my life. Wayne, being a caring educator, has listened to my problems with endless patience, never reluctant to offer helps. David has been extremely helpful either as a brilliant lecturer in class, or as an observing critics during our appointments. I thank him for trying hard to make senses out of my self-indulgent narration and not so illustrious illustrations.

I am equally grateful to Irene Heim, James Higginbotham, Michael Kenstowicz, Alec Marantz, and Shigeru Miyagawa. As a complete stranger of formal semantics, I have been picking up my semantics training in Irene's classes. Her meticulously prepared handouts have become legendary (for that matter, we should thank Angelika Kratzer as well, who coauthors the handouts). In spite of my slowness and syntax-centricism, she has always been kind and ready to help, particularly in providing invaluable insights into the issues of existential closure and syntax-semantics mapping. Jim Higginbotham is one of a handful of people who can play the double role as a syntactician-semanticist, and plays it well. He matches my stereotypical image of a "professor" most perfectly, and is inspiring in every way. It is Jim and Irene who convinced me the necessity of converging syntax and semantics. I learned from Michael not only the cream of recent accomplishments in phonology, but also his methodological approach of problem-solving. I think anyone around Building 20 would agree that Alec has made himself available as often as one can get. I thank him for disentangling my impossible reasoning thread by thread, and for the disillusion of my self-assertion, now a nostalgic remembrance of my reckless youth. Shigeru has always been encouraging and supportive. He is not only a wonderful teacher, but also a caring friend.

Furthermore, I would like to express my admiration of Lisa Cheng, Audrey Li, and Jane Tang, whose influences will be evident as our plot unfolds. When I first came to Boston, Lisa took me, an "intellectual brother" in Chinese terms, under her wings. Since then, I have been benefiting tremendously from her example, both in terms of academics and real life. I thank her for the guidance and timeless friendship. Audrey has pioneered the research of several major issues of this thesis. We agree and disagree. But we always share the same intuition as to which direction we should proceed and which methodology we should be equipped with. I thank her for seeing things in wonder eyes. For the past four years, Jane has been an inexhaustible source of comforting and encouragement. She is not only constructive in comments, but also resourceful in suggestions. I thank her for being a devoted friend and comrade.

I am eternally grateful to Masa Koizumi, Masayuki Oishi, Asako Uchibori, and Hiro Ura for their support in the process of completing this thesis. I will never forget our little tea party, the feast at Cape Cod, and the incident of "German cake". I too benefit greatly from discussions with John Frampton, Sarah "Brenda" Kennelly, and Tanya Reinhart during their visits at MIT. I thank John for his penetrating insights. Brenda has always been there for me when things got tough, whose friendship I will cherish for life. Tanya's works has been the inspiration of numerous proposals of this thesis. I was particularly impressed by her elegance in presentation and tenacity in argumentation.

Moreover, I would like to say thanks to Jun Abe, Andrew Carnie, Danny Fox, Naoki Fukui, Elly van Gelderen, Sabine Iatridou, Toru Ishii, Alessandro Lenci, Marta Luján, Martha McGinnis, Anoop Mahajan, Orin Percus, Toshi Oka, Colin Phillips, Norvin Richards, Uli Sauerland, Yuji Takano, Hubert Truckenbrodt, Sarma Vaijayanthi, Akira Watanabe for their invaluable comments in various occasions, and to Chris Collins, Hamida Demirdash, Koji Fujita, Tom Green, Heidi Harley, Doug Jones, Yasuhiko Kato, Utpal Lahiri, Paul Law, Kumiko Murasugi, Renate Musan, Pierre Picard, Jason Stanley, Hiroaki Tada, Chris Tancredi for their friendship.

Special thanks to Jim Harris for his understanding and encouragement. Baby-sitting my class must have been giving him a lot of headaches. I thank Allen Katherine, Rachel Pearl and Jamie Young for their patience and kindness in arranging the seemingly impossible defence date.

Finally, my most sincere gratitude goes to my classmates: Pilar Barbosa, Jonathan Bobaljik, Tony Bures, Diana Cresti, and Seth Minkoff. From the first day we were summoned to do the registration, which reminds me of a kindergarten assembly, our destinies are bound together. In those bittersweet days, we protested and we conspired, boasting about Bresnan's piano in our office and offering each other a shoulder to cry on. Of course we argued. Over smoking or non-smoking. Over astrology or astronomy. Still, nothing sticks but our friendship and mutual appreciation. I thank them for making MIT a second home for me, and for the fun and craziness throughout all these years.

Abbreviations

CL: classifier
DE: postverbal complement marker
DUR: durative aspect
EXP: experiential aspect
INC: incoative aspect
PNM: prenominal modifier marker
PRF: perfective aspect
PRG: progressive aspect

On Economizing the Theory of A-Bar Dependencies

CHAPTER ONE

From Lexicon to LF

Do nothing. Then you have done everything.
—Lao Tze

0. To Move or Not to Move—That is the Question

The past decade has seen a persistent evolution toward a minimal design of grammar, or the theory of grammar to the same effect, within the principles-and-parameters framework. A part of the intuitive content of this "minimalist" approach, as proclaimed by Chomsky (1993), is to take interface levels to be the only levels involved in derivation of linguistic expressions, with the notion of "interface" strictly defined within the domain of (virtual) conceptual necessity. It is suggested that the only levels needed are PF and LF, which serve as the doorways from linguistics proper (including nothing more than a lexicon and a computational system) to the articulatory-perceptual and conceptual-intentional systems respectively. The bottom line is that the interface conditions on PF and LF are satisfied in conformity with the economy principles.

An intriguing prospect of this approach concerns the fact that with the theoretical status of D-structure nullified, nothing prevents Merge operation from blocking Chain formation along the "least effort" guideline in Chomsky's (1991) sense. This is because lexical insertion need not be done all at once at a level between the lexicon and S-structure, and because Merger, being a binary operation, does not increase the "length" of a formal object, whereas Chain formation does. Other things being equal, a recast base-generation account should be preferable to a movement one in deriving certain syntactic dependencies.

Now consider a formal object which is by definition a pair, as is the case of operator-variable constructions. There are essentially two ways to construct a operator-variable pair under the minimalist approach. Take *wh*-questions for example. The first one invloves Merger (also called binary substitution), which targets X', and substitutes a Q(uestion)-operator for an empty position Δ external to X'. The operator in turn binds a *wh-in-situ* without resorting to Chain formation, as illustrated in (1):

(1) a. $[_{X''}\ \Delta\ [_{X'}\ ...\ wh\ ...\ ]] \rightarrow [_{X''}\ Op_{[Q]}\ [_{X'}\ ...\ wh\ ...\ ]]$

$\rightarrow [_{X''}\ Op_{i\ [Q]}\ [_{X'}\ ...\ wh(i)\ ...\ ]]$

b. $[_{X''}\ \Delta\ [_{X'}\ ...\ wh\ ...\ ]] \rightarrow [_{X''}\ wh_i\ [_{X'}\ ...\ t_i\ ...\ ]]$

The second one involves Chain formation (i.e., singular substitution), moving the *wh-in-situ* into Δ. (1a) is therefore preferable to (1b), since movement is employed only as a last resort (cf Chomsky 1993). We may formulate the intuitive idea in the following terms:[1]

(2) *Lexical Courtesy Hypothesis (LCH):*

If a language may introduce an operator by Merger, it will not resort to Chain formatin.

On conceptual grounds, there are also a few good reasons why this should be the case. First, the computational system of our linguistic faculty must have something to operate upon. It is thus still within the conceptual necessity to employ Merger. Besides, since Merger is the only way to weave phrase markers into one single piece, and to satisfy the minimal requirement for a legitimate PF representation, it should be preferable to Chain formation. Therefore, the "courtesy" in considering Merger costless is really a built-in part of Economy: We may not minimize the linguistic design into "saying nothing" for the sake of communication, but "moving nothing" is certainly a minimalist goal to achieve.

The main purpose of this chapter is to explore the consequences of the above hypothesis, and its relation to the theory of A'-dependencies in general. We would like to sketch three preliminary proposals with a view to characterizing syntaco-semantic properties of operator-variable pairs. Section two proposes that Merger has intrinsic priority over Chain Formation, as stated in the LCH (2). We will argue from a cross-linguistic point of view that there is an optimal design of the architecture of *wh*-dependencies, which works in very much the same way as (1a) does. In section three, we will argue that only categories which introduce variables in situ are subject to unselective binding. This move leads to a noun-adverb distinction among *wh*-phrases with respect to their extraction behavior in LF. Section four puts forward the claim that operator features are not universally strong: Procrastination of *wh*-movement is independently motivated by the noun-adverb asymmetry in construing Chinese *wh's-in-situ*, and by LF Subjacency/CED effects displayed by Hindi *wh's-in-situ*.

1. Toward a Minimalist Design of *Wh*-Dependencies

Under the minimalist approach, it is conceptually undesirable to associate independent properties with S-Structure, which proves to be a significant departure from the EST (Extended Standard Theory) model. The level of S-Structure, a derivative concept in essence, is understood as a SPELL-OUT point of a particular derivation to PF. Consequently, nothing should hinge upon the notion of S-Structure. Nor, it seems, can we take locality conditions such as Subjacency to be a matter of overt Syntax (i.e., the mapping from D-Structure to S-Structure in the sense of EST), as originally proposed by Huang (1982), because this amounts to saying that Subjacency ceases to be relevant after the level of S-Structure.

The empirical motivation for Huang's proposal is well known, as illustrated by the following argument-adjunct asymmetry of Chinese *wh's-in-situ*:

(3) Akiu kan-bu-qi [$_{DP}$ [$_{CP}$ Op$_i$ [$_{IP}$ e$_i$ zuo shenme]] de ren$_i$]?
  Akiu look-not-up   do what PNM person
  What is the thing/job x such that Akiu despises [people [who do x]]?

(4) * Akiu xihuan [$_{DP}$ [$_{CP}$ Op$_i$ [$_{IP}$ Luxun weishenme xie e$_i$]]
Akiu like   Luxun why   write
de shu$_i$]?
PNM book
What is the reason x such that Akiu likes [books [that Luxun wrote for x]]?

Both (3) and (4) involve *wh's-in-situ* embedded in complex-NP islands. The differences are that (3) contains a *wh*-argument, i.e., *shenme* 'what', whereas (4) contains a *wh*-adjunct *weishenme* 'why', and more importantly, that question formation is blocked in (4), but not in (3). As Huang (1982) points out, (4) can be ruled out along with its English counterpart (5), given that *weishenme* undergoes abstract movement to the matrix Comp, and creates the offending LF representation (6):

(5) * Why$_j$ does John like [$_{DP}$ books$_i$ [$_{CP}$ which$_i$ [$_{IP}$ Bill wrote t$_i$ t$_j$]]]?

(6) * weishenme$_j$ Akiu xihuan [$_{DP}$ [$_{CP}$ Op$_i$ [$_{IP}$ Luxun t$_j$ xie e$_i$]]
why   Akiu like   Luxun   write
de shu$_i$]?
PNM book

The deviance of (2), therefore, is identified with the kind of locality effects typically associated with the ECP and Subjacency. The beauty of this analysis lies in the parallelism that it envisions among languages: Sooner or later, a *wh*-phrase must be related to a [+wh] Comp by movement. Consequently, Chinese and English *wh*-questions look exactly alike at LF.

Nevertheless, there remains a non-trivial problem to tackle. Let's consider the following LF representation of (3) given the abstract movement hypothesis:

(7)   Shenme$_j$ Akiu kan-bu-qi [$_{DP}$ [$_{CP}$ Op$_i$ [$_{IP}$ e$_i$ zuo t$_j$]] de ren$_i$]?
what   Akiu look-not-up   do   PNM person

The object trace of *shenme* 'what' is lexically governed by the embedded verb *zuo* 'do', thus satisfying the disjunctive version of the ECP (Chomsky 1981, Huang 1982, Lasnik & Saito 1984, 1992). On the other hand, both DP and CP count as barriers in Chomsky's (1986b) sense, since the relative clause (i.e., the CP node) is not L-marked, and the DP node in turn inherits barrierhood from the CP node. Although the Chain (*shenme*, t) does not violate the ECP in its disjunctive formulation, the Chain-formation involved undoubtedly violates Subjacency, with both DP and CP crossed in one link. However, no deviance is detected in (3). For this very reason, Huang concludes that Subjacency holds in (overt) Syntax but not in LF.

In the following sections, we would like to offer an alternative to accommodate the asymmetry between (3) and (4) without compromising the global status of Subjacency, which may well be an instantiation of the Economy of derivation in the sense that crossing more than one barrier in forming one Chain-link is considered an intolerable cost.[2] On the one hand, we will characterize the long-distance construal in (3) as an instance of unselective binding (cf. Heim 1982, Pesetsky 1987, Nishigauchi 1986, 1990), and hence an operator-variable pair (see also Li 1992, Aoun & Li 1993a,b), and to some extent, Cheng (1991) for proposals in the same vein). On the other hand, we would also like to maintain the insight behind Huang's treatment of (4), i.e., characterizing its deviance as the kind of locality effect associated with improper Chain formation.

2. Merger vs. Chain Formation

2.1. Disintegrate Lexical Integrity

Our first proposal concerns the two fundamental operations of shaping phrase structures under the minimalist approach. Namely, Merge operation of (8a) has intrinsic priority over Chain formation of (8b):

(8) a. $[_{X''} \Delta [_{X'} ... wh ...]] \rightarrow [_{X''} Op_{[Q]} [_{X'} ... wh ...]]$

   b. $[_{X''} \Delta [_{X'} ... wh ...]] \rightarrow [_{X''} wh_i [_{X'} ... t_i ...]]$

On the ground of Economy, UG should always prefer (8a) to (8b), since movement is employed only as a last resort. (8a) thus represents the optimal design of *wh*-dependencies, which is unlikely to vary across languages. It also follows from the LCH (2) that if we ever find (8b) in operation, then (8a) must have already been implemented somehow. If this reasoning proves to be a sound one, then the key question to ask is probably not why the Chinese sentence (3) does not display Subjacency effects, but why its English counterpart (9) is never allowed:

(9) * Akiu despises people who do what?

If we take the question literally, potential answers are abundant: Aoun (1986) suggests that Comp-indexing applies at S-structure in English, and at LF in Chinese. Since the matrix [+wh] Comp is not filled by *what* at S-structure, (9) is ruled out in not complying with the selectional restriction. Similar solutions can be sketched easily in terms of Spec-head agreement in the IP-CP system (vs. the S-S' system adopted by Aoun). For instance, we may postulate to the same effect that *Wh*-Criterion (10), as formulated in Rizzi (1991) (see also Pesetsky 1982, May 1985), applies at S-structure in English:

(10) a. A *wh*-operator must be in a Spec-head configuration with an $X^0_{[+wh]}$.

b. An $X^0_{[+wh]}$ must be in a Spec-head configuration with a *wh*-operator.

Chomsky (1986b:52), on the other hand, maintains that selectional properties are satisfied universally at LF, by appealing to the positive setting of the parameter (11) in English, based on the assumption that vacuous movement is optional at S-structure:

(11) At LF, *wh*-phrases move nonvacuously only to a position occupied by *wh*-.

Under (11), *what* is not allowed to undergo (nonvacuous) LF movement in (9), since the matrix CP Spec is not occupied by another *wh*-phrase. As a result, the sentence is correctly ruled out. It is also possible to sketch a minimalist solution without resorting to the notion of S-sketch a minimalist solution without resorting to the notion of S-structure: Given that operator features such as [+wh] are strong in English, procrastination of *wh*-movement is not allowed. Consequently, the derivation of (9) crashes at PF, because the [+wh] feature on *what* is visible but unchecked.

Our question, however, has a quite different connotation in the face of the LCH, which amounts to asking why English never takes advantage of the design represented by (8a). The answer, in our opinion, is that English does implement the design, but in a miniature scale. To see this, let's compare the following paradigms:

(12)　a.　*wh*-words　　　　　　b.　pronominals

wh-o	wh-en	th-ey	th-en
wh-om	wh-ere	th-em	th-ere
wh-at		th-at	

By comparing (12a) with (12b), it is not difficult to see that English *wh*-words and pronominals are more or less built on the same materials except that the prefix for pronominals is *th*- instead of *wh*-.[3] Nevertheless, there is a crucial distinction between these two morphemes: *Th*-, for obvious reason, should be regarded as a reduced form of English definite article *the*, capable of licensing the indefinite morphemes it attaches to (i.e., *ey, en, em, ere,* and *at*). *Wh*- , on the other hand, does not seem to act as a determinant of quantificational force, as evidenced by the free relative construals of *wh*-words:[4]

(13)　a.　free relative *wh's*　　　b.　pronominals

wh-o-ever	wh-en-ever	* th-ey-ever	* th-en-ever
wh-om-ever	wh-er(e)-ever	* th-em-ever	* th-er(e)-ever
wh-at-ever		* th-at-ever	

(13a) shows that *wh*- does not block binding from the suffix -*ever*, which contributes universal force to the indefinites, as illustrated by (14a). As a result, *whoever* can be paraphrased directly as 'anyone',

contrast, pronominals cannot be suffixed by *-ever*, as shown by (13b). This indicates that *th-* blocks the binding construal between *-ever* and the indefinite in (14b), just as its determiner counterpart might do in a full DP:

(14) a.   b.

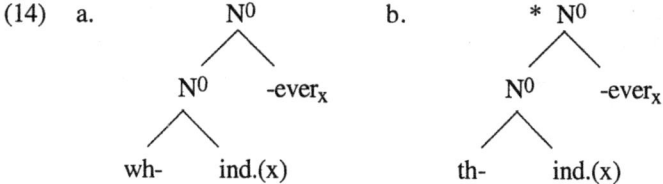

A similar pattern can also be found in a class of adverbials built on *wh-* words:

(15) a. *wh*-adverbials   b. pronominals

some-wh-at   * some-th-at
some-wh-ere   * some-th-ere

Here the binding relation holds between the existential operator *some* and the indefinite morphemes (i.e., *at* and *ere*), as shown by (15a). As it turns out, *somewhere* can be read as 'in some place' *somewhat* 'to some extent' (though it can also be construed in parallel with *whatever*, meaning 'something', as in *He is somewhat of an artist*). The same construal is not available to the corresponding pronominals in (15b). The cause of this asymmetry again seems to lie in the (strong) quantifier status of *th-*, which render *-ever* and *some-* vacuous quantifiers, as in (14b) and (16b) respectively:

(16) a.   b.

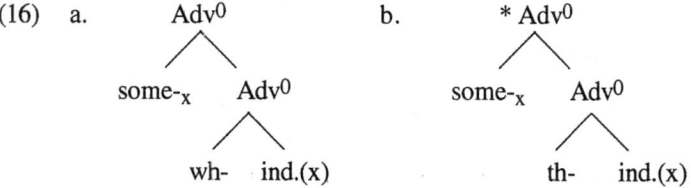

The contrast between (13a,b), as well as that between (16a,b) is

From Lexicon to LF

therefore reminiscent of Reinhart's (1992) observation that DPs headed by *which* may be treated as a function variable subject to unselective binding, which option is never available for definite DPs. We will elaborate on this point later.

With the prospect created by (14a) in mind, we may put the design (8a) into work. A natural suggestion here is that interrogative *wh's* have a Q(uestion)-operator instead of *-ever* as the relevant binder, as illustrated by (17):

(17)
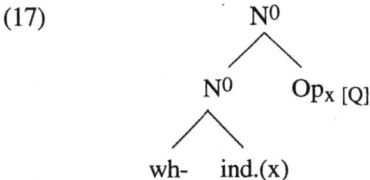

This move can be achieved by employing Merger, which targets the lower N^0, and extends the target by inserting a Q-operator as its specifier. We then have a ready answer for why (9) is not a possible English sentence. As illustrated by (18a), since *what* in itself is an operator-variable pair (recall that (8a) has been implemented below the X^0-level, as in (17)), and Merger is thus uncalled-for.[5] Even if it does apply, as it is costless, the Q-operator dangling alone in the CP Spec results in vacuous quantification:

(18) a. [$_{CP}$ Δ [$_{IP}$ ... what-Op$_{[Q]}$ ...]]

—x→ [$_{CP}$ Op$_{[Q]}$ [$_{IP}$ ... what-Op$_{[Q]}$ ...]]

b. [$_{CP}$ Δ [$_{IP}$ ... what-Op$_{[Q]}$ ...]]

→ [$_{CP}$ [what-Op$_{[Q]}$]$_i$ [$_{IP}$ ... t$_i$ ...]]

The rest of the story is essentially the same: Since the [wh] feature is strong in English, *wh*-movement must apply before SPELL-OUT to make sure that *what* is in the matrix CP Spec for feature-checking, as illustrated by (18b). (9) is thus ruled out in failing to check the strong feature of *what* in overt syntax.

As for relative *wh*-words, we may either leave the structure as it is, in which case relative *wh's* are essentially null operators plus a set of f-features, or insert a null operator in the specifier position, serving as a medium for identification (cf. Chomsky 1986a), as illustrated below:

(19)

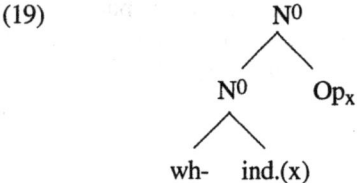

Either way we make the right prediction that relative *wh's* are not quantifiers. Rather, they take scope positions for defining the domain of (syntactic) predicates. It is also in this sense that "free relatives" is an ironic term for *wh*-words like *whoever*, since they are really "bound" relatives, as much as ordinary relative *wh's* are free.

To sum up, if our position proves to be defendable, then the feature [wh] should be conceived as a purely morphological device, whose function is to create configurations for both predication and question-formation through feature-checking on the Spec of CP.

2.2. *Dou*, *Dou*, *Dou*, and *Dou*

As a suggestive comparison, we would like to point out that Chinese *dou* 'all' has a few different types of usages, each of which roughly corresponds to one of the following English words: *all, always, already,* and *also* :

(20) a. tamen / *ta   dou   zou-le.
          they / (s)he   all   leave-Prf
          They all left.

      b. zheli   shei dou bu   xihuan   Akiu.
          here   who all not   like   Akiu
          Here nobody likes Akiu.

(21) Akiu dou qu   nali   nao   geming?
      Akiu all go   where incite revolution
      Where does Akiu go to incite revolution all (the time)?

(22) (zhe-ci   geming),   Akiu dou   qu-le   na-li?
      This-CL   revolution Akiu all   go-Prf   where
      Where has Akiu already been to (in this revolution)?

(23) Akiu   (lian) yi-fen   qian   dou / ye   yao.
      Akiu   even   one-penny   money   all / also want
      Akiu also wants (even) one penny.

The most common usage of *dou* is acting as a universal operator quantifying over plural NPs or *wh*-NPs to its left, as shown by (20a,b) respectively.[6] But what is more intriguing in the context of our discussion concerns the adverbial construals presented above. Let's start with (21) and (22). First note that there is no plurality restriction on the subject *Akiu*. It is thus unlikely for *dou* to quantify over individuals. Rather, the aspectual interpretations indicate that *dou* actually induces universal quantification over time segments (or temporal-spatial slices of an event in terms of intensional semantics). The difference is that the reading tends to be collective in (21), but distributive in (22), as illustrated by (24a,b) respectively:

(24) a. For all x, x a time, where does Akiu go to incite revolution at x?
     b. For each x, x a time (during the period of this revolution), where has Akiu been to at x?

This move captures the fact the answer to (21) has to be a unique place, while that to (22) is expected to be a list of locations, since the speaker is asking for a choice for each set of propositions associated with one distinct time segment.[7]

(23), on the other hand, is a totally different story. As shown above, *dou* alternates with *ye* 'also', often in conjunction with an optional focusing adverb *lian* 'even'. Here *dou* certainly does not quantify over the object *yi-fen quian* 'one penny'. Namely, (23) does not mean 'Akiu wants even every penny'. Rather, there seems to be a universal quantification over the contrast (pre-established) set implicated by the semantics of *lian* 'even' (see also Rooth 1985). As noted by Jim Huang (p.c.), the smallness of the amount of money (merely one penny) is emphasized by contrasting it with all the larger amounts of money which *Akiu* would also love to have. According to Horn (1988), the English counterpart of (23) has the following semantics:

(25) a. John wants even one penny.

   b. Even (x=the amount of one penny, want (John,x))
   Presupposition: $(\exists_y)$ (y≠x & want (John,y))
   Assertion: want (John,x)

We may then treat *dou* and *ye* as the triggers of universal quantification over the contrast set associated with the presupposition of *lian*. As a matter of fact, as Alec Marantz (p.c.) points out, the practical interpretation of (25a) comes very close to that of its Chinese counterpart, as illustrated by (26b):

(26) a. Akiu lian yi-fen qian dou / ye yao.
   Akiu even one-penny money all / also want

   b. Lian (x=the amount of yi-fen, yao (Akiu,x))
   Presupposition: $(\forall y)$ (y≠x & yao (Akiu,y))
   Assertion: yao (Akiu,x)

Namely, *one penny* is contrasted with ALL the larger amounts of money, rather than just SOME amount of money. If the above semantics proves to hold across languages, then *dou* and *ye* may well be the syntactic reflexes, rather than the actual triggers, of the universal quantification at issue here.

In this light, English adverbs such as *always*, *already*, and *also* may well be analyzed as miniature operator-variable pairs, in that they are all prefixed by *al-*, a reduced form of *all*.[8] Although this line of speculation still calls for a fine-grained lexical semantics, the pattern is already there. That is, while English implements the design (8a) word-internally, Chinese does it at a sentential level.

2.3. Interrogative construals in Chinese bare conditionals

If our analysis is on the right track, Chinese *wh*-questions may well embody the optimal design in its grandest scale. That is, (3) has (27) instead of (7) as its LF:[9]

(27) [$_{CP}$ Op$_{x\ [Q]}$ [$_{IP}$ Akiu kan-bu-qi [$_{DP}$ [$_{CP}$ Op$_i$ [$_{IP}$ e$_i$ zuo
 Akiu look-not-up do
shenme(x)]] de ren$_i$]?
what PNM person
What is the thing/job x such that Akiu despises [people [who do x]]?

Since the operator-variable pair (Op$_{[Q]}$, *shenme*) is built by Merger and unselective binding, and since Move-α is not involved, naturally we do not expect any Subjacency effect. As a result, nothing hinges upon the notion of S-structure in this solution.

Probably the most solid showing of this sentence level of binding comes from Chinese bare conditionals. As noted by Cheng & Huang (1993), a pair (or pairs) of *wh's-in-situ* separately located in two clauses induces a conditional construal without any lexical marker like *ruguo* 'if' or *yaoshi* 'in case that':

(28) a. shei lai, shei chi.
 who come who eat
 If x comes, x eats (it).

 b. shei xian lai, shei (jiu) xian chi.
 who first come who then first eat
 If x comes first, x eats first.

Since this type of conditional can be so "bare" as (28a,b), it is not difficult to see that there must be an abstract (necessity) operator which binds both the *wh's-in-situ* and enables the construal. The resulting logical representations thus have a classical *donkey* outlook (cf. Heim 1982):

(29) a. $\forall_x$ (x comes $\rightarrow$ x eats it)

b. $\forall_x$ (x comes first $\rightarrow$ x eats first)

They further point out that the second *wh-in-situ* in the consequent clause cannot be treated as an E-type pronoun in Evans' (1980) sense, since it is in complementary distribution with typical pronominals and demonstratives, as evidenced by the contrast between the bare conditional (30a) and the *ruguo*-conditional (30b):

(30) a. shei chi-dao, shei/*na-ge-ren/*ta/*pro jiu yao
       who late-come who/that-CL-preson/(s)he then must
       qing-ke.
       invite-guest
       If x comes late, then x must pay the bill.

b. ruguo shei chi-dao, na-ge-ren/ta/pro/*shei jiu
   if   who late-come that-CL-person/(s)he/who then
   yao   qing-ke.
   must invite-guest

As a result, (28) is most likely to be an instance of unselective binding, just as Heim (1982) originally proposes for *donkey* sentences. Their position is supported by the fact that the pairing not only can be multiple, but also can be interchangeable, as long as the *wh's-in-situ* involved are indentical:

(31) shei qin-le   shei, shei jiu   yao
     who   kiss-Prf who   who   then must
     qu   shei.
     marry (male to female) who
     a. If x has kissed y, then x (male) must marry y (female).
     b. If x has kissed y, then y (male) must marry x (female).

This is fully expected since the binders in question are claimed to be unselective. We may thus assign the following two logical representations to (31a,b) respectively:

(32) a. $\forall_x \forall_y$ (x has kissed y → x must marry y)

b. $\forall_x \forall_y$ (x has kissed y → y must marry x)

By incoporating the notion of tripartite structure (Kemp 1981, Heim 1982, Chierchia 1992) into the Parallelism Constrain on Operator Binding (PCOB) in Safir's (1985) sense,[10] they propose the following principle further to capture the identity condition on the pair(s) of *wh's-in-situ* :

(33) *Revised PCOB:*
In a tripartite structure of quantification Q [A] [B], [x_1, x_2, ... x_n],where n≥1, are variables in A. For every variable in A, there must be an identical variable in B.

For the purpose of this paper, let's twist the bare conditionals a little bit, i.e., making the numbers of *wh's-in-situ* uneven in the antecedent and consequent clauses. The result is most curious. Sentences such as (34) and (35) are not ruled out, with the "stranded" *wh's-in-situ* construed as interrogative:

(34) shei ying-le shei, shei jiu dei qing-ke (ne)?
who defeat-Inc who who then must treat-guest Q_{wh}
   a. Who is the person x such that if x defeats y, then y must pay for the treat? (The first *wh* stranded)
   b. Who is the person y such that if x defeats y, then x must pay for the treat? (The second *wh* stranded)

(35) shei ying-le, shei jiu dei qing shei (ne)?
who win-Inc who then must treat who Q_{wh}
   a. Who is the person x such that if y wins, then x must treat y? (The second *wh* stranded)
   b. Who is the person y such that if x wins, then x must treat y? (The third *wh* stranded)

In (34), we have two *wh's-in-situ* in the antecedent clause, but only one in the conseqent clause. Either the first *wh* or the second *wh* may induce a matrix question, with the other paired with the third *wh* in the consequent clause, forming a bare conditional, as illustrated by (34a,b) respectively. The situation with (35) is the other way around. There is only one *wh-in-situ* in the antecedent clause, but two in the consequent clause: Either the second *wh* or the third *wh* may induce a matrix question, with the other paired with the first *wh* in the antecedent clause, as illustrated by (35a,b) respectively.

In the light of our view presented in (27), this phenomenon is hardly surprising, since there is neither worry about Sujacency or the CED associated with the adjunct island (i.e., the *ruguo*-clause), nor concern about Relativized Minimality or the ECP in the matrix. The situation, on the other hand, becomes less clear when we reconsider sentences like (28b) in the new light:

(36) a. shei xian lai, shei jiu keyi xian chi ne?
    who first come who then can first eat Q_{wh}
    Who is the person x such that if x comes first, then x is allowed to eat first?

   b. Akiu xiang-zhidao [shei xian lai, shei jiu
    Akiu want-know who first come who then
    keyi xian chi].
    can first eat
    Akiu wonders [who is the person x such that if x comes first, x is allowed to eat first].

When a touch of "privilege" is added to the predicate *xian chi* 'eat first', the interrogative reading becomes salient with the conditional construal remaining intact, as shown by (36a). This reading is most salient when the bare conditional is embedded as an indirect question, as shown by (36b).

The solution, in our opinion, lies in a more articulated logical representation of (28b) offered by Cheng & Huang (1993), as illustrated below:

(37) For all (x, s(ituation)) (if x comes first in s), (x eats first in s)

From Lexicon to LF

Here the situation or spatiotemporal variable is spelled out, and the semantics shared by bare conditionals and *ruguo*-conditionals is also captured. More importantly, this analysis allows us to solve the puzzle straightforwardly. That is, by delegating the conditional construal to the pair of situation variables, there is plenty of room left for the interrogative construal on the part of *wh's-in-situ*. As a result, the proposed Q-operator is able to "cut in" and license the question readings of (36a,b) in the following manner:

(38) Q_x [x a person] $\forall_s$ [s a situation] if x comes first in s, x is allowed to eat first in s

Our observation thus lends strong support to the analysis of (37) in turn.

At this stage, it is tempting to suggest that maybe the conditional construal has nothing to do with the *wh'-in-situ*, since they appear to have their own life. In fact, this position is not totally hopeless at first glance:

(39) a. laoshi shang-ke renzhen, xuesheng *(jiu)
teacher give-lecture attentatively student then
will exert-effort
hui yong-gong.
If teachers teach attentively, then students will study hard.

b. Akiu yong-gong, ta/pro*(jiu) shang-de-liao daxue.
Akiu exert-effort he then go-can-finish college
If Akiu studies hard, then he can get into college.

(39a,b) show that without any conditional marker or *wh-in-situ*, conditional construals are still possible. However, the presence of *jiu* 'then' becomes obligatory, which seems to be a physical reminder of the missing conditional marker. Similar situations also obtain in some apparent violation of the revised PCOB, as originally observed by Yü (1965):

(40) shei yong-gong, na-ge-ren/ta/pro *(jiu) shang-de-liao
 who exert-effort that-CL-person/(s)he then go-can-finish
 daxue.
 college
 If anyone/someone studies hard, then (s)he can get into college.

The fact that (39a,b) are well-formed therefore does not indicate that universal quantification over situations alone can license the conditional construal in quesiton. Rather, it confirms Cheng & Huang's conjecture that Chinese allows an abstract conditional operator. Consequently, (39a,b), as well as (40), should be interpreted as if there is a conditional marker *ruguo* 'if' standing in the sentence-initial position. Furthermore, while an indefinite *wh-in-situ* may occur unpaired in an antecedent clause, as in (40), presumably licensed by the unseen *ruguo*, consequent clauses in general block this construal, as exemplified below:

(41) Akiu yong-gong, shei jiu shang-de-liao daxue?
 Akiu exert-effort who then go-can-finish college
 a. # If Akiu studies hard, then anyone/someone can get into ollege.
 b. Who can get into college if Akiu studies hard?

As a result, (41) can only be construed as interrogative. It is then not surprising to see that the interrogative construal in (38) does not allow a "paired" reading (i.e., with the pair of variables referring to distinct persons). In other words, representations like (42) are never possible for (36a,b):

(42) $Q_{x,y}$ [x,y a person] $\forall_s$ [s a situation] if x comes first in s,
 y is allowed to eat first in s

This suggests that even though the *wh's-in-situ* in question are subject to independent construals, their licenser (i.e., the Q-operator) still observes the same principle as the necessity operator (i.e., the revised PCOB (33)).

To get the whole picture, we need to further consider constructions such as (43), where paired interrogative readings are actually possible.

From Lexicon to LF

For ease of exposition, we will omit situation variables, and reserve the formulae "$Q_{x,z}$" and "$Q_{y,z}$" exclusively for paired construals of distinct *wh's* from different clauses. In addition to the expected double conditional readings (cf. (32)), (43) has the following interrogative readings:

(43)   (cai-cai-kan) shei ying-le shei, shei jiu dei
        try-to-guess who defeat-Inc who who then must
        qing shei (ne)?
        treat who Q_{wh}

    a. $\forall_x Q_y$ (if x defeats y, then x must treat y)

    b. $Q_x \forall_y$ (if x defeats y, then x must treat y)

    c. $\forall_x Q_y$ (if x defeats y, then y must treat x)

    d. $Q_x \forall_y$ (if x defeats y, then y must treat x)

    e. $\forall_x Q_{y,z}$ (if x defeats y, then x must treat z)

    f. $Q_{x,z} \forall_y$ (if x defeats y, then z must treat y)

    g. $\forall_x Q_{y,z}$ (if x defeats y, then z must treat x)

    h. $Q_{x,z} \forall_y$ (if x defeats y, then y must treat z)

    i. $Q_x Q_y$ (if x defeats y, then x must treat y)

    j. $Q_x Q_y$ (if x defeats y, then y must treat x)

    k. $Q_x Q_{y,z}$ (if x defeats y, then x must treat z)

    l. $Q_{x,z} Q_y$ (if x defeats y, then z must treat y)

    m. $Q_x Q_{y,z}$ (if x defeats y, then z must treat x)

    n. $Q_{x,z} Q_y$ (if x defeats y, then y must treat z)

As one might expect, it is not all that easy to get all of the readings of (43e-h) and (43k-n) due to ensured complexity. Nevertheless, it is quite possible to pin down each reading with carefully constructed scenarios. For instance, the answers to (43g) and (43m) could be (44a) and (44b) respectively, where *Wangyun* and *Lübu* are conspirators against *Dongzhuo*:

(44) a. shei ying-le Dongzhuo, Wangyun jiu dei
 who defeat-Inc Dongzhuo Wangyun then must
 qing shei.
 treat who
 If x defeats Dongzhuo, then Wangyun must treat x.

 b. Lübu ying-le Dongzhuo, Wangyun jiu dei
 Lübu defeat-Inc Dongzhuo Wangyun then must
 qing Lübu.
 treat Lübu
 If Lübu defeats Dongzhuo, then Wangyun must treat Lübu.

On any account, our main purpose here is to point out that paired question construals (i.e., construals involving distinct *wh*-variables) are allowed only if at least one pair of indentical *wh*-variables is licensed, either by a necessity operator or by a Q-operator. In other words, abstract situation variables do not have independent status in licensing bare conditionals, and the following representations are blocked along with (42):

(45) a. $Q_{x,z} Q_{y,k}$ (if x defeats y, then k must treat z)

 b. $Q_{x,z} Q_{y,k}$ (if x defeats y, then z must treat k)

 c. $Q_{x,z} Q_{y,k}$ (if y defeats x, then k must treat z)

 d. $Q_{x,z} Q_{y,k}$ (if y defeats x, then z must treat k)

The implication is far-reaching. As we have seen in (34) and (35), the question construal does not observe the revised PCOB when the conditional construal is not at stake.[11] The same observation applies to (36a,b) and (43). This indicates that there is no "archetype" behavior for unselective binding: Everything is conditioned by logical necessity imposed by principles such as the revised PCOB, which happens to apply on the sentence level due to the morpho-syntactic makeup of Chinese. In other words, unselective binding is just binding, definable in terms of the notion of c-command. By reflecting upon the specficity effects manifested by lexical binding in English (cf. the contrasts between (13a,b)), we find similar traits. That is, lexical binding is just binding, subject to general principles such as the specificity condition (Fiengo & Higginbotham 1981), and definable in an optimal and minimal way. We will allude to this point later when we are prepared to sort out some potential problems with the LCH.

2.4. Japanese *Mo*-quantification and Chinese *Dou*-quantification

Along the line sketched above, we would expect to find languages in between, where the Q-operator is located in the vicinity of regular determiners, say, the Spec of DP. This possibility has actually been entertained by Watanabe (1991), based on the variety of indefinite contruals of Japanese *wh's-in-situ*. First consider the following paradigms:

(46) a. interrogative construals   b. universal construals

dare	'who'		dare-mo	'everyone'
nani	'what'	?	nani-mo	'everything'
doko	'where'		doko-mo	'everywhere'
itsu	'when'		itsu-mo	'whenever'
naze	'why'		-----------	

c. polarity construals   d. existential construals

dare-mo	'anyone'	dare-ka	'someone'
nani-mo	'anything'	nani-ka	'something'
doko-mo	'anywhere'	doko-ka	'somewhere'
-----------		itsu-ka	'sometime'
-----------		naze-ka	'for some reason'

Built upon Kuroda's (1965) observation that Japanese *wh*-words (indeterminate pronominals in his terms) behave rather like unbound variables, Nishigauchi (1986,1990) makes the proposal that morphemes such as *-mo* and *-ka* should be analyzed as unselective binders in the sense of Lewis (1975) and Heim (1982). He further demonstrates that these morphemes behave rather like prepositions or determiners than part of a word. For instance, *ka* may switch its word order with prepositions like *kara* 'from', inducing subtle semantic distinction:

(47)   a.   dare-ka-kara   henna   tegami-ga   todoi-ta.
            who-some-from   strange   letter-Nom   arrived
            A strange letter came from somebody.

       b.   dare-kara-ka   henna   tegami-ga   todoi-ta.
            who-from-some   strange   letter-Nom   arrived
            A strange letter came from god knows who.

Mo, on the other hand, can be attached to adjunct clauses and complex NPs:

(48)   a.   [dare-ga   ki-te]-mo,   boku-wa   aw-a-nai.
            who-Nom   come all   I-Top   meet-not
            For all x, if x comes, I will not meet x.

       b.   [[dare-ga   kai-ta] tegami]-ni-mo onazi   kota-ga
            who-Nom   wrote   letter in-all same   thing-Nom
            kai-te-at-ta
            written-was
            For all x,y, x a person, y a letter x wrote, the same thing
            was written in y.

The conditional construals of (48a,b) are reminiscent of a variety of bare conditionals in Chinese, which patterns with *ruguo*-conditionals in disallowing a *wh-in-situ* in the consequent clause (cf. Cheng & Huang 1993):

(49)   shei xian lai,   na-ge-ren/ta/pro/*shei   dou yao qing-ke.
       who first come   that-CL-preson/(s)he/who   all must invite-guest
       If x comes first, x must play the host.

As shown above, the only difference between the *dou*-conditional (49) and a genuine bare conditional is that the optional connective *jiu* 'then' is replaced by *dou* 'all'. Their semantics nonetheless differ drastically: Only demonstratives and E-type pronominals, but not *wh's-in-situ*, are allowed in the consequent clause of (49). Moreover, the other two usages of *mo* also remind us of the peculiar behavior of *dou* mentioned above (data from Nishigauchi 1990):

(50) a. John   mo   ki-ta.
             John   also   came
             (In addition to other persons,) John also came.

       b. John-ga   ki-te   mo, ...
           John-Nom come even-if
           Even if John comes, ...

As exemplified below, *dou* has an obscure usage hidden behind the usual universal interpretation:

(51) ni-men   dou   lai   ba!
       you (pl.) all   come Exc
       a. Come! All of you!
       b. Come along! you guys!

(51a) represents a typical reading of *dou*, quantifying over plurals. It is the second reading (51b) which bears resemblance to (50a). The difference is that *dou* requires a plural subject in both readings. When a singular subject is substituted, only *ye* 'also' may appear:

(52) ni   ye   lai   ba!
       you also come Exc
       You come along!

(Lian) ... *dou* 'even ... all' constructions such as (23) also allow construals parallel to (50b), where the focus position is occupied by a CP instead of a DP:

(53) Dongzhuo (a), (lian) [$_{CP}$ Lübu lai] dou/ye tai-bu-dong.
Dongzhuo Top even Lübu come all/also lift-not-move
Even if Lübu comes, (he) cannot lift Dongzhuo.

Here universal quantification again applies over the contrast set of the proposition *Lübu lai*, resulting in the focus construal. (53) thus can be paraphrased as 'Even *Lübu* cannot lift *Dongzhuo*, let alone all the others'. The same analysis seems to hold for its Japanese counterpart (50b) as well.

This parallelism seems to break down when we consider the contrast between (55a,b): As Nishigauchi observes, corresponding to the distinction between *every* and free-choice *any* in (54a,b) (cf. Hornstein 1984), there is an asymmetry between *mo-* and *demo-* quantification with respect to their ability to license pronominals across sentence boundaries:

(54) a. Take every number. *I will divide it$_i$ by three.
b. Take any number$_i$. I will divide it$_i$ by three.

(55) a. Dono sakana$_i$-mo mot-te ki-te kudasai.
which fish all carry come please
* Sore$_i$-o ryoori-si-te agemasu kara.
it-Acc cook-for-you because
Bring in every fish$_i$: I will cook it$_i$ for you.

b. Dono sakana$_i$-demo mot-te ki-te kudasai.
which fish even carry come please
Sore$_i$-o ryoori-si-te agemasu kara.
it-Acc cook-for-you because
Bring in any fish$_i$: I will cook it$_i$ for you.

The contrast in question thus bear some resemblance to the asymmetry between bare conditionals and *duo*-coditionals in Chinese.

On the other hand, although *mo*-conditionals appear to pattern with bare conditionals in (55b), *mo* does not license an extra *wh-in-situ* in the main clause, as in (56) (cf. (48a)), any more than its Chinese counterpart *dou* does in (57) (cf. (49)):

(56) * [dare$_i$-ga ki-te]-mo, boku-wa dare$_i$-ni aw-a-nai.
       who-Nom come all   I-Top   who-Dat meet-not
       For all x, if x comes, I will not meet x.

(57) * [shei$_i$ lai], wo dou bu jian shei$_i$.
       who come I all not meet who
       For all x, if x comes, I will not meet x.

Therefore, *mo* and *dou* behave similarly at least in two respects: First, they may license a *wh-in-situ* from a detached position. Second, they only take scope over the antecedent clause in a conditional construction. In other words, they never license a *wh-in-situ* in a consequent clause. This point can also be illustrated by comparing the following two constructions:

(58) a. na-ge ren$_{j/*k}$ / ta$_{j/*k}$ / shei$_{j/*k}$ [$_{CP}$ shei$_k$ lai] dou
         that-CL person/(s)he/who   who come all
         hui   lian-hong.
         will face-red
         Whoever$_i$ comes to visit, that person$_i$ /(s)he$_i$ will flush.

     b. [$_{CP}$ shei$_k$ lai]$_i$, na-ge ren$_{j/k}$ / ta$_{j/k}$ / shei$_{j/*k}$ t$_i$ dou
         who come that-CL person/(s)he/who   all
         hui   lian-hong.
         will face-red
         Whoever$_i$ comes to visit, that person$_i$ /(s)he$_i$ will flush.

First we leave out null subjects, since there is no way to tell their positions relative to the focused constituent in question. As shown by (58a), definite subjects such as *na-ge ren* 'that person' and *ta* '(s)he' cannot be coreferential with the *wh-in-situ* in the adjunct (antecedent) clause, presumably due to Principle C violations. In contrast, when the antecedent clause is preposed to the sentence-initial position, as in (58b), referential contruals become available. Unselective binding construals, on the other hand, are blocked in both cases,[12] which suggests that *dou* never widens its scope by undergoing LF QR to license a genuine bare conditional. In other words, (58a,b) can never have the following *donkey*-type representation:

(59) dou$_x$ (x comes →   x will flush)

It is also instructive to note that this "scope rigidity" follows straightforwardly from the Syntax-LF isomorphism in Huang's (1982) sense.

Besides, as pointed out by Hiro Ura and Masa Koizumi (p.c.), (55b) improves when we replace the singular pronoun *sore* with its plural counterpart or an empty pronominal. Consequently, the reading of *mo* might be collective rather distributive in this particular case, which in turn suggests that the similarity between (55b) and Chinese bare conditional is only apparent.

The real difference, it seems, still lies in their structural properties. *Ka* and *mo* behave like determiners or prepositions (cf. Nishigauchi 1986,1990): They cannot be stranded by scrambling the constituents over which they take scope, as evidenced by the contrast between (60b,c), as well as that between (61b,c):

(60) a. Dare-mo-ga   nani-ka-o   tabe-te-iru.
          everyone-Nom something-Acc   eating-be
          Everyone is eating something.

       b. [Nani-ka-o]$_i$ dare-mo-ga   t$_i$ tabe-te-iru.
           something-Acc   everyone-Nom   eating-be

       c. * Nani$_i$ dare-mo-ga   t$_i$ -ka-o   tabe-te-iru.
            what   everyone-Nom some-Acc   eating-be

(61) a. Dare-ka-ga   dare-mo-o   aisi-te-iru.
          someone-Nom   everyone-Acc   love-be

       b. [Dare-mo-o]$_i$ dare-ka-ga   t$_i$ aisi-te-iru.
           everyone-Acc   someone-Nom   love-be

       c. * Dare$_i$ dare-ka-ga   t$_i$ -mo-o   aisi-te-iru.
            who   someone-Nom every-Acc   love-be

In contrast, *dou* can be and in fact must be stranded in the presence of focus movement, as shown by the contrast between (62b,c), as well as that between (63b,c):

(62) a. Akiu shei dou xiangxin.
       Akiu who all trust
       Akiu trusts everyone.

    b. shei$_i$, Akiu t$_i$ dou xiangxin.
       who Akiu all trust

    c. * [shei dou]$_i$, Akiu t$_i$ xiangxin.
       who all Akiu trust

(63) a. Akiu [$_{CP}$ shei lai] dou hui lian-hong.
       Akiu who come all will face-red
       Whoever comes to visit, Akiu will flush.

    b. [$_{CP}$ shei lai]$_i$, Akiu t$_i$ dou hui lian-hong.
       who come Akiu all will face-red

    c. * [[$_{CP}$ shei lai] dou]$_i$, Akiu t$_i$ hui lian-hong.
       who come all Akiu will face-red

As shown by (62a) and (63a), *dou* usually takes scope over a constituent immediately to its left. Apparent exceptions to the above generalization such as (62b) and (63b) thus can be attributed to local focus movement. (62c) and (63c) indicates that *dou* may behave like a clitic, but it is not a morphological suffix or a determiner.

    A side comment here concerns an interesting comparison between *dou*-constructions and *(lian) . . . dou* constructions. The first noticable thing is that the presence of *lian* 'even' becomes obligatory when the focus position is occupied by a *wh-in-situ*, as in (64a), or by a CP containing a *wh-in-situ*, as in (64b):

(64) a. Akiu *(lian) shei dou/ye xiangxin (ne)?
Akiu even who all/also trust Q$_{wh}$
Who is the person x such that Akiu trusts even x?

b. Akiu *(lian) [$_{CP}$ shei lai] dou/ye hui lian-hong (ne)?
Akiu even who come all/also will face-red Q$_{wh}$
Who is the person x such that Akiu will flush even if x comes?

The cause could be functional, since (64a,b) can only be construed as interrogative, in contrast to (62) and (63). The obligatory presence of *lian* thus disambiguates the potential confusion. The exclusive interrogative construal also lends support to our view that *dou* actually quantifies over the contrast set of the focused constituent in *(lian)* . . . *dou* constructions (cf. section 2.2), not the constituent itself. Otherwise, the readings of (64a,b) should be universal, just like (62) and (63).

The conclusion thus appears to be that while Japanese *(de)mo*-quantification patterns with Chinese *dou*-quantification in almost every aspect of its semantics, they differ in morpho-syntactic terms: *(De)mo* behaves as a part of the constituent over which it takes scope, whereas *dou* appears to a sentential adverbial cliticized leftward to whatever it can quantify over (see also Lee 1986, Cheng 1991,1993).

The asymmetry becomes even clearer when we consider the fact that Chinese-style bare conditionals are nowhere to be found in Japanese, as evidenced by (65):

(65) * dare$_i$-ga ki-te, boku-wa dare$_i$-ni aw-a-nai.
who-Nom come I-Top who-Dat meet-not
For all x, if x comes, I will not meet x.

This suggests that Japanese does not allow an abstract necessity operator on the sentence level, which in turn substantiates our conjecture that Japanese stands in between Chinese and English in tems of the maneuverability of (unselective) binding. Given the equation that the degree of binding maneuverability refects the structural height of binders, we may well hypothesize that Japanese Q-operators locate in

From Lexicon to LF

the Spec of PP or DP, in the vein of Watanabe (1991), Tsai (1992), and Aoun & Li (1993b).

2.5. A Conceptual Problem and an Empirical Solution

A conceptual problem with the Lexical Courtesy Hypothesis (2), as raised by Noam Chomksy (p.c.) is that although Merger has initial advantage over Chain formation in not increasing the length of a formal object, it does need some "add-on" linking mechanism to make the (unselective) binding relation work. The analysis represented by (66a) thus appears to follow from a richer theory which requires unselective binding in addition to LF *wh*-movement:

(66) a. $[_{X''} \Delta \; [_{X'} \; ... \; wh \; ... \;]] \rightarrow [_{X''} Op_{[Q]} \; [_{X'} \; ... \; wh \; ... \;]]$

$\rightarrow [_{X''} Op_{i \; [Q]} \; [_{X'} \; ... \; wh(i) \; ... \;]]$

b. $[_{X''} \Delta \; [_{X'} \; ... \; wh \; ... \;]] \rightarrow [_{X''} wh_i \; [_{X'} \; ... \; t_i \; ... \;]]$

Conseqently, (66a,b) may not be subject to comparison on the ground of Economy, even if some languages do prefer (66a) to (66b).

This observation has inspired us to look further into various types of unselective binding construal on different levels in different languages. The result can be visualized in the following diagram (word orders irrelevant):

(67)

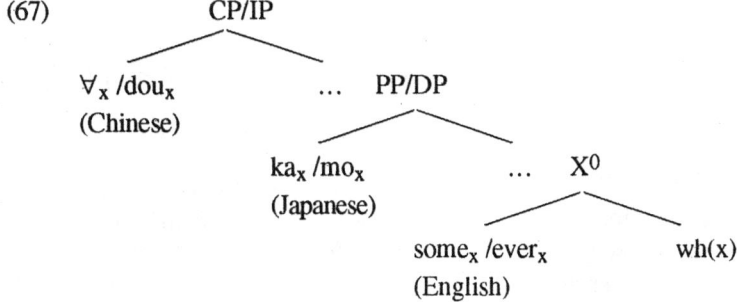

Our observation, though by no means infallible, seems to lead to an interesting conclusion: Unselective binding is an augmentation of lexical binding (or, in a sense, an equal of pronominal binding). In other words, the relation between *shei* 'who' and *dou* 'all' in Chinese, as well as that between *dare* 'who' and *-mo* 'all' in Japanese, is no different from the relation between *who* and *-ever* in English. Under this view, the distinction between external and internal binding in Nishigauchi's (1990) sense is only an illusion, created by morphological makeups of individual languages and imposed by principles associated with particular configurations (e.g., the revised PCOB; cf. section 2.3).

We thus expect that interrogative construals also display the same trait across languages. First let's consider Japanese *wh*-questions. Although it is still under debate whether Japanese displays genuine *wh*-island effects (cf. Lasnik & Saito 1984,1992 vs. Nishigauchi 1986,1990, Pesetsky 1987, and Watanabe 1991), it is generally agreed that Japanese lacks Complex NP (i.e., strong island) effects. Let's assume that there does exist such an asymmetry between Complex NPs and *wh*-islands in Japanese, and see what our theory may say about it. The solution turns out to be quite straightfoward, as illustrated below (data from Watanabe 1991, categorial labels attached to the right in Japanese for ease of exposition):

(68) a.?? [[[John-wa   [[Mary-ga   [[$nani_i$ $_{NP}$] t_i $_{DP}$]-o   katta $_{IP}$]
John-Top   Mary-Nom   what   -Acc   bought
ka-dooka $_{CP}$] Tom-ni   tazuneta $_{IP}$]   no $_{C'}$] Op_i $_{[Q]}$ $_{CP}$] ?
whether   Tom-Dat   asked   Q
What is the thing x such that John asked Tom whether Mary bought x?

b.?? [$_{CP}$ $What_i$ [$_{C'}$ did [$_{IP}$ John ask Tom [$_{CP}$ whether [$_{IP}$ Mary bought t_i]]]]] ?

Following Watanabe (1991), we may assume that a Q-operator originates from the Spec of DP in Japanese, as in (68a). Consequently, it patterns with English *wh*'s (i.e., full *wh*-phrases containing a Q-operator, cf. section 2.1) in displaying *wh*-island effects, as in (68b). On the other hand, since the Q-operator is already in the Spec of DP, any *wh-in-situ* within its c-command domain (and hence within a

Complex NP) can be licensed by unselective binding, as shown below:

(69) [[[John-wa   [[[[t_k dare(x) -o   aisiteiru $_{IP}$]   Op$_k$ $_{CP}$]
     John-Top   who-Acc   loves
     onna$_k$ $_{NP}$] t_i $_{DP}$]-o   nagutta $_{IP}$] no $_{C'}$] Op$_x$ $_{[Q]}$ $_{CP}$] ?
     woman   -Acc   hit   Q
     Who is the person x such that John hit the woman who loves x?

This is exactly what we would expect in view of the lack of locality effects in *mo*-quantification, as exemplified below ((48b) repeated here):

(70) [[[dare(x) -ga t_k kai-ta $_{IP}$] Op$_k$ $_{CP}$]   tegami$_k$ $_{DP}$]-ni-mo$_x$ $_{PP}$]
     who-Nom   wrote   letter   -in-all
     onazi kota-ga   kai-te-at-ta.
     same thing-Nom   written-was
     For all x,y, x a person, y a letter x wrote, the same thing was written in y.

This analysis of the lack of strong island effects in Japanese carries over to Chinese directly, except that the position of Chinese binders is probably much higher than PPs or DPs, as mentioned above. As evidenced by the parallel between the long-distance interrogative construal in (71) and *dou*-quantification in (72), this class of A'-dependency does not observe Subjacency or the ECP:

(71) [$_{CP}$ Op$_x$ $_{[Q]}$ [$_{IP}$ [$_{DP}$ [$_{CP}$ Akiu de   piping [$_{PP}$ dui   shei(x)]
                             Akiu PNM   criticism about who
     zaocheng] de shanghai] zui   da]]?
     cause   PNM damage   most   great
     Who is the person x such that [the damage [which Akiu's criticism caused x]] is greatest?

(72)   [DP [CP Akiu de   piping [PP dui   shei(x)] zaocheng]
            Akiu PNM criticism about who   cause
       de   shanghai] dou$_x$ henda.
       PNM damage   all   great
       For every x, x a person, [the damage [which Akiu's criticism
       caused x]] is great.

The difference between Chinese and Japanese therefore lies in the fact that the former clearly lacks *wh*-islands effects, as evidenced by the following classic example from Huang (1982):

(73)   ni   xiang-zhidao [shei   mai-le   shenme] (ne/ma)?
       you want-know   who   buy-Prf what $Q_{wh}/Q_{yes/no}$
       a. Who is the person x such that you wonder what x bought?
       b. What is the thing x such that you wonder who bought x?
       c. Do you wonder who bought what?

For skeptics who question the wide scope question construals of (73), we may further consider the following examples. The idea is to single out the wide scope readings by invoking the incompatibility between *wh*-questions and yes/no-questions:

(74)   ni   xiang-zhidao [shei   lai-bu-lai]   (ne)?
       you want-know   who   come-not-come Q_{wh}
       a. Who is the person x such that you wonder whether x will come?
       b. #Do you wonder who will come?

(75)   ni   xiang-zhidao [Akiu mai-bu-mai   shenme] (ne)?
       you want-know   Akiu buy-not-buy   what Q_{wh}
       a. What is the thing x such that you wonder whether Akiu will buy x ?
       b. #Do you wonder what Akiu will buy?

The judgement is clear-cut. Native speakers who usually have trouble in processing (73) pick up the wide scope readings without much difficulty.

From Lexicon to LF 35

The distribution of locality effects in the three types of language may thus be summarized as follows:

(76)

	English	Japanese	Chinese
Wh-island effects	yes	yes	no
Complex NP effects	yes	no	no

This is exactly what we would expect from the distinct positions of Q-operators in these languages, as illustrated below (word orders irrelevant):

(77) a. Chinese-type:

$[_{CP} Op_{x\ [Q]}\ [_{IP} ... wh(x) ...]]$

b. Japanese-type:

$[_{CP} Op_{x\ [Q]}\ [_{IP} ... [_{PP/DP}\ t_x\ [... wh(x) ...]] ...]]$

c. English-type:

$[_{CP}\ [_{PP/DP}\ wh(x)\text{-}Op_{x\ [Q]}\ ]_k\ ]\ [_{IP} ... t_k ...]]$

Since Chinese Q-operators are inserted in the CP Spec, no movement is involved. In contrast, since Japanese Q-operators are inserted in the DP Spec, the "half-way" movement to the CP Spec evades Complex NP effects, but still respects the *wh*-island constraint, or whatever principle it might be reduced to. As for English, since the whole *wh*-phrase must move to check its feature on the CP Spec, both Complex NP and *wh*-island constraints are to be observed.

If our analysis proves to be on the right track, then the linking mechanism required in (66a) is only an annotation of the general binding relationship behind any operator-variable pair, definable by the notion of c-command. Since the relationship can be realized in such a minimal way, it manifests itself maximally across languages. Along this line, the basic intuition behind the LCH seems to hold, and the intrinsic priority of (66a) over (66b) can still be made to follow from a broader notion of Economy.

3. Nouns vs. Adverbs

As a reflection, we have been pursuing an ideal design at the cost of a popular assumption; that is, all *wh*-phrases are created equal. As a matter of fact, it is crucial for our purpose here that *wh*-phrases vary in their internal structures, not only across languages, but also across categories. Although it is not clear so far that this is indeed the case, [13] our analysis is essentially in line with the spirit of the minimalist approach; namely, languages differ only in the lexicon and PF.

In the same vein, our next proposal is to follow Tsai (1992, 1997) in claiming that the argument-adjunct asymmetry in question is essentially a noun-adverb asymmetry under the assumption that only nouns may introduce pure (i.e., [-pronominal]) variables in situ. [14] This move captures the essence of Higginbotham's (1983, 1985) proposal that N is generated with an index-argument, which must be "discharged" in terms of binding from a determiner. For instance, a definite DP such as *the donkey* is analyzed as an operator-variable pair based on its internal structure (78):

(78) a.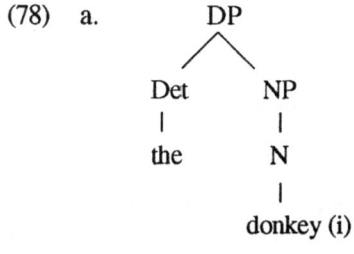

  b. the$_x$ (donkey (x))

(78a) can then be mapped straightforwardly into the usual logical representation for the DP, i.e., (78b). Reinhart (1992, 1993) extends this plot further to *which*-NPs, with a view to deriving the well-known asymmetry between them and *wh*-pronominals in regard to superiority and/or crossing effects (cf. Pesetsky 1987):

(79) a.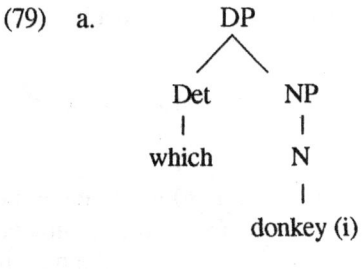

b.   f { x | donkey (x) }

Here *which* is treated as a weak determiner, which by definition is defective in serving as an operator. As an alternative, Reinhart suggests that together with a set introduced as the translation of N, it forms a (choice-) function variable, as in (79b). As a result, *which*-NP may be interpreted in situ given Baker's (1970) Q-morpheme hypothesis (see also Katz & Postal 1964, Pesetsky 1987). In contrast, *who* and *what* are categorized as determiners, which project directly to DP:

(80)   DP
          |
          Det
          |
          who/what

The difference is that although *who* and *what* may in theory be translated as functions, there is no N-set in (80) for them to apply to. Consequently, the only way to realize their quantificational force is to undergo *wh*-movement. In the light of the structural distinction between *wh*-pronominals and *which*-NPs, Reinhart (1992) proposes that *which man* in (82b) does not undergo LF movement, since it introduces an N-set, and is therefore eligible for unselective binding from the matrix Q-morpheme:

(81) a.   Who$_i$ did you persuade t$_i$ to read what?

b. ?? What$_j$ did you persuade whom to read t$_j$?

(82) a. [$_{Comp}$ Q$_{<i,j>}$ which man$_i$] did you persuade t$_i$ to read which book(j) ?

b. [$_{Comp}$ Q$_{<i,j>}$ which book$_j$] did you persuade which man(i) to read t$_j$?

In contrast, its pronominal counterpart in (i.e, *whom*) has to move in LF, and hence the crossing effects displayed by (81b). Her treatment thus captures Baker-Pesetsky's insight without resorting to the notion of D(iscourse)-linking.

On the other hand, we are not to dismiss the intuition that a *which*-NP tends to be D-linked (cf. Pesetsky 1987). From our point of view, the D-linking effect is essentially a result rather than the cause of the asymmetry between *which*-NPs and *wh*-pronominals. Namely, when *which* does function as a strong determiner (i.e., undergoing *wh*-movement), the head noun of (79a) readily provides a restrictive clause, inducing the presuppositional (D-linked) reading (also cf. Heim (class lecture), Kroch 1989, Diesing 1991). Under this view, what is responsible for the D-linkedness of (82a,b) is the fronted *which*-phrase rather than the in-situ one. As a result, we not only come very close to Cinque's (1989) original conception of referentiality and its connection with nominality, but also capture the cross-linguistic generalization that *which*-questions typically come with a pre-established set of answers.

One drawback here is that neither the structural solution nor the D-linking account provides a satisfactory explanation of the long-distance construal in multiple *wh*-questions. First consider the following contrast:

(83) a. Who remembers [where we bought what]?

b.?? What$_i$ does John remember [where we bought t$_i$]?

It has been widely noted that the wide-scope reading of *what* in (83a) is licensed by the presence of another *wh*-phrase in the main clause. If *what* has to undergo LF movement, as it is a *wh*-pronominal and/or a non-D-linked *wh*-phrase, we would expect the same locality effect displayed by (83b). This prediction, as evidenced by (83a), is not borne out. Consequently, we are led back to exactly where we began, i.e., the postulation that Subjacency does not hold in LF.

A possible way out is to follow Reinhart's (1993) refinement, replacing (80) with a structure parallel to (79a), i.e., [$_{DP}$ who/what [$_{N'}$ e(i)]]. As a matter of fact, this analysis of *wh*-pronominals is virtually equivalent to those represented by (17) and (19), except that it is conceived in terms of phrasal syntax. She proposes to derive the crossing effect of (81b) under Economy considerations: Since it is always the c-commanding *wh*-phrase which crosses fewer nodes, the derivation of (81a) is less costly than that of (81b), although it still remains to be seen why (82a) does not block (82b) under the same consideration.

We can then account for the lack of locality effects in (83a) by recasting the Baker-Pesetsky's analysis in terms of the IP-CP system, as illustrated by the following LF representation:

(84) [$_{CP}$ who$_i$ [$_{C'}$ Q$_{<i,k>}$ [$_{IP}$ t$_i$ remembers [$_{CP}$ where$_j$ [$_{C'}$ Q$_{<j>}$ [$_{IP}$ we bought what(k) t$_j$]]]]]]?

Under this analysis, the relevant unselective binder in (84) is the matrix Q-Comp, which remains inactive until being "turned on" by Spec-head agreement with the moved-in *wh*-phrase (that is, by morphological checking in Chomsky's sense). Since the wide-scope construal of *what* in (84) is achieved by unselective binding instead of Chain formation, no Subjacency and/or relativized minimality violation is expected. This move, in a sense, also provides a more explicit mechanism for the Scope Absorption analysis (Chomsky 1986b, 1993).[15]

Along the line sketched above, we then expect Chinese *wh*-phrases to pattern with *which*-NPs (and*wh*-pronominals in the new light) in terms of their status as (function) variables. This possibility has already been explored by Cheng (1991) and Li (1992) with fruitful results: Chinese *wh*-phrases appear to lack their own quantificational properties, and behave in line with polarity items in Klima's (1964) sense. (See also Huang (1982:241-253) for original discussions of indefinte *wh*-construals under negation, A-not-A questions, conditionals, and *dou*-quantification).

Our prediction, however, is not entirely borne out. As we have seen in (4), *wh*-adjuncts such as *weishenme* 'why' apparently do not fit into the picture. They display both strong and weak island effects when wide-scope question formation is involved, and in general resist indefinite construals. For example, while *shenme* 'what' can be embedded within conditionals and read as 'something', as in (85), the same construal is impossible for *weishenme*, as evidence by (86):

(85) ruguo Akiu mai-le shenme, ta iding hui lai
      if Akiu buy-Prf what he surely will come
      gaosu wo.
      tell me
      If Akiu bought something, he surely will come to tell me.

(86) * ruguo Akiu weishenme buneng jiao zuoye,
      if Akiu why cannot hand-in homework
      ta yiding hui lai gaosu wo.
      he surely will come tell me
      If for some reason Akiu cannot hand in homework, he surely will come tell me.

Nevertheless, the asymmetry is not so surprising if again we put English *wh*-words under the microscope: While we can easily pick out *some-what*, *what-ever*, or even *what-so-ever* in the dictionary, (non-)words like **some-why* and **why-ever* are never to be found.[16] This in turn suggests that *why*, unlike *who* and *what*, is not subject to binding construals, as illustrated below:

(87) a.   b.

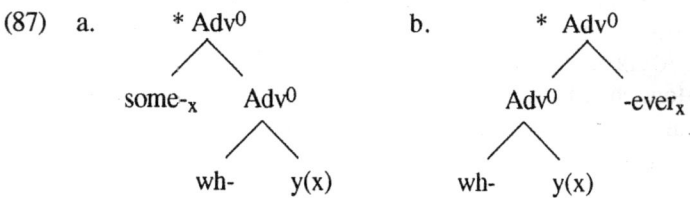

Nor does Japanese allow universal quantification over *naze* 'why': **naze-mo*, which would mean 'for any/every reason' if well-formed, is not a possible combination.[17]

All in all, we find that it is quite safe to assume that adverbs, as intrinsic operators, do not enter into unselective binding as variables. Rather, being denied access to Merger, they appeal to Chain formation to avoid vacuous quantification. The traces which they leave behind then count as variables for binding purpose. Given Huang's (1982) LF movement analysis, we thus have a principled account of why (4) displays ECP/Subjacency effects, and why LF representations like (6) are impossible.

The same analysis applies to the contrast between (85) and (86). As observed by Cheng & Huang (1993), the existential construal of the *wh-in-situ* in (85) results from existential closure ($\exists$-closure) triggered by *ruguo* 'if', given that Chinese *wh*-phrases count as polarity items (cf. Cheng 1991, Li 1992), as illustrated by (88):[18]

(88)   [$_{CP}$ ruguo $\exists_x$ [$_{IP}$ Akiu   [$_{VP}$ mai-le   shenme(x)]]], ...
         if   Akiu   buy-Prf what

Here a technical problem has to be solved before we proceed. For typical indefinites like *yi-ge ren* 'a person', $\exists$-closure appears to stick to VP (cf. Diesing 1992) or syntactic predicates (cf. chapter 3), as evidenced by the obligatory presence of *you* 'have' in (89), which contributes existential force to the subject indefinite:

(89)   * (you)   yi-ge   ren   ($\exists$) [$_{VP}$ lai-le].
         have   one-CL   person   come-Prf
         One man came.

This holds for Chinese *wh's-in-situ* when the trigger in question occurs between IP and VP, as in the case of negation and probability operators:

(90)   Akiu   bu $\exists_x$ [$_{VP}$ yao   shenme(x)].
         Akiu   not   want   what
         a. Akiu does not want anything.
         b. What doesn't Akiu want?

(91)   Akiu   dagai/keneng $\exists_x$ [$_{VP}$ yao   shenme(x)].
         Akiu   probably/possibly   want   what
         a. Akiu probably/possibly wants something.
         b. What does Akiu probably/possibly want?

As shown above, the object *wh's-in-situ* can be construed as either indefinite or interrogative (see chapter 3 for detailed discussion). On the other hand, these triggers do not license subject *wh's-in-situ* in the same configurations, as evidenced by the lack of indefinite readings in the following examples:

(92) shei   bu   yao   kafei?
      who   not   want   coffee
   a. # Someone/Anyone does not want coffee.
   b. Who does not want coffee?

(93) shei   dagai/keneng   yao   kafei?
      who   probably/possibly   want   coffee
   a. # Someone probably/possibly wants coffee.
   b. Who probably/possibly wants coffee?

This indicates that, as far as polarity items are concerned, the scope of ∃-closure is determined by the structural position of its trigger. Our observation is further supported by the fact that a subject *wh-in-situ* does get licensed within *ruguo*-conditionals, in contrast to its counterparts in (92) and (93):

(94) ruguo $\exists_x$ [$_{IP}$ shei(x) mai-le chezi], Akiu yiding hui
      if   who   buy-Prf car   Akiu surely will
      lai   gaosu   wo.
      come   tell   me
      If someone bought a car, Akiu surely will come to tell me.

Consequently, a line has to be drawn between Chinese indefinites and *wh's-in-situ* with respect to the domain of ∃-closure.

With this knowledge in mind, we may account for the deviance of (86) in a straightforward manner. On the one hand, *weishenme* 'why' cannot be targeted by unselective binding from $-closure on the IP node, as illustrated below:

(95) * [$_{CP}$ ruguo $\exists_x$ [$_{IP}$ Akiu weishenme(x) bu-neng
              if   Akiu why   can-not
      [$_{VP}$ jiao   zuoye]]] ...
              hand-in   homework

On the other hand, since there is no intermediate scope position for *wh-*

phrases in (95), *weishenme* have to move all the way to the matrix CP Spec. As a result, (86) is ruled out by Subjacency, the ECP, and possibly Relativized Minimality.

4. Strong vs. Weak Operator Features

An issue which we have not touched upon so far concerns the status of Chinese Comp in regard to feature checking; namely, whether its operator feature is strong or not. We did not concern ourselves with this aspect mainly because, given that the design (8a) is realized in an IP-CP magnitude, the Q-operator in question should satisfy the checking requirement vacuously. Nonetheless, since we have introduced the noun-adverb distinction in terms of their ability to enter into binding construals, it becomes necessary to spell out the inevitable: Operator features are weak in Chinese, and the procrastination principle applies accordingly to block overt *wh*-extraction. In other words, Chomsky's (1993) generalization that operator features are universally strong is probably too strong for our purposes here.

For one thing, there does not seem to be an *a priori* reason why languages should agree on the status of operator features, while they diverge with respect to N-features and V-features, as generally assumed to be the case with English and French head movement (cf. Chomsky 1991). The issue, as it turns out, is really an empirical one. So let's start with the null hypothesis that languages vary in regard to the strong/weak status of their operator features, and see how far it can go.

First note that if operator features are strong across languages, the claim that Subjacency holds only in overt Syntax still serves as an adequate descriptive generalization. Our task, therefore, is to find out if there exists a language where *wh*-phrases are in general allowed to stay in situ, but nonetheless display Subjacency effects. Hindi *wh*-questions seem to be a promising candidate, as evidenced by (96a,b) (All Hindi data below from Mahajan 1990):

(96) a.* raam-ne socaa ki [$_{DP}$ yah baat [$_{CP}$ ki mohan-ne kis-ko
Ram-erg thought   this fact   that Mohan-erg who
maaraa] galat   hE
hit   wrong   is
Who is the person x such that Ram thought that [the fact
[that Mohan hit x]] is wrong?

b.* raam-ne [$_{DP}$ us aadmii-ko [$_{CP}$ jis-ko ravii-ne kyaa ciiz
Ram-erg   that man   who   Ravi-erg what thing
dii]] baazaar jaate dekhaa
gave   market going saw
What is the thing x such that Ram saw [the man [who
Ravi gave x]] going to the market?

As Mahajan points out, the deviance in question poses non-trivial problems for S-structure Subjacency. He then proposes that Hindi *wh*-phrases do not undergo LF wh-movement; rather, they are quantifier-raised (QRed) to adjoin to the immediately dominating IPs (see also Kim 1991). By restating the *Wh*-Criterion in terms of government (originally defined in terms of dominance in May (1985)), (96a,b) is then ruled out by selectional restrictions on the matrix [+wh] Comp, in that the government relation between $C^0_{[+wh]}$ and the wh-phrase in question is blocked by the DP and CP node, both barriers in Chomsky's (1986b) sense (see also Nishigauchi (1986) for a similar treatment in terms of *wh*-feature percolation). Consequently, there is no need to reject S-structure Subjacency under Mahajan's analysis, since no movement is involved in assigning scope to the adjoined *wh*-phrase.

This approach, though plausible in its own right, is incompatible with the checking mechanism developed by Chomsky (1993), where selectional restrictions are satisfied in a Spec-head configuration. Nor does it fit into Rizzi's (1992) formulation of *Wh*-Criterion (cf. (10)) for exactly the same reason. A simple way out, as we might expect from the discussion at the beginning of this section, is to claim that operator features are weak in Hindi. Consequently, overt *wh*-movement is blocked by the principle of procrastination. When Move-a does apply in LF, it induces a strong Subjacency violation since two barriers (i.e., DP and CP) are crossed. We then have a compatible account within the minimalist framework.

Another related fact comes from CED effects associated with extraposed complements: As Mahajan (1990) observes, a finite clausal complement always extraposes in Hind (and hence is located to the right of the main verb), and an extraposed clause does not allow an in-situ *wh*-phrase, as shown by (97a). To make the question licit, the *wh*-phrase must undergo overt fronting, as shown by (97b). In contrast, when a clausal complement does not extrapose (i.e., remaining to the left of the main verb), as is the case of infinitivals like (98), *wh's-in-situ* are allowed:

(97) a. * raam-ne t_i socaa [$_{CP}$ ki mohan-ne kis-ko dekhaa]$_i$
Ram-erg   thought that   Mohan-erg who   saw
Who did Ram think Mohan saw?

   b. kis-ko$_j$ raam-ne t_i socaa [$_{CP}$ ki mohan-ne t_j dekhaa]$_i$
   who   Ram-erg   thought that   Mohan-erg   saw
   Who did Ram think Mohan saw?

(98) raam-ne [PRO kis-ko dekhnaa] caahaa
Ram-erg   who   to see   want
Who did Ram want to see?

First consider (97b). Since the extraposed clause is an ungoverned domain, it is unlikely for the embedded subject *kis-ko* 'who' to move after extraposition, in violation of the CED (Huang 1982) or Subjacency (Chomsky 1986b). Therefore, *wh*-fronting must have preceded extraposition in (97b).[19] In case *wh*-fronting does not apply at all, as in (97a), the wide-scope construal is blocked. This deviance is totally expected, because, under our approach, Subjacency works in exactly the same way in LF as it does in overt Syntax. The delayed LF movement in (97a) is thus ruled out along with that in (96a) (also cf. Srivastav 1991). On the other hand, since the infinitive complement is still L-marked by the verb *caahaa* 'want' in (98) (recall that extraposition of infinitivals is not obligatory), LF movement does not induce any CED effect. The procrastination analysis thus makes the right prediction again.

The story, however, does not quite end here. A notable problem with Watanabe's (1991) analysis with respect to Hindi *wh*-questions concerns cases like (97a). Here we expect that the *wh*-operator generated in the DP Spec of *kis-ko* moves in overt Syntax, and thereby escapes the CED effect in exactly the same fashion as the full *wh*-phrase does in (97b).[20] Nevertheless, as Masa Koizumi (p.c.) points out, this will not be a necessary conclusion if we assume that (pure) *wh*-operators are not subject to scrambling, which is a common practice for full *wh*-phrases in both Hindi and Japanese. Under this view, the *wh*-operator has to move all the way to the local CP Spec before extraposition applies, to avoid a CED violation. When extraposition does apply, presumably adjoining the *wh*-phrase to the right "roof" of IP, strict cyclicity is violated, since the IP-adjunction in question does not extend its target, i.e., the matrix CP (cf. Chomsky 1993), as illustrated below:

(99) [$_{CP}$ Op$_i$ [Q] [$_{IP}$ raam-ne [$_{CP}$ ki mohan-ne [$_{DP}$ t$_i$ [$_{NP}$ kis-ko]]
    Ram-erg   that Mohan-erg   who
dekhaa] socaa]]
saw   thought

—x→ [$_{CP}$ Op$_i$ [Q] [$_{IP}$[$_{IP}$ raam-ne t$_k$ socaa] [$_{CP}$ ki mohan-ne
[$_{DP}$ t$_i$ [$_{NP}$ kis-ko]] dekhaa]$_k$]]

(97a) is thus ruled out correctly. On the other hand, since the whole *wh*-DP in (97b) has been scrambled out of the finite complement before extraposition, the so-called "invisible" *wh*-movement (i.e., movement of the pure *wh*-operator) may be postponed until extraposition applies, and thereby observe strict cyclicity. The derivation is given as follows:

(100) [$_{CP}$ [$_{IP}$ [$_{DP}$ Op$_{[Q]}$ [$_{NP}$ kis-ko]]$_i$ raam-ne [$_{CP}$ ki mohan-ne t$_i$
                         who   Ram-erg   that Mohan-erg
dekhaa] socaa]]
saw   thought
→ [$_{CP}$ [$_{IP}$ [$_{IP}$ [$_{DP}$ Op$_{[Q]}$ [$_{NP}$ kis-ko]]$_i$ raam-ne t$_k$ socaa]
[$_{CP}$ ki mohan-ne t$_i$ dekhaa]$_k$]]
→ [$_{CP}$ Op$_j$ [Q] [$_{IP}$ [$_{IP}$ [$_{DP}$ t$_j$ [$_{NP}$ kis-ko]]$_i$ raam-ne t$_k$ socaa]
[$_{CP}$ ki mohan-ne t$_i$ dekhaa]$_k$]]

As noted by Koizumi, there is still a technical problem to tackle in this solution: The *wh*-DP, when scrambled, becomes an ungoverned domain, and supposedly constitutes an island for the ensuring invisible *wh*-movement according to the CED. The same observation applies to Japanese scrambling under strict cyclicity. Namely, scrambling cannot occur after invisible *wh*-movement. As a result, scrambling has to be undone in LF (cf. Saito 1989). This move, however, renders invisible *wh*-movement an LF operation, and results in a dilemma. We will leave the issue open here.

Now let's take a step back from the technical details, and look at the big picture. First, as confirmed by Mahajan (p.c.), Hindi does not have the parallel morphology which Japanese employs in licensing indefinite *wh's* (cf. Kuroda 1965, Nishigauchi 1986, 1990, Watanabe 1991, among others), which is one of the major motivations for Watanabe's proposal. The null hypothesis, therefore, is that Hindi *wh*-phrases move as a whole due to their morphological makeups. The burden of proof is thus shifted to the pure *wh*-operator hypothesis: Unless there exists evidence in Hindi showing that the "invisible" movement analysis explains something which the "covert" movement analysis cannot, our position is defendable.

Second, Hindi and Japanese also differ with regard to strong island effects. Namely, Japanese allows long-distance construals of *wh*-arguments embedded in complex NPs. This point can be made clear by comparing (101a,b) with (96a,b) respectively (Data from Lasnik & Saito 1992):

(101) a. kimi-wa [$_{DP}$ [$_{CP}$ Taroo-ga nani-o te-ni ireta] koto]-o
you-top   Taroo-nom what-acc obtained fact-acc
sonnani   okotteru   no?
so much   angry   Q
What is the thing x such that you are so angry about [the fact [that Taro obtained x]]?

b. kimi-wa [$_{DP}$ [$_{CP}$ e$_i$ nani-o katta] hito$_i$]-o sagasite iru no?
you-top   what-acc bought person-acc looking-for Q
What is the thing x such that you are looking for [the person [who bought x]]?

Watanabe (1991) observes that the lack of locality effects in (101a,b) can be explained if we assume that there is a *wh*-operator located in the DP Spec of the entire complex NP, which serves as a binder of the *wh*-

in-situ down below (i.e., *nani* 'what'). Consequently, if the strict cyclicity account goes through (that is, if *wh*-operators indeed cannot scramble), it still remains to be seen why Japanese allows insertion of a *wh*-operator in the topmost Spec of a complex NP, while Hindi does not.

Finally, there is a potential paradox between the strict cyclicity account and the extension of the pure *wh*-operator analysis to *kyaa*-questions. If we are to identify *kyaa* as an overt *wh*-operator in Hindi, then the analysis presented by (98) cannot be carried over to examples like (102), where *kyaa* appears to undergo successive cyclic movement (i.e., leaving overt copies in intermediate adjunction sites) before extraposition, and escape from the CED effect:

(102) raam-ne kyaa socaa [$_{CP}$ ki ravil-ne kyaa kahaa
 Ram-erg KYAA thought that Ravil-erg KYAA said
 [$_{CP}$ ki kOn sa aadmii aayaa thaa]].
 that which man come
 Which is the man x such that Ram think [that Ravi say [that x came]]?

It is also instructive to note that the extension cannot hold if Srivastav Dayal (1993) is correct about her indirect dependency analysis, where *kyaa* is related to *kOn sa aadmii* 'which man' through semantic composition of two local *wh*-dependencies.[21] Under this approach, *kyaa* is treated syntactically as an expletive in an argument position, linked to an "extraposed" indirect question, and semantically as a scope marker, quantifying over propositions (i.e., possible answers). More importantly for us, *kyaa* undergoes LF movement to the matrix CP Spec to fulfill feature checking. Her view thus neatly dovetails our analysis of Hindi question formation.

5. An Overview

So far we have sketched three basic proposals: First, Merger enjoys intrinsic priority over Chain formation. Second, only nominals, but not adverbs, are subject to unselective binding. Third, languages vary in regard to the strong/weak status of their operator features. Now we can see how these three could combine to derive the linguistic variations at

From Lexicon to LF 49

issue, not only across languages but also across categories. Putting the last thing first, we may group Hindi and Chinese together in terms of the status of their operator features: Since operator features are weak in these two languages, *wh*-movement procrastinates until LF. In contrast, their English and Japanese counterparts are strong (though the observation is still subject to debate on the part of Japanese). And hence overt movement of *wh*-phrases in English and that of empty *wh*-operators in Japanese, as illustrated below:

(103)

	English	Japanese	Chinese	Hindi
Operator features	strong	(?)strong	weak	weak
LF *wh*-movement	no	(?)no	yes	yes

On the other hand, as we have demonstrated throughout section 1, Chinese and Japanese should be grouped together with respect to their relatively high maneuverability of (unselective) binding. Namely, both Japanese and Chinese allow long-distance indefinite construals of *wh's*, as exemplified in *(de)mo*-conditionals and *dou*-conditionals respectively (cf. section 2.4), and only Chinese allows bare conditionals (cf. section 2.3). We may thus employ the following criterion to capture the above intuition:

(104) *The Watchtower Criterion:*

   a. The higher a binder is, the farther the binding will be.

   b. The farther a binding is, the higher the binder should be.

(104) therefore provides a rationale for the descriptive generalization which we have been depicting in the last tree sections, as illustrated in the following table:

(105)

	English	Japanese	Chinese	Hindi
Non-quantificational *wh's*	no	yes	yes	no
(De)mo/dou-conditionals	(?)no	yes	yes	(?)no
Bare conditionals	no	no	yes	no
Binding construals of operator-variable pairs	lexical	phrasal	sentential	lexical

It is instructive to note that (105) only provides a general outline of patterning and contrasting, and there do exist some overlaps among these languages. For intance, English *no matter*-constructions bear partial resemblance to *(de)mo-* and *dou*-quantification, in that they only license E-type pronoun construals in consquent clauses. The difference is that *(de)mo* and *dou* may take scope over either DPs or CPs (hence qantifying over either individuals or propositions), while *no matter* only takes scope over CPs, quantifying over propositions or situations. We will return later to elaborate on the syntactic aspects of this distinction.

The interaction between the above two sets of factors thus produces the now familiar pattern of interrogative construals in regard to locality effects:

(106) Single *Wh*-questions

	English	Japanese	Chinese	Hindi
Wh-island effects	yes	(?)yes	no	yes
Complex NP effects	yes	no	no	yes

Since English *wh*-phrases are neither subject to procrastination nor subject to indefinite construals above the X^0 level, overt *wh*-movement applies and locality conditions are observed strictly. Hindi follows similar patterns except that *wh*-movement applies in LF due to the weak status of its operator features. Like Hindi, Chinese *wh*-movement applies only in LF. But unlike Hindi, it applies only on the part of *wh*-adverbs, which cannot introduce variables in-situ and therefore are not subject to binding. Japanese, on the other hand, displays mixed behavior, because of the structural position of its Q-operator (i.e., the

Spec of DP/PP), which allows the evasion of Comlex NP islands, but not *wh*-islands.

Furthermore, the Lexical Courtesy Hypothesis (2) also sheds new light on the way we look at cross-linguistic variation. That is, languages may appear to specialize in some specific type of operation (hence the traditional distinction between syntactic and abstract *wh*-movement languages). Nonetheless, they all share the basic design as to how an operator-variable pair should be constructed, and only diverge because of the tension between Syntax and Morphology, the logical necessity imposed by particular configurations, and the idiosyncracies resulted from historical changes and regional influences.

CHAPTER TWO

Some Asymmetries between Chain Formation and Unselective Binding

If a name can be named, it is only nominal.
—Lao Tze

1. Long-Distance Construals of Amount *Wh's*

So far we have demonstrated that there is a principled way to determine where and when unselective binding applies with respect to a fairly restricted set of factors, resulting in a noun-adverb asymmetry. What we haven't shown is whether this move is to characterize a distinct type of A'-dependency, or just to provide an alternative taxonomy of *wh*-construals. To begin with, Chain formation can be further divided into two categories, i.e., successive cyclic movement and long movement (Cinque 1989,1990, Rizzi 1990), with the latter being understood as an instance of long-distance binding (or individual variable binding in the sense of Heim (1987) and Frampton (1990)).[1] The hallmark of long movement construals is that they display Subjacency/CED effects, but do not observe the (conjunctive) ECP and Relativized Minimality. This point is illustrated by the following contrast:

(1) a. ? [How many fish]$_i$ do you wonder whether John weighed t$_i$?

   b. * [How many pounds]$_i$ do you wonder whether John weighed t$_i$?

(2) a. [How many fish]$_i$ do you think John weighed t$_i$?

   b. [How many pounds]$_i$ do you think John weighed t$_i$?

53

As Cinque (1989) points out, although both *how many fish* in (1a) and *how many pounds* in (1b) are q-marked by the verb *weigh*, only the former, but not the latter, escapes from the ECP effect. This point can be made clear by comparing the *wh*-island constructions (1a,b) with the bridge-verb constructions (2a,b) respectively.

The reason, as provided by Cinque, is that the amount *wh*-phrase *how many pounds* is not referential, and therefore not eligible for binding construals (see also Koopman & Sportiche 1988, Rizzi 1990). As a result, it must undergo successive cyclic movement, and accordingly observe both the ECP and Subjacency. In contrast, only referential expressions such as *how many fish* may undergo long *wh*-movement, by definition immune to the antecedent-government requirement.

On the other hand, our characterization of unselective binding dictates an absolute absence of Subjacency and ECP effects, as long as *wh*-phrases involved introduce variables in situ. This prediction is indeed borne out by the following wide scope construal of Chinese amount *wh*-nominals:

(3) ni xiang-zhidao [shei zhong`duoshao/ji`bang] ne?
     you want-know   who weigh how-many pound Q_{wh}
     a. Who is the person x such that you wonder how many
        pounds x weighs?
     b. What is the number/amount x such that you wonder who
        weighs x pounds?

As evidenced by (3b), *duoshao bang* and *ji bang* pattern with argument NPs in not displaying *wh*-island effects in wide-scope question formation (cf. Huang 1982). It is also instructive to note that *zhong* 'weigh' is construed only as stative (vs. agentive) in Chinese, as evidenced by (4a):

(4) a. * Akiu   zhong   liang-tiao   yu.
          Akiu   weigh   two-CL   fish
          Akiu weighs two fishes.

     b. Akiu   zhong   *(liang-bai   bang).
         Akiu   weigh   two-hundred   pound
         Akiu weighs two hundred pounds.

The deviance of (4a) indicates that the amount NP in question is lexically selected. As pointed out by Howard Lasnik, the same pattern applies to English multiple *wh*-questions:

(5) a. * How many pounds does [who remember whether John weighed t]?

b. Who remembers [whether John weighed how many pounds]?

Since there is no referential DP (or DP ranging over individuals) such as *how many fish* involved in (3b) and (5b), it is clear that this lack of *wh*-island effects in LF calls for independent treatment other than the long movement analysis.

One might suspect that the bond between *zhong* and *duoshao/ji bang* in (3) is much stronger than that between their English counterparts in (1b): It is not impossible that *zhong* both lexically selects and q-marks *duoshao/ji bang*, whereas *weigh* lexically selects but does not q-mark *how many pounds*.. A closer inspection reveals that even this stipulation does not solve the problem. For one thing, *zhong* can also be read as 'gain weight', when suffixed by the perfective aspect *-le*, as exemplified below:

(6) a. Akiu zhong-le.
Akiu weigh-Prf
Akiu has gained some weight.

b. Akiu zhong-le liang bang
Akiu weigh-Prf two pound
Akiu has gained two pounds.

Here the amount phrase *liang bang* 'two pounds' is optional, and hence neither lexically selected nor q-marked by *zhong-le*. Nonetheless, there is still no locality effect what-so-ever when *wh*-island constructions are involved, as in (7):

(7) ni xiang-zhidao [shei zhong-le duoshao/ji bang] ne?
you want-know who gain-Prf how-many pound Q_{wh}
   a. Who is the person x such that you wonder how many pounds x has gained?
   b. What is the number/amount x such that you wonder who has gained x pounds?

The parallel between *zhong* 'weight' and *zhong-le* 'gain weight' again emerges in the long-distance question construals of (8-11), where Complex NP islands are violated, but still no deviance is detected:

(8) [$_{DP}$ [$_{CP}$ zhong duoshao/ji bang] de zhu] cai keyi canjia
           weigh how-many pound PNM pig just can join
bisai ne?
competition Q_{wh}
What is the number/amount x such that pigs which weigh x pounds just can join the competition?

(9) [$_{DP}$ [$_{CP}$ zhong-le duoshao/ji bang] de zhu] cai keyi
           gain-Prf how-many pound PNM pig just can
canjia bisai ne?
join competition Q_{wh}
What is the number/amount x such that pigs which have gained x pounds just can join the competition?

(10) [$_{DP}$ [$_{CP}$ Akiu zhong duoshao/ji bang] de shuofa]
           Akiu weigh how-many pound PNM story
bijiao kexin ne?
more believable Q_{wh}
What is the number/amount x such that the story that Akiu weighs x pounds is more believable?

(11) [$_{DP}$ [$_{CP}$ Akiu zhong-le duoshao/ji bang] de shuofa]
Akiu gain-Prf how-many pound PNM story
bijiao kexin ne?
more believable Q$_{wh}$
What is the number/amount x such that the story that Akiu
has gained x pounds is more believable?

Similarly, English multiple *wh*-questions also allow long-distance construals of amount *wh's-in-situ* in Complex NP constructions, as evidenced by the following contrast (data due to Howard Lasnik):

(12) a. * How many pounds does who remember [$_{DP}$ a man [$_{CP}$ who weighed t]]?

b. Who remembers [$_{DP}$ a man [$_{CP}$ who weighed how many pounds]]?

We may therefore rule out q-marking as a factor in deriving the absence of LF locality effects. In fact, there is substantial evidence indicating that q-marking does not play a role in licensing Chain-formation either: As Rizzi (1990:77) observes, there is an unexpected asymmetry between French *wh*-adverbials *avec qui* 'with whom' and *comment* 'how'. First note that adverbs like *bien* 'well' are lexically selected (or q-marked) by *se comporter* 'behave', while PPs like *avec les amis* 'with friends' are not, as evidenced by (13):

(13) Jean se comporte *(bien) (avec les amis).
Jean behaves well with friends.

However, the locality effects displayed by their corresponding *wh*-forms are totally unexpected given the q-government requirement:

(14) a. ?Avec qui$_j$ ne sais-tu pas [comment$_i$ [PRO te comporter t$_i$ t$_j$]?
With whom don't you know how to behave?

b. *Comment$_i$ ne sais-tu pas [avec qui$_j$ [PRO te comporter t$_i$ t$_j$]?
How don't you know with whom to behave?

As shown by the contrast between (14a,b), the adverb *comment*, though lexically selected, undergoes successive cyclic movement, and observes both the ECP and Subjacency accordingly. In contrast, the extraction of the adjunct PP *avec qui* counts as long *wh*-movement due to its referentiality (or individuality in Heim-Frampton's sense). And hence the minor Subjacency violation in (14a). We may thus summarize the whole pattern of contrasts in the following table:

(15)	Successive cyclic *wh*-mvt	Long *wh*-mvt	Unselective binding
Subjacency/CED	yes	yes	no
ECP/R. Minimality	yes	no	no

The noun-adverb asymmetry, on the other hand, plays an important role in construing amount *wh's*: First compare the following examples to (3b) and (5b) (Chinese and English data due to Jim Huang and Noam Chomsky respectively):

(16) ni xiang-zhidao [shei (you) duo zhong] ne?
      you want-know   who   have how heavy Q$_{wh}$
      a. Who is the person x such that you wonder how heavy x is?
      b. #What is the degree x such that you wonder who is x heavy?

(17) a. *How much does who remember [whether John weighed t]?

b. *Who remembers [whether John weighed how much]?

As shown by (16), *zhong* can also be construed as a stative adjective when modified by adverbs such as *duo* 'how' and *hen* 'very' (as in *Akiu hen zhong* 'Akiu is very heavy'). Although the subject reading (16a) is as good as (3a), the wide scope construal of the *wh*-adverb *duo* is in fact blocked, as evidenced by (16b). This is exactly what we would expect from the noun-adverb distinction explored in chapter 1. That is, only *wh*-nominals introduce variables in situ, whereas *wh*-adverbs must move to create operator-variable pairs. Moreover, the parallel between (17a,b), in contrast to the asymmetry between (5a,b), also lends cross-linguistic support to our position: Only nominals such as *how many pounds*, but not adjectivals such as *how much*, are subject to long-distance in-situ construals.[2]

A descriptive generalization is thus in order: The availability of long movement is determined by the referentiality or individuality of the *wh*-phrases involved, whereas the availability of unselective binding hinges upon their nominality, as illustrated in the following table:

(18)

	Successive cyclic *wh*-mvt	Long *wh*-mvt	Unselective binding
wh-adverb	yes	no	no
non-referential *wh*-DP/PP	yes	no	yes
referential *wh*-DP/PP	yes	yes	yes

On technical grounds, there are essentially two ways to look at the wide scope construals of amount *wh's* along the unselective binding approach. One is to treat *duoshao/ji bang* as objectual/individual variables (vs. amount/degree variables), in that numbers count as formal objects. As pointed out by Noam Chomsky and Jim Huang (p.c.), the matrix Q-operator in (3b) may well quantify over a set of numbers, as shown by the following derivation:

(19) $[_{CP} Op_k [_{C'} Q_k [_{IP}$ ni   xiang-zhidao $[_{CP} Op_j [_{C'} Q_j$
                                        you   want-know
      $[_{IP}$ shei(j) zhong duoshao/ji bang(k)]]]]]]?
               who   weigh how-many pound

   → $[_{CP} [_{C'} Q_k [_{IP}$ ni   xiang-zhidao $[_{CP} [_{C'} Q_j$
                                  you   want-know
      $[_{IP}$ shei(j) zhong duoshao/ji bang(k)]]]]]]?
               who   weigh how-many pound

Here we may assume either that a Q-operator transfers its binding relation to a Q-Comp through operator feature checking (i.e., Spec-head agreement), or that the Q-Comp may enter into the binding relation by itself after feature checking. The crucial point here is that, once the [Q] feature is "checked off" in the CP Spec, the Q-operator is free to delete, since its only lexical content has been nullified and there is no concern with the recoverability condition. It is thus possible to avoid the scenario where a variable is bound by two operators (i.e., the Q-operator and the Q-comp).[3]

Given the copy theory developed in Chomsky (1993), the same analysis carries over to English multiple *wh*-questions, as shown by the following derivation of (5b):

(20) LF: $[_{CP}$ who$_i$ $[_{C'}$ Q$_i$ $[_{IP}$ who$_i$ remembers $[_{CP}$ whether$_j$ $[_{C'}$ Q$_j$ $[_{IP}$ John weighed how many pounds]]]]]]?

→ $[_{CP}$ $[_{C'}$ Q$_{i,k}$ $[_{IP}$ who(i) remembers $[_{CP}$ $[_{C'}$ Q$_{yes-no}$ $[_{IP}$ John weighed how many pounds(k)]]]]]]?

First we will put aside the exact treatment of *whether* in the intermediate Spec of CP. It suffices to note that *whether* ranges over two opposite cases or situations, inducing an indirect yes-no question. We then apply upward deletion to the subject Chain of the matrix clause, as the [Q] feature on the head *who* is checked off. This move also prevents the copy *who* from being bound by two operators. The matrix Q-Comp thus licensed further serves as a binder and the only binder of the amount *wh-in-situ*, because the intermediate Q-Comp (expressing a yes-no question) is incompatible with the *wh*-question construal of *how many pounds*.

The other alternative is to analyze the *wh-in-situ* as a functional variable (or a D variable in Chomsky's terms; see also Engdahl 1980, Reinhart 1992, 1993), as illustrated below:

(21) [$_{CP}$ Op$_{G [Q]}$ [$_{C'}$ Q [$_{IP}$ ni   xiang-zhidao [$_{CP}$ Op$_{F [Q]}$ [$_{C'}$ Q
                                      you want-know
       [$_{IP}$ F(shei) zhong G(duoshao/ji   bang)]]]]]]?
             who   weigh   how-many   pound

  → [$_{CP}$ [$_{C'}$ Q$_G$ [$_{IP}$ ni   xiang-zhidao [$_{CP}$ [$_{C'}$ Q$_F$
                                 you   want-know
       [$_{IP}$ F(shei)   zhong G(duoshao/ji bang)]]]]]]?
             who   weigh how-many   pound

Under this view, the Q-Comp in question ranges over a set of functions which apply to the noun head (cf. chapter 1, section 3), inducing an amount or degree reading. The English multiple *wh*-question can be treated in a similar way:

(22) LF: [$_{CP}$ who$_i$ [$_{C'}$ Q$_i$ [$_{IP}$ who$_i$ remembers [$_{CP}$ whether$_j$ [$_{C'}$ Q$_j$
          [$_{IP}$ John weighed how many pounds]]]]]]?

  → [$_{CP}$ [$_{C'}$ Q$_{i,G}$ [$_{IP}$ who(i) remembers [$_{CP}$ [$_{C'}$ Q$_{yes-no}$
       [$_{IP}$ John weighed G(how many pounds)]]]]]]?

or → [$_{CP}$ [$_{C'}$ Q$_{F,G}$ [$_{IP}$ F(who) remembers [$_{CP}$ [$_{C'}$ Q$_{yes-no}$
       [$_{IP}$ John weighed G(how many pounds)]]]]]]?

Because, as far as *duoshao/ji bang* and *how many pounds* are concerned, the difference between the number-objectual reading and the amount-functional reading is too subtle to justify an argument in favor of either of the two approaches, we will leave the choice open here.

A natural prediction along our line is that Chinese measure *wh*-phrases should be able to undergo indefinite construals, which is again borne out. First compare (8a,b) and (11a,b) with (23a,b) and (24a,b) respectively. The two sets of sentences are near minimal pairs: In the former, we have an optional *wh*-question marker *ne* and an adverb like *cai* 'just' or *bijiao* 'more' in the matrix clauses; in the latter, we have the universal binder *dou* instead, ranging over either numbers or amounts (see above):

(23) a. [$_{DP}$ [$_{CP}$ zhong duoshao/ji bang] de zhu] dou keyi
weigh how-many pound PNM pig all can
canjia bisai.
join competition.
For every number/amount x, pigs which weigh x pounds
can join the competition.

b. [$_{DP}$ [$_{CP}$ zhong-le duoshao/ji bang] de zhu] dou keyi
gain-Prf how-many pound PNM pig all can
canjia bisai.
join competition.
For every number/amount x, pigs which have gained x
pounds can join the competition.

(24) a. [$_{DP}$ [$_{CP}$ Akiu zhong duoshao/ji bang] de shuofa]
Akiu weigh how-many pound PNM story
dou bu kexin.
all not believable
For every number/amount x, the story that Akiu weighs
x pounds is not believable.

b. [$_{DP}$ [$_{CP}$ Akiu zhong-le duoshao/ji bang] de shuofa]
Akiu weigh-Prf how-many pound PNM story
dou bu kexin.
all not believable
For every number/amount x, the story that Akiu has gained
x pounds is not believable.

As expected, the noun-adverb asymmetry also show up in *dou*-quantification: When we substitute *(you) duo zhong* '(have) how heavy' for *zhong(-le) duoshao/ji bang*, the sentences degrade considerably, as evidenced by the deviance of (25) and (26):[4]

(25) * [$_{DP}$ [$_{CP}$ you   duo zhong] de   zhu]   dou   keyi canjia
              have howheavy PNM pig   all   can   join
    bisai.
    competition.
    For every degree x, pigs which are x heavy can join the
    competition.

(26) * [$_{DP}$ [$_{CP}$ Akiu (you) duo zhong] de   shuofa] dou bu
              Akiu   have howweigh   PNM   story   all not
    kexin.
    believable
    For every degree x, the story that Akiu is x heavy is not
    believable.

A precaution here is that cases like (25) and (26) should not be confused with sentential subject constructions such as (27a) or bare conditionals such as (27b), which in general allow predicative *duo zhong*, as exemplified below:

(27) a.   [$_{CP}$ Akiu (you)   duo zhong] dou wu-quan-jinyao.
              Akiu   have   howheavy   all not-concern-matters
         It doesn't matter [how heavy Akiu is].

    b.   Akiu (you) duo zhong,   wo jiu (you) duo zhong.
         Akiu   have   howheavy   I then have   howheavy
         However heavy Akiu is, I am (exactly) that heavy.

As pointed out by Jim Huang (p.c.), what undergoes *dou*-quantification in (27a) is not *duo zhong* 'how heavy', but the whole sentential subject. In other words, *dou* ranges over questions (or more precisely, answers to the questions) in (27a). Similarly for the bare conditional, it is the antecedent and consequent clauses which undergo universal quantification in (27b), not the predicates which they contain (also cf. chapter 1, section 2.3): A necessity operator quantifies over two sets of questions in a tripartite style, each of which corresponds to one clause of (27b):

(28) For every x, if x is an answer to how heavy Akiu is, then x is an answer to how heavy I am.

Our position is further supported by the fact that *wh*-elements which usually resist indefinite construals also occur in the same environments. For instance, A-not-A questions and *wh*-adverbs like *weishenme* 'why' as a rule resist *dou*-quantification:

(29) * [DP [CP Akiu lai-bu-lai]   de   shuofa] dou bu kexin.
          Akiu come-not-come PNM story   all not believable
     Both the story that Akiu comes and the story that Akiu does not come are not believable.

(30) * [DP [CP weishenme   zhong-le]   de   zhu]   dou keyi
          why   gain-weight-Prf PNM pig   all can
     canjia bisai.
     join competition.
     For every reason x, [pigs [which have gained weight for x]] can join the competition.

However, just as *duo zhong* 'how heavy' in (27a,b), they are allowed in bare conditionals and in sentential subjects under the scope of *dou*, as illustrated below:

(31) a. [CP Akiu   lai-bu-lai]   dou wu-quan-jinyao.
          Akiu   come-not-come   all not-concern-matters
     It doesn't matter [whether Akiu comes or not].

     b. Akiu weishenme gaoxing, wo jiu weishenme   shang-xin.
        Akiu why   happy   I then   why   hurt-feeling
     I am hurt for whatever reasons Akiu is pleased.

Cases like (27a,b) and (31a,b), therefore, not only do not count as counterexamples of the noun-adverb asymmetry, but also shed new light on the intriguing nature of *dou*-quantification and bare conditionals.

Finally, there are a few mysteries which deserve mention. First of all, for some reason A-not-A questions are incompatible with bare conditionals, as shown below:

(32) * Akiu qu-bu-qu, wo jiu qu-bu-qu.
　　　Akiu go-not-go I then go-not-go

(32), if grammatical, would mean 'If Akiu goes, I will go; if Akiu does not go, I will not go'. This suggests that there is still some fundamental difference between yes-no questions and *wh*-questions in conditional construals. Second, *duo-shao*, literally translated as 'many-few', differs from *ji* in resisting indefinite construals in existential contexts:

(33) a. Akiu shi-bu-shi zhong-le ji bang?
　　　　Akiu is-not-is gain-Prf a few pound
　　　　Isn't it the case that Akiu has gained a few pounds?

　　b. ruguo Akiu zhong-le ji bang, ...
　　　　if Akiu gain-Prf a few pound
　　　　If Akiu has gained a few pounds, then ...

(34) a. * Akiu shi-bu-shi zhong-le duo-shao bang?
　　　　 Akiu is-not-is gain-Prf many-few pound
　　　　 Isn't it the case that Akiu has gained a few pounds?

　　b. * ruguo Akiu zhong-le duo-shao bang, ...
　　　　 if Akiu gain-Prf many-few pound
　　　　 If Akiu has gained a few pounds, then ...

Since A-not-A questions are incompatible with *wh*-questions, *ji bang* can only be licensed by existential closure, and hence the indefinite construal as 'a few pounds' in (33a). *Duo-shao bang*, in contrast, is denied this option. Consequently, both interrogative and indefinite construals are blocked, as shown by the deviance of (34a). Similarly, the most prominent reading of *ji bang* embedded within a *ruguo*-conditional is indefinite, as shown by (33b).[5] The same construal is not available for *duoshao bang*, as evidenced by (34b).

This asymmetry should be further compared with cases where no triggers like A-not-A questions and *ruguo* are involved:

(35) Akiu zuotian mai-le ji-ben shu (ne)
     Akiu yesterday buy-Prf a few-CL book Q_{wh}
   a. Akiu bought a few books yesterday.
   b. How many books did Akiu buy yesterday?

As shown above, *ji* can also be construed as a genuine indefinite (vs. polarity items), in alternation with its question construal. Here again *duo-shao* is denied the indefinite option, and only the interrogative reading survives, as illustrated by the contrast between (36a,b):

(36) Akiu zuotian mai-le duo-shao-ben shu (ne)
     Akiu yesterday buy-Prf many-few-CL book Q_{wh}
   a. #Akiu bought a few books yesterday.
   b. How many books did Akiu buy yesterday?

As we can tell from the English translation, *duo-shao* 'many-few' is really a disjunctive compound, which might account for its remote resemblance to the A-not-A question in (32). This intrinsic property is most prominent when *duo-shao* is used as a sentential adverbial, meaning 'more-or-less':

(37) Akiu duo-shao zuo-le yixie hao shi.
     Akiu many-few do-Prf some good thing
     Akiu more or less has done some good deeds.

Since this adverbial usage is the only case where *duo-shao* can be said to be existential (roughly an equivalent of 'in some cases'), it may well be the case that existential *duo-shao* has been "specialized" into its present adverbial form, while existential *ji* is "generalized" to cover even genuine indefinite construals.

In sum, we have shown that we do have a case where neither the lack of referentiality nor the absence of q-marking makes any difference as to the licensing of long-distance A'-dependencies. The implication is significant: There is an entire different breed of long-distance construals, namely, unselective binding, which cannot be leveled with long *wh*-movement. We will continue to examine some suggestive facts in the following sections.

2. Interrogative Construals in *Dou-* and *Mo-*Quantification

As we assimilate interrogative construals of *wh's-in-situ* to typical cases of unselective binding like *dou*-quantification, we also commit ourselves to the prediction that the interaction between both should not display the ECP and/or Relativized Minimality effects. This prediction appears to be false at first glance:

(38) [$_{CP}$ shei zai shafa-shang shui] dou ke-yi (*ne)
       who at sofa-on sleep all will-do Q_{wh}
   a. Whoever sleeps on the sofa, it will do.
   b. # Who is the person x such that it will do if x sleeps on the sofa?

As shown above, the wide-scope question construal (38b) appears to be blocked by *dou*. A similar observation is also made by Nishigauchi (1990:148) concerning *mo*-quantification in Japanese, as exemplified below:

(39) kimi-wa [$_{CP}$ dare-ge ki-te]-mo ik-a-nai no?
     you-Top who-Nom come-all go-not Q
   a. Are you not going, whoever may come?
   b. # For which x, x a person, are you not going if x is coming?

First note that unlike the necessity operator which licenses bare conditionals, *dou* and *mo* only take scope over the embedded CPs of (38) and (39) respectively. As a result, when *shei* 'who' and *dare* 'who' undergo long-distance construals, *dou* and *mo* becomes vacuous quantifiers. Besides, according to the "answer variable" hypothesis presented in the last section, the embedded CPs are actually indirect questions. The wide scope question construals (38b) and (39b) thus fail to satisfy the selectional restrictions on the embedded CPs, resulting in the following nonexistent readings:

(40) # Who is the person x such that if for every y, y satisfies the property of [x sleeps on the sofa], it will do?

(41) # Who is the person x such that if for every y, y satisfies the property of [x is coming], you are not going?

Either way, (38b) and (39b) are correctly ruled out. Along this line, a natural question is why question construals are ever allowed in bare conditionals such as (42b):

(42) shei xian lai, shei jiu keyi xian chi (ne)
 who first come who then can first eat Q_{wh}
 a. Whoever comes first, then (s)he is allowed to eat first.
 b. Who is the person x such that if x comes first, x is allowed to eat first?

The solution to this puzzle is where the answer variable analysis really shines: The "across-the-board" behavior of universal quantification in (42a) and that of the question construal in (42b) can be both attributed to the fact that it is answers that matter here. This point is illustrated by (43a,b), which correspond to (42a,b) respectively (situation variables omitted):

(43) a. For every x, if x is an answer to the question who comes first, then x is the answer to the question who is allowed to eat first.

 b. What is x such that if x is an answer to the question who comes first, then x is the answer to the question who is allowed to eat first?

The above move in turn yields another prediction: if there is more than one *wh-in-situ* in *dou-* and *mo*-clauses (i.e., antecedent clauses), the wide scope construals in question should be possible, which is indeed the case in Chinese:

(44) [CP (tamen) shei zai nali   shui] dou ke-yi   (ne)
      they   who at where sleep all will-do Q_wh
   a. No matter (among them) who sleep where, it will do.
      (If for every x, x is an answer to the question who sleeps
      where, it will do.)
   b. Who is the person x such that it will do wherever x sleeps?
   c. Where is the place y such that it will do whoever sleeps at y?

As shown above, in addition to the paired indirect question reading (44a), each of the *wh's-in-situ* may assume the wide scope, as in (44b) and (44c). Also as expected, (44) does not allow a paired matrix question like (45), for reasons just mentioned:

(45) * Who is the person x and where is the place y such that if for
       every y, y is an answer to the question [x sleeps at y], it will
       do?

We can further eliminate the (a) clause reading by embedding (44) as a an indirect question, as shown by (46):

(46) Akiu xiang-zhidao [[CP shei zai nali   shui] dou ke-yi].
     Akiu want-know   who at where sleep all will-do
   a. Akiu wonders who is the person x such that it will do
      wherever x sleep.
   b. Akiu wonders where is the place y such that it will do
      whoever sleeps at y.

Here the long-distance question construals (46a) and (46b) stand out as the only two readings available.

As for Japanese, the prediction is only partially borne out, as exemplified below (data due to Masa Koizumi):

(47) [CP dare-ga   nani-o   tabe-te]-mo ii   (no)
         who-Nom what-Acc eat-Infl]-all good   Q
   a. No matter who ate what, it will do.
   b. Who is the person x such that it will do whatever x eat?
   c. #What is the thing y such that it will do whoever eat y?

Just as its Chinese counterpart *shei* in (44), the subject *wh-in-situ dare* may assume the wide scope in (47b), in addition to its narrow scope construal (47a). In contrast, the object *nani* 'what' only allows the narrow scope reading. Consequently, there seems to be a subject-object asymmetry with respect to unselective binding. But as Masa Koizumi (p.c.) points out, the (c) clause reading becomes available when the object is scrambled to the left of the subject:

(48) [$_{CP}$ nani-o   dare-ga   tabe-te]-mo   ii   (no)
      what-Acc who-Nom   eat-Infl]-all   good   Q
    a. No matter who ate what, it will do.
    b. # Who is the person x such that it will do whatever x eat?
    c. What is the thing y such that it will do whoever eat y?

This indicates that the asymmetry may have something to do with (anti-)superiority effects in Japanese: The embedded CP, being an indirect question, may well involve invisible *wh*-movement, since the selectional restriction must be fulfilled by feature-checking before SPELL-OUT (recall our assumption that operator features are strong in Japanese (cf. chapter 1, section 4); see also Watanabe 1991). As a detailed account is beyond the scope of this chapter, we will drop the issue here.

Another factor which can be isolated in (38) concerns the presence of indirect questions under the scope of *dou*. Recall that *dou* takes scope over not only CPs, but also DPs, where the noun-adverb asymmetry holds, and answer/situation variables are irrelevant (cf. section 1). In the latter cases, long-distance construals should be available even when there is only one *wh-in-situ* within the scope of *dou*, as long as the ban against vacuous quantification is observed. This is indeed the case, as evidenced by (49):

(49) [$_{DP}$ [$_{CP}$ Dufu zai nali xie] de shi] dou shi
    Dufu at where write PNM poem all be
yiliude (ne)
first-rate Q$_{wh}$

a. For every x, x a place, for every y, y a poem which Dufu wrote at x, y is first-rate.
b. Where is the place x such that for every y, y a poem which Dufu wrote at x, y is first-rate.

As shown above, *dou* may either quantify over both *zai nali* 'at where' and the head noun (i.e., the bare indefinite *shi* 'poem'), as in (49a), or quantify over the head noun alone, as in (49b). It is in the latter option that a direct question is possible.

Our observation is further consolidated by the fact that even paired question readings are allowed when there are more than one *wh-in-situ* in the same configuration. Take (50) for example, where *Dufu* is replaced by *shei* 'who': *dou* may quantify over *shei*, *zai nali*, and the head noun *shi* in one swipe, as in (50a). Alternatively, either one of the *wh's-in-situ* may assume the wide scope, as in (50b,c). And most importantly, a paired direct question is also possible when *dou* quantify over the head noun alone, as in (50d):

(50) [$_{DP}$ [$_{CP}$ shei zai nali xie] de shi] dou shi yiliude (ne)
    who at where write PNM poem all be first-rate Q$_{wh}$

a. For every x, x a person, for every y, y a place, for every z, z a poem which x wrote at y, z is first-rate.
b. Who is the person x such that for every y, y a place, for every z, z a poem which x wrote at y, z is first-rate?
c. Where is the place y such that for every x, x a person, for every z, z a poem which x wrote at y, z is first-rate?
d. Who is the person x and where is the place y such that for every z, z a poem which x wrote at y, z is first-rate?

Again, if we further embed the whole sentence as an indirect question, the "free relative" reading (50a) is suppressed due to the selectional restriction imposed by the matrix verb, and the long-distance question construals parallel to (50b-d) stand out most clearly, as shown below:

(51) Akiu xiang-zhidao [$_{CP}$ [$_{DP}$ [$_{CP}$ shei zai nali xie]   de   shi]
Akiu want-know   who at where write PNM poem
dou shi yiliude].
all be first-rate

    a. Akiu wonders who is the person x such that for every y,
       y a place, for every z, z a poem which x wrote at y, z is
       first-rate?
    b. Akiu wonders where is the place y such that for every x,
       x a person, for every z, z a poem which x wrote at y, z is
       first-rate?
    c. Akiu wonders who is the person x and where is the place y
       such that for every z, z a poem which x wrote at y, z is
       first-rate?

    To sum up, we have demonstrated that the interaction between *dou*-quantification and *wh*-question formation displays the same characteristics as that among *wh's-in-situ* themselves. Namely, neither Subjacency or the ECP/relativized minimality effects are detected. Although the situation is less clear on the part of Japanese *mo*-quantification, it seems safe to attribute the difference to the strong status of its operator features.

3. A'-Bound Pro or Pure Variable?

Given our observation so far, one might sketch a working hypothesis based on Cinque's (1990) analysis of parasitic gaps and *tough*-constructions: That is, Chinese allows an extensive A'-bound (resumptive) pro strategy, not in syntax, but in LF. Along this line, all *wh's-in-situ* undergo LF movement in Chinese. Since only *wh*-nominals have corresponding proforms, the resumptive pro strategy is not available for *wh*-adverbs. And hence the noun-adverb asymmetry. The proposal, though stipulative in nature, appears to be technically sound. Therefore, we should look further into other factors to determine whether it is consistent with the general properties of Chinese *wh*-construals.

On conceptual grounds, an immediate concern is that we are to lose the generalization that Chinese interrogative and indefinite *wh*-construals are two instances of one type of A'-dependency, i.e., unselective binding (or simply binding in the context of the Lexical Courtesy Hypothesis). In other words, we have to stipulate two classes of *wh*-nominals: One with intrinsic quantificational force, and the other without. Moreover, Subjacency again has to be ordered before SPELL-OUT, which in turn renders our account of Hindi *wh*-questions irrelevant. Most importantly, as Huang (1984) observes, Chinese allows an empty pronominal only to the extent that it is associated with the closest potential controller:

(52) * zhe-ge ren$_k$, Akiu xihuan [$_{DP}$ hao-ji-ben [$_{CP}$ e$_k$ xie e$_j$]
     this-CL person Akiu like   quite-a few-CL   write
     de   shu$_j$].
     PNM book
     This person, Akiu likes quite a few books that (he/she) wrote.

As shown above, the control relation between the topic and the embedded empty subject is blocked by the matrix subject *Akiu*, a potential controller for the subject EC. When we shift the complex NP to the subject position, the deviance disappears, as evidenced by (53):

(53) zhe-ge ren$_k$, [$_{DP}$ hao-ji-ben [$_{CP}$ e$_k$ xie e$_j$] de shu$_j$] dou
    this-CL person   quite-a few-CL   write PNM book all
    de-le   jiang.
    win-Prf award
    This person, quite a few books that (he/she) wrote has won awards.

This is because the original blocking factor is eliminated. The only exception to this minimality requirement (the Generalized Control Rule (GCR) in Huang's terms) occurs when the controller is inanimate or inhuman. This point can made clear by comparing (52) with (54), where we have *zhe-ben shu* 'this book' instead of *zhe-ge ren* 'this person' as the topic:

(54) zhe-ben shu$_k$, Akiu renshi [$_{DP}$ hao-ji-ge [$_{CP}$ e$_j$ xihuan e$_k$]
    this-CL book Akiu know   quite-a few-CL   like
    de   ren$_j$].
    PNM person
    This book, Akiu knows quite a few people who like (it).

In other words, a resumptive pro, which behaves more like a lexical pronoun and does not observe the GCR, can only be associated with an inanimate/inhuman antecedent in Chinese. However, there is no such restriction in construing Chinese *wh's-in-situ*, as exemplified below:

(55) Akiu xihuan [$_{DP}$ [$_{CP}$ shei xie e$_j$] de shu$_j$] ne?
    Akiu like   who write PNM book Q$_{wh}$
    Who is the person x such that Akiu likes books that (he/she) wrote?

On empirical grounds, first we would like to point out that the control relation, as well as (lexical) pronominal binding, does not display specificity effects:

(56) zhe-ge ren$_k$, [$_{DP}$ naxie [$_{CP}$ ta$_k$/e$_k$ xie e$_j$] de shu$_j$] dou
 this-CL person those (s)he write PNM book all
 de-le jiang.
 win-Prf award
 This person, those books that (s)he wrote has won awards.

(57) zhe-ben shu$_k$, Akiu renshi [$_{DP}$ naxie [$_{CP}$ e$_j$ xihuan e$_k$] de ren$_j$].
 this-CL book Akiu know those like PNM person
 This book, Akiu knows those people who like (it).

As shown above, the presence of an intervening demonstrative such as *naxie* 'those' does not affect long-distance control and pronominal binding. In contrast, long-distance *wh*-construals out of complex NPs are in general blocked by demonstratives:

(58) * [$_{DP}$ naxie [$_{CP}$ shei xie e$_j$] de shu$_j$] dou de-le
 those who write PNM book all win-Prf
 jiang ne?
 award Q$_{wh}$
 Who is the person x such that those books that x wrote has won awards?

(59) * Akiu xihuan [$_{DP}$ naxie [$_{CP}$ shei xie e$_j$] de shu$_j$] ne?
 Akiu like those who write PNM book Q$_{wh}$
 Who is the person x such that Akiu likes those books that x wrote?

This contrast thus lends strong support to the distinction between pronominal variables and so-called "pure" (i.e., [-pronominal]) variables in Cinque's sense.

Another piece of evidence comes from double island constructions. As Cinque (1990) points out, A'-bound pro construals are not entire island-free: They are capable of violating one complex NP island, as evidenced by the following Italian examples (see also Longobardi 1983, Kayne 1984):

(60) ? Carlo, che$_k$ abbiamo ricoverato t$_k$ [con la speranza di
Carlo who we hospitalized with the hope of
poter salvare e$_k$], ...
being able to save

(61) ? Carlo, che$_k$ abbiamo discusso più volte [la
Carlo who we discussed several times the
possibilità di ammettere e$_k$ nel nostro club], ...
possibility of admitting to our club

But when there are more than one island involved, the construals in question are blocked, as illustrated below:

(62) * Carlo, che$_k$ abbiamo ricoverato t$_k$ [con la speranza di
Carlo who we hospitalized with the hope of
aumentare [le probabilità di salvare e$_k$]], ...
increasing the probabilities of saving

(63) * Carlo, che$_k$ ci siamo presentati [con la speranza di
Carlo who we turned up with the hope of
aumentare [le probabilità di salvare e$_k$]], ...
increasing the probabilities of saving

Cinque proposes that the object pro may either undergo *wh*-movement or pied-piping in LF, and it is the latter option that evades strong island effects in (60) and (61) by moving the entire complex NP. On the other hand, even LF pied-piping cannot escape from double islands such as those in (62) and (63), since the higher complex NP blocks its way. The same observation, in contrast, does not obtains for Chinese *wh's-in-situ*, as evidenced by the well-formedness of the following double island constructions:

(64) [$_{DP}$ [$_{CP}$ e$_k$ xihuan [$_{DP}$ [$_{CP}$ shei xie e$_i$] de   shu$_i$]] de
              like   who write   PNM   book   PNM
ren$_k$] zui   rongyi   jiao-dao   pengyou?
person most easily   make-reach   friend
Who is the person x such that [people [who like [books [x wrote]]]] make friends most easily?

(65) ni   bu   xiangxin [$_{DP}$ [$_{CP}$ [$_{DP}$ [$_{CP}$ shei xie e$_i$] de   shu$_i$]
you not   believe   who write PNM book
zui   chang-xiao]   de   shuofa]?
most well-selling PNM   story
Who is the person x such that you do not believe [the story [that [the book [which x wrote]] is best-selling]]?

This again confirms our view that neither LF movement nor pied-piping involves in construing Chinese *wh*-nominals, which in turn casts doubt upon any effort to reduce unselective binding to A'-bound pro binding.

Even more interestingly, Japanese *wh*-questions, which are often cited as typical instances of large-scale LF pied-piping (see, for example, Nishigauchi 1986,1990), pattern with their Chinese counterparts instead of their Italian counterparts, in not displaying double strong island effects, as exemplified below (data due to Masa Koizumi):

(66) [$_{DP}$ [$_{CP}$ [$_{DP}$ [$_{CP}$ dare-ga   kaita] hon-o   sukina] hito-ga
                              who-Nom wrote book-Acc like person-Nom
tomodati-o iti-ban   tukuri   yasui   no?
friend-Acc most   make   easy   Q
Who is the person x such that [people [who likes [books [x wrote]]]] makes friends most easily?

(67) [DP [CP [DP [CP dare-ga   kaita] hon-ga]   itiban-yoku
              who-Nom wrote book-Nom most-good
      urete-iru toyuu] uwasa-o]   sinzite-i-nai   no?
      sell-be that   rumor-Acc believe-be-not Q
      Who is the person x such that you do not believe [the rumor
      [that [the book [which x wrote]] is best-selling]]?

Consequently, Watanabe's (1991) invisible *wh*-movement hypothesis does have advantage over the traditional pied-piping approach at least in one respect: It correctly predicts the well-formedness of (66) and (67). This is because the Q-operators responsible for the long-distance construals can be generated in the upmost DP Spec, and undergo subsequent cyclic movement to the matrix CP Spec without violating either one of the complex NP islands (cf. chapter 1, section 2.5). On the other hand, Nishigauchi's feature-percolation hypothesis makes the same prediction as Cinque's analysis, which is based on the notion of g-projection in Kayne and Longobardi's sense. As a result, (66) and (67) are wrongly ruled out under the LF pied-piping approach.

4. *Wh*-Extraction from Derived Nominals

Another difference between chain formation and unselective binding lies in wh-extraciton from derived nominals. As Stowell (1989) observes, the following contrast can be explained if we assume that the DP Spec in (68b) is filled by the subject of the picture-NP, i.e., *Mary*, while it is left empty in (68a) before extraction applies:

((8)) a.   Who$_k$ did you sell [DP t'$_k$ [D' a [N' picture of t$_k$]]?

       b. * Who$_k$ did you sell [DP Mary [D' 's [N' picture of t$_k$]]?

Consequently, the object of the picture-NP can extract freely in (68a) through the "escape hatch", i.e., the DP Spec. On the other hand, since the escape hatch is not available in (68b), subsequent extraction is blocked by the ECP and Subjacency.

The above contrast does not seem to hold in Chinese long-distance question construals, as evidenced by (69a,b):

(69) a. ta   caina-le [$_{DP}$ yi-xiang [$_{D'}$ [$_{PP}$ dui shei]   de   piping]?
       (s)he adopt-Prf   one-CL   about whom PNM   criticism
       Who$_k$ did (s)he adopt a criticism of t?

    b. ta   caina-le [$_{DP}$ Akiu (de) [$_{D'}$ [$_{PP}$ dui shei] de   piping]]?
       (s)he adopt-Prf   Akiu Poss   about whom PNM criticism
       *Who$_k$ did s/he adopt Akiu's criticism of t$_k$?

Here the syntactic configuration of (69b) is almost identical to that of (69b), except that the PP complement occurs to the left of the head noun. However, the long-distance construal of *shei* 'who' does not display any ECP/Subjacency effect.

In addition, there is a further contrast between the English example (70a) and its Chinese counterpart (70b), where the DPs in question are headed by so-called strong determiners:

(70) a. * Who$_k$ did you sell [$_{DP}$ every/several/all/most [$_{D'}$ [$_{N'}$ picture(s) of t$_k$]]]?

    b. ta   caina-le [$_{DP}$ mei-yi-xiang/hao-ji-xiang/suoyou/daduoshu
       (s)he adopt-Prf   every-one-CL/quite-a few-CL/all/most
       [$_{D'}$ [$_{PP}$ dui   shei]   de   piping]]?
              about whom PNM criticism
       *Who$_k$ did (s)he adopt every/quite a few/all/most criticism(s) of t?

By assuming that a strong determiner either occupies the Spec itself or does not project a Spec position, we correctly rule out (70a). The same observation, however, does not apply to (70b).

Note that the absence of locality effects in (69b) and (70b) cannot be totally subdued by claiming that the CED/Subjacency does not hold in LF. Let's consider first the contrast between (71a,b):

(71) a. Akiu [$_{PP}$ dui   shei] bu   manyi?
         Akiu   about who   not   satisfied
         Who is the person x such that Akiu is not satisfied with x?

   b. * shei$_k$, Akiu [$_{PP}$ dui   t$_k$] bu   manyi?
        who   Akiu   about   not   satisfied

As shown by (71b), overt *wh*-fronting over the PP node results in strong deviance. In comparison, the deviance caused by extraction out of adjunct clauses is relatively minor:

(72) a. ? shei$_k$, Akiu [$_{CP}$ Op$_i$ [$_{IP}$ t$_i$ yi   jian t$_k$]] jiu bu
         who   Akiu   once meet   then not
         zou-le?
         leave-Inc
         Who is the person x such that Akiu didn't leave once he met x?

   b. ? shei$_k$, Akiu [$_{CP}$ Op$_i$ [$_{IP}$ t$_i$ jian-ye-mei-jian t$_k$]]
        who   Akiu   meet-also-not-meet
        jiu zou-le?
        then leave-Inc
        Who is the person x such that Akiu left without meeting x?

This indicates that the ECP is at least partially responsible for the strong deviance of (71b): On the one hand, *dui* 'about' does not count as a q-governor; on the other, antecedent government is blocked by the PP node. In contrast, since *shei* is licensed by the verb *jian* 'meet' in (72a,b), the extraction in question only crosses one barrier (i.e., the CP node), inducing the CED/Subjacency effect.

As a result, if (69b) and (70b) involves LF *wh*-extraction, we would detect deviance at least stronger than that of (72a,b) due to an ECP violation. This prediction, as we have seen above, is not borne out.

5. Reflection on a Syntax-LF Asymmetry

As far as *wh*-construals are concerned, there is a recent trend in the literature to reduce argumentality to referentiality (see, among others, Aoun 1986, Cinque 1989, Rizzi 1990, Tsai 1994), or nominality to pronominality (cf. Cinque 1990). These proposals, though extremely useful in accounting for a wide range of data, do not seem to fully capture a curious generalization observed in Huang (1982): That is, *when* and *where* pattern with *why* and *how* in syntax, while they pattern with *who* and *what* in LF. Here the paradox is that if *when* and *where* are referential (or leave [+pronominal] variables to a similar effect), they should pattern with arguments throughout derivation, either in undergoing long movement, or in binding resumptive pro's. If not, they should only be subject to cyclic movement, patterning with adjuncts. Therefore, other factors have to be introduced to derive this syntax-LF asymmetry.

There are essentially two ways to approach the problem. One is based on Huang's (1982) intuition that *when* and *where* behave like PPs in syntax, but like NPs in LF. In other words, they are syntactically PPs, but semantically NPs. Huang proposes that this is because *when* and *where* are NPs with empty prepositions, as in [PP [P e] *wh*]. Consequently, they may extract freely from the "bare" PP node in LF, given that the CED/Subjacency holds only in syntax. The other is to follow WHAL's (1987) split ECP approach, attributing the adjunct behavior of *when* and *where* to the head-government requirement in PF, and their argument behavior to the (generalized) binding requirement in LF (see also Tsai 1994).

Nevertheless, the problem is compounded by the fact that this marginal behavior of *wh*-adjuncts is not limited to *when* and *where*. As observed by Lin (1992), there is a *how-why* asymmetry in construing Chinese *wh's-in-situ*: *Zenmeyang* 'how' patterns with arguments, while *weishenme* 'why' retains its adjunct characteristics. Tsai (1994) further points out that the *how-why* asymmetry is a subcase of a more general asymmetry between instrumental *how* and purpose *why* on the one hand, and manner *how* and reason *why* on the other. The whole pattern of contrasts is summarized in the following tables (see below for some detailed discussions):

Table 1.

Chinese in-situ Wh-construal	Strong Islands Wh-Islands	Non-Bridge Verb	Others
who	ok	ok	ok
what	ok	ok	ok
where	ok	ok	ok
when	ok	ok	ok
how many-DP	ok	ok	ok
how-AP (predicative)	*	*	ok
resultative how	ok	ok	ok
instrumental how	ok	ok	ok
purpose why	ok	ok	ok
manner how	*	*	ok
reason why	*	*	ok

This paradigm should be further compared with overt wh-fronting in Chinese:

Table 2.

Chinese Wh-fronting	Simple Sentence	Bridge Verb	Others
who	ok	ok	*
what	ok	ok	*
where	*	*	*
when	ok with modals	ok with modals	*
how many-DP	*	*	*
how-AP (predicative)	*	*	*
resultative how	ok	ok	*
instrumental how	*	*	*
purpose why	*	*	*
manner how	ok postverbally	ok postverbally	*
reason why	*	*	*

Given what we have said in chapter 1, the above syntax-LF asymmetry may well reflects a fundamental distinction between Chain-formation and unselective binding in the context of the LCH. That is, *wh*-fronting is subject to Economy considerations such as "minimizing Chain links" in the sense of Chomsky & Lasnik (1991), while in-situ *wh*-construals are relatively cost-free. This can be seen by comparing the far more rigid locality displayed by *wh*-fronting with the unbounded in-situ construals of all but a few *wh*-adverbs.

To reduce ensued complexity, we will single out the most problematic cases such as *zenmeyang* 'how' and *weishenme* 'why'. In the following discussion, we essentially reproduce the observations made in Tsai (1994, 1997), and see how the asymmetries can be accommodated in the current framework.

Let's start with *zenmeyang*, which is three-way ambiguous. When construed with a manner reading, it acts like an adjunct, displaying island effects; when construed with an instrumental reading, it patterns with arguments, lacking any island effect. This point is illustrated by the contrast between (73a) and (73b), where a complex NP island is involved. Only PPs like *yong xiao huo* 'with low heat' and *yong shaguo* 'with a sand pot', but not manner adverbs like *xiaoxinyiyi-di* 'very carefully', are possible answers to (73). In contrast, both readings are valid in simple sentences like (74):

(73) ni   zui xihuan [$_{NP}$ [$_{CP}$ Op$_i$ [$_{IP}$ ta zenmeyang duen t$_i$]]
     you most like   she how   stew
     de   niurou$_i$]?
     PNM beef
   a. What is the means x such that you like best [beef [which she stewed by x]]?
   b.# What is the manner x such that you like best [beef [which she stewed in x]]?

(74) ta   shang-ci   zenmeyang dun   niurou?
     she last-time how   tew   beef
   a. By what means did she stew beef last time?
   b. In what manner did she stew beef last time?

Futhermore, it is not uncommon for *zenmeyang* to function like a predicate, either intransitive as in (75a) or transitive as in (75b): In (75a), *zenmeyang* questions the current state of the subject; in (75b), it questions the consequence affecting the object:

(75) a. Lisi zenmeyang   le?
       Lisi   how   Inc
       What happened to Lisi?

   b. nimen   neng [$_{PP}$ ba wo] zenmeyang?
      you(pl.) can   BA me   how
      What can you do to me?

This predicate usage is also responsible for the resultative reading of postverbal *zenmeyang* in (76a), while the adverbial usage leads to the manner reading in (76b):

(76) a. ta niurou$_i$ duen-de [pro$_i$ zenmeyang]?
       she beef   stew-DE   how
       Till what state did she stew beef?

   b. ta   niurou duen-de   zenmeyang?
      she beef   stew-DE   how
      In what manner did she stew beef?

Also note that postverbal *zenmeyang* is exclusively introduced by the V-*de* complex, which, for some reason, suppresses the instrumental reading and introduces the resultative reading (see below).

Interestingly enough, when postverbal *zenmeyang* is further embedded in a relative clause, only the resultative reading emerges. That is, it patterns with instrumental *zenmeyang* (and hence arguments) rather than manner *zenmeyang*, as shown by the contrast between (77a) and (77b):

(77) ni   zui   xihuan [$_{NP}$ [$_{CP}$ Op$_i$ [$_{IP}$ ta t$_i$ duen-de
      you most   like   she   stew-DE
      zenmeyang]] de   niurou$_i$]?
      how   PNM   beef
      a. What is the state x such that you like best [beef [which she stewed till x]]?
      b. # What is the manner x such that you like best [beef [which she stewed in x]]?

This observation is reflected by the fact that the only possible type of answers to (77) is an AP like *lan-yi-dian de* 'a little more mushy', but never a manner adverb like *xixin-yi-dian-di* 'a little more attentively'. The same pattern of contrasts obtains for other instances of strong islands, such as the sentential subject in (78) and the appositive clause in (79):

(78) [zhe-jian shi, women yao zuo-de zenmeyang] cai
 this-CL matter we need handle-DE how just
 ling-ren-manyi?
 make-people-satisfied
 a. What is the state x such that it is just satisfying [for us to handle this matter till x]?
 b.# What is the manner x such that it is just satisfying [for us to handle this matter in x]?

(79) ni bijiao xiangxin [[na-dao cai, tamen zuo-de zenmeyang]
 you more believe that-CL dish they cook-DE how
 de shuofa]?
 PNM story
 a. What is the state x such that you believe more [the story [that they cooked that dish till x]]?
 b.# What is the manner x such that you believe more [the story [that they cooked that dish in x]]?

What should be further included in this discussion is overt extraction of postverbal *zenmeyang*. Generally speaking, Chinese *wh*-fronting patterns with topicalization to the extent that no control (non-movement) construal is allowed. Namely, it observes Subjacency and the head-government requirement. As we can tell from (80) and (81), the object *shei* 'who' may move as long as Subjacency and the CED are respected; in contrast, preverbal *zenmeyang* cannot undergo *wh*-fronting even in a simple sentence, no matter what reading it is associated with:

(80) a. shei$_i$, ni zui xihuan t$_i$?
 who you most like
 Who do you like most?

    b. shei$_i$, ni kan [tamen zui   xihuan t$_i$]?
       who you think they most like
       Who do you think they like most?

(81) a. * zenmeyang$_i$, tamen yinggai t$_i$ zuo   zhedao cai?
        how   they   should   cook this-CL dish
        How should they cook this dish?

    b. * zenmeyang$_i$, ni kan [tamen yinggai t$_i$ zuo zhedao cai]?
         how   you think they should   cook this-CL dish
         How do you think they should cook this dish?

On the other hand, overt extraction of postverbal *zenmeyang* is allowed, with both manner and resultative readings valid:

(82) ? zenmeyang$_i$ (a), ta   niurou dun-de   t$_i$?
        how   Top   she beef   stew-DE
        a. What is the state x such that she stewed beef till x?
        b. What is the manner x such that she stewed beef in x?

(83) ? zenmeyang$_i$ (a), ni   kan [ta niurou dun-de t$_i$]?
        how   Top   you think she beef   stew-DE
        a. What is the state x such that you think [she stewed beef till x]?
        b. What is the manner x such that you think [she stewed beef in x]?

It is quite clear that this asymmetry is a matter of extraction sites in the syntactic projection. An immediate answer comes from Huang (1991), in which an illuminating picture of Chinese postverbal complementation has been sketched in the spirit of Larson (1988). In the relevant discussion, Huang adopts McConnel-Ginet's (1982) distinction between Ad-VP and Ad-Verb, and translates it into a VP-shell-type analysis. Essentially, there are two types of manner adverbs: the "outer" one is a modifier of a verb phrase, while the "inner" one is a stative predicate which may form a complex predicate with the verb. This distinction is reflected by the contrast between the inner Ad-Verb in (84a) and the outer Ad-VP in (84b):

(84) a. John finished the job quickly/ real fast.

b. John quickly/* fast finished the job.

The distribution of Chinese manner adverbials, as illustrated in (85), fall neatly under the inner/outer pattern:

(85) a. Zhangsan pao-de hen kuai.
 Zhangsan runs fast.

b. Zhangsan hen-kuai-di pao le.
 Zhangsan quickly ran away.

Here I will take the null hypothesis that this pattern holds for their interrogative counterparts as well. A specific view of the distribution of *zenmeyang* is thus in order:

(86)
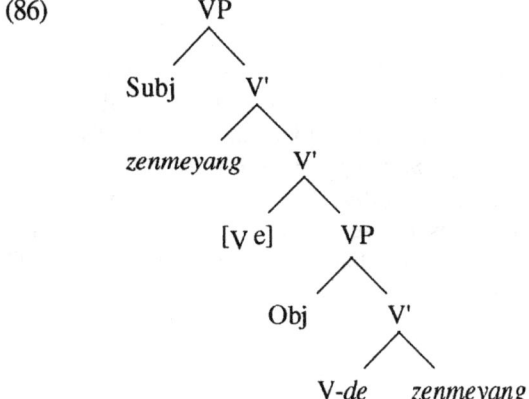

As illustrated by (86), perverbal *zenmeyang* is protected by the higher VP node from being governed by any functional head, while postverbal *zenmeyang* is always head-governed by the lower V node. This move provides a straightforward account of the contrast between (81a,b) and (82,83).

The semantics of *zenmeyang* also follows in a natural way: On the one hand, since the inner position is restricted to a stative predicate, there is no way to introduce the instrumental reading for postverbal *zenmeyang*. Accordingly, the resultative reading comes by default due to the predicate usage of *zenmeyang*. On the other, since preverbal *zenmeyang* is in a modifier position, the resultative reading is suppressed and the instrumental reading pops out.

Under the unselective binding approach outlined in chapter 1, the capability of introducing variables is essential to the survival of long-distance *wh*-construals in a given island construction. For one thing, *zenmeyang* consists of two morphological units: an adverb *zenme* 'how' and a noun head *yang* 'manner/way'. It is thus plausible to assume that instrumental *zenmeyang* projects to an DP, as sketched in (87):

(87)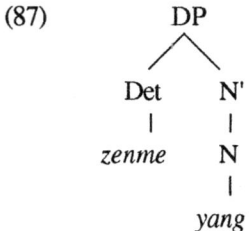

Manner *zenmeyang*, on the other hand, appears to be a genuine adverb, patterning with *zenme* in regard to locality effects. This sort of category-shifting is not uncommon among languages, as the distinction between *some times* and *sometimes* suggests in English.

Furthermore, given Huang's (1991,1992) analysis of postverbal complementation (cf. (86)), resultative *zenmeyang* may well be treated as a predicate nominal in a small clause, i.e., the result clause (RC) itself, as illustrated below:

(88)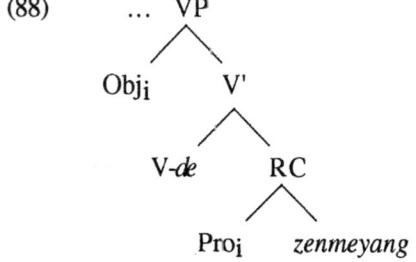

Asymmetries between Chain Formation and Unselective Binding 89

This way, we are able to relate instrumental and resultative *zenmeyang* in terms of their categorical status. Namely, they both count as nominals, and accordingly introduce variables when interpreted in-situ.

Additional support comes from the contrast between purpose and reason *why*: *wei(-le) shenme* 'for what' contrasts with *weishenme* 'why' not only in their readings (i.e., purpose vs. reason), but also in their behavior with respect to strong islands, as shown below:

(89) a. ni zui xihuan [[wei(-le) shenme gongzuo] de ren]?
you most like for what work PNM people
What is the purpose x such that you like best [people [who work for x]]?

b.* ni zui xihuan [[weishenme gongzuo] de ren]?
you most like why work PNM people
What is the reason x such that you like best [people [who work for x]]?

(90) a. ni bijiao xiangxin [[tamen wei(-le) shenme cizhi]
you more believe they for what resign
de shuofa]?
PNM story
What is the purpose x such that you believe more [the story [that they resigned for x]?

b. * ni bijiao xinagxin [[tamen weishenme cizhi] de shuofa]?
you more believe they why resign PNM story
What is the reason x such that you believe more [the story [that they resigned for x]?

(91) a. [women wei(-le) shenme nianshu] cai you yiyi?
we for what study just have meaning
What is the purpose x such that it is just meaningful [for us to study for x]?

b. * [women weishenme nianshu] cai you yiyi?
we why study just have meaning
What is the reason x such that it is just meaningful [for us to study for x]?

(89-91) represent relative, appositive, and subject clause constructions respectively. As we can tell from the contrast between the (a)- and (b)-clauses, only purpose *wei(-le) shenme* gets valid wide-scope readings. Unless we stress the preposition *wei* 'for' or separate *wei* from *shenme* with a suffix *-le*, *weishenme* as a whole counts as a genuine adverb associated with the reason reading. A similar case is also found in French. The distinction between *pour quoi* 'for what' and *pourquoi* 'why' is reflected in the writing system: Only the former is granted the in-situ option and interpreted as purposive (cf. Aoun 1986).

As for *wh*-fronting, both *weishenme* and *wei(-le) shenme* behave exactly like preverbal *zenmeyang*. Namely, they never extract overtly. The head-government requirement thus seems to be a promising candidate for blocking Chinese adjunct fronting in general.

This dichotomy based on the categorical status of *wh*-expressions enjoys a further advantage over that based on referentiality, in that people sharing the same locality judgement of (73), (77-79), and (89-91) do not necessarily agree on our semantic distinction. In particular, the line between reason *why* and purpose *why* is indeed very thin, and at least some of the native speakers consulted feel that *wei(-le) shenme* 'for what' could be either causal or purposeful. On technical grounds, it is also hard to spell out why purpose *why* is more "referential" than reason *why*.

In comparison, the nominality account outlined in chapter 1 (also cf. Huang 1982, Higginbotham 1983, 1985, Reinhart 1992, 1993, Tsai 1994, 1997, and to some extent, Cinque 1990) is relatively uncontroversial. Moreover, since one of defining characteristics of nominals is their ability to refer (or their capability of naming in a more traditional term), the somewhat vague intuition about referentiality is also accounted for.

Finally, In view of the diversity displayed by Chinese *wh*-adjuncts, it is hardly surprising to find that there are sporadic idiosyncrasies in languages with more "agglutinating" *wh*-morphology, such as the asymmetries between **why-ever* and *how-ever* in English, and that between **naze-mo* 'why-ever' and *naze-ka* 'why-some' in Japanese (cf. chapter 1).

As a result, before we can conduct a comprehensive research on the origin of these *wh*-expressions, it suffices to note that *why* in **why-ever* behaves more like Chinese reason *why*, while *how* in *how-ever* behaves more like Chinese instrumental and resultative *how*. Along the same line, *naze* in **naze-mo* patterns with Chinese reason *why*, whereas *naze* in *naze-ka* patterns with Chinese purpose *why* (or more accurately, *for what*).

6. Aftermath

In this chapter, we continue to explore the consequences of the LCH largely on empirical grounds. We have pointed out the inadequacy of characterizing long-distance *in-situ* construals as some kind of long movement in LF. While they do share some properties such as the lack of ECP effects, they differs in the relevance of Subjacency/CED, and in the possibility of construing amount *wh's*. To strengthen our position, we further demonstrate that Chinese *wh*-questions and *dou*-quantification do not interact to display any minimal binding effects (Aoun & Li 1989) or relativized minimality effects (Rizzi 1990), as long as no vacuous quantification is involved.

It is also argued that the A'-bound pro strategy (cf. Cinque 1990) may not play a role in shaping the peculiar behavior of Chinese *wh's-in-situ*, and unselective binding should be identified neither with (resumptive) pronominal binding nor with generalized control in Huang's (1984) sense. Evidence from specificity, inanimacy, and double island effects has testified the substantial discrepancy between unselective binding and A'-pro binding.

As we proceed to consider the asymmetries among Chinese *wh*-adjuncts, as well as those between syntactic and LF operations, it becomes clear that our proposals, though simplistic at first glance, do cover a wide range of data without tolling on the original insight behind the LCH. We demonstrate that the seemingly random distribution and interpretations of Chinese *wh*-adjuncts are actually systematic manifestation of their nominality and certain fundamental properties of binding.

In the next chapter, we will take a step further into the border between syntax and semantics.

CHAPTER THREE

Toward LF Interface

> *If you get the meaning, forget about the words.*
> —Chuang Tze

0. ∃-Closure Extensions

One of the current issues concerning the Syntax-Semantics interface is whether syntactic structures can be related to their logical representations by a fairly explicit mechanism, as sketched in Diesing (1992a,b):

(1) *Mapping Hypothesis:*
  a. Material from VP is mapped into the nuclear scope.
  b. Material from IP (excluding VP) is mapped into a restrictive clause.

Diesing demonstrates that, by splitting a syntactic tree in correspondence with the tripartite representations developed by Kamp (1981) and Heim (1982) (consisting of a quantifier, a restrictive clause, and a nuclear scope), the Syntax-Semantics mapping can be implemented in a straightforward manner, as illustrated the following derivation:[1]

(2) [$_{IP}$ Every donkey [$_{VP}$ kicks a man]]

  → $\forall_x$ [x is a donkey] $\exists_y$ y is a man ∧ x kicks y
     quantifier restrictive clause ∃-closure   nuclear scope

She further argues that this approach sheds light on a number of mysteries around the issue of specificity, whose accounts crucially

93

relies on the assumption that the Existential closure (∃-closure) closes off VP, rather than IP.[2]

A significant consequence of the proposal is that any variable outside the nuclear scope has to be licensed in a marked way, e.g., by strong quantifiers, by generic tense, or by sentential adverbials such as *always* and *usually*. It follows that the IP Spec and the VP Spec have different status in regard to the interpretation of indefinites: An indefinite in the IP Spec must be quantificational, whose interpretation is determined by the type of operator available in a given sentence. On the other hand, an indefinite in the VP Spec is licensed by ∃-closure, yielding a non-specific existential reading. In this case, the indefinite is treated as a cardinal predicate within the nuclear scope (cf. (2)). The IP-VP distinction is backed by two S-structure positions for German subjects, each of which corresponds to one of the readings mentioned above. Take the bare plural *Linguisten* 'linguists' in (3) for example (data from Diesing 1992a):

(3) a. ... weil ja doch [$_{VP}$ Linguisten Kammermusik spielen].
    since Prt Prt   linguists chamber music play
    ... since there are linguists playing chamber music.

b. ... weil [$_{IP}$ Linguisten$_i$ ja doch[$_{VP}$ e$_i$ Kammermusik spielen]].
    since   linguists Prt Prt   chamber music play
    ... since (in general) linguists play chamber music.

As Diesing points out, the bare plural in question is associated with a cardinal (non-specific existential) reading when located lower than the particles *ja* and *doch*, presumably in the VP Spec of (3a). In contrast, the bare plural is interpreted as generic (i.e., quantified over by an implicit generic operator) when located higher than *ja* and *doch*, presumably in the IP Spec of (3b) after raising. The contrast thus follows directly from the mapping hypothesis (1) plus the assumption that ∃-closure applies only to the VP node.

Given the elegant way the theory works out, one may wonder whether the whole conception of the Syntax-Semantics mapping can be further extended to the topic-comment configuration, in view of the cross-linguistic generalization that a topic has to be definite or generic. This point is illustrated by the contrast between (4a,b) in English and that between (5a,b) in Chinese:[3]

(4) a. John, I like.
   b. * A man, I like.

(5) a. Akiu, wo hen xihuan.
      Akiu I very like
      Akiu, I like very much.

   b. * yi-ge ren, wo hen xihuan.
      one-CL person I very like
      * A man, I like very much.

Furthermore, a bare plural is disambiguated when it is topicalized, as shown by the contrast between (6) and (7):

(6) I always salute firemen.
   a. Always$_x$ [x is a fireman]   I salute x
   b. Always $_t$ [t is a time] $\exists_x$ (x is a firemen $\wedge$ I salute x)

(7) Firemen, I always salute.
   a. Always$_x$ [x is a fireman]   I salute x
   b. # Always$_t$ [t is a time] $\exists_x$ (x is a firemen $\wedge$ I salute x)

Both the quantificational reading (6a) and the cardinal reading (6b) are available when the bare plural *firemen* remains in the object position at S-structure.[4] In contrast, the quantificational reading survives the cardinal one in (7), where the bare plural stands in the topic position.

As a starting point, we would like to adopt Chomsky's (1977) view that topicalization involves a base-generated topic and a comment clause containing an empty operator, as illustrated below:

(8) Topic, [Comment Op$_i$ [... e$_i$ ...]].

The extraction of the empty operator creates an open sentence, which is in turn predicated on the "topic-in-situ". The role of the empty operator can be compared to that of a lambda operator in formal semantics. Now let's assume that the empty operator undergoes IP-adjunction in the sense of Lasnik & Saito (1992). An account immediately suggesting itself would be to assimilate the topic-comment structure to the subject-predicate structure in the following terms:

(9) a. Material from IP is mapped into the nuclear scope.

    b. Material from CP (excluding IP) is mapped into a restrictive clause.

As a result, (7) is correctly mapped into the logical representation (7a), where $\exists$-closure would apply vacuously, and hence does not apply to avoid vacuous quantification, as sketched by (10):

(10)   [$_{CP}$ Firemen, [$_{IP}$ Op$_i$ [$_{IP}$ I always admire e$_i$]]]

$\rightarrow$ Always$_x$ [x is a fireman] l$_y$ (*$\exists$)   I admire y
      quantifier   restrictive clause $\exists$-closure   nuclear scope

At first glance, the mapping hypothesis appears to be trivialized under our approach. In the following discussion, we will show that (1) and (9) can be made to follow from a more general algorithm, according to which $\exists$-closure is associated with the notion of "nuclear scope", rather than a specific category like VP, while the syntactic corespondent of a nuclear scope is defined locally by the notion "syntactic predicate" in a cyclic manner, as sketched below:

(11) *Extended Mapping Hypothesis (EMH):*

    a. Mapping applies cyclically, and vacuous quantification is checked derivationally.

    b. Material from a syntactic predicate is mapped into the nuclear scope of a mapping cycle.

    c. Material from XP immediately dominating the subject chain of a syntactic predicate (excluding that predicate) is mapped outside the nuclear scope of a mapping cycle. A subject chain is an A-chain containing a subject (nominative case-marked) position.

    d. Existential Closure applies to the nuclear scope of a mapping cycle, and should be employed only as a last resort.

A syntactic predicate is defined as a (one-place) predicate inducing predication rather than modification.

Section 1 will spell out some general problems which have to be dealt with by anyone who commits herself/himself to the mapping hypothesis. Particularly, we will show that the mapping mechanism is a sort of cyclic operation, presumably working side by side with semantic composition. In section 2, we will show that there are substantial reasons to return to Heim's (1982) original position, i.e., associating ∃-closure with the nuclear scope. This move opens the otherwise closed class of candidates which might be mapped into the nuclear scope (according to Diesing's formulation, there is only one member, namely, VP). On empirical grounds, we will show that non-restrictive relatives and a certain type of secondary predicate display crucial characteristics of the comment clause in (8): they count as syntactic predicates and induce specificity effects on the subject of predication. We will then propose to reformulate the mapping hypothesis in a broader term. Section 3 demonstrates that linguistic variations of indefinite construals, as well as the distinction between individual-level and stage-level predicates, can be accounted for in terms of the copying mechanism developed by Chomsky (1993), without resorting to lowering and VP-external subjects. The claim is that languages (and predicates) differ in the possibility of leaving copies in chain formation: only when a copy is left in the VP Spec can the relevant subject be interpreted within the nuclear scope, and hence licensed by ∃-closure.

1. Mapping as a Cyclic Operation

1.1. The Cyclic Hypothesis

A notable problem with the mapping hypothesis (1) is that it is not entirely clear how it works when a bi-clausal structure is involved, as illustrated below:

(12)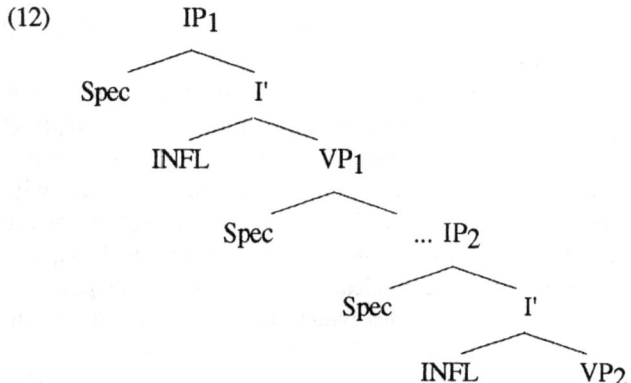

There are three logical possibilities. The first one is to implement the mapping in a top-down manner, which we will reject on empirical grounds, since it wrongly predicts that a variable in the IP$_2$ Spec can be licensed by $\exists$-closure on the VP$_1$ node in (12). As evidenced by (13), embedding a clause with an individual-level predicate like *admirable* does not add to its subject, i.e., *firemen*, an extra cardinal reading:[5]

(13) [IP I [VP think [IP firemen [VP are admirable]]]].

An even more robust argument comes from Chinese indefinite subjects. As Cheng (1991) observes, the well-known specificity/definiteness restriction on Chinese subjects (cf. Li & Thompson 1981, Lee 1986, among others), as shown by the contrast between (14) and (15a,b), is best explained by adopting the mapping hypothesis, given that Chinese indefinites, unlike their English counterparts, lack intrinsic quantificational properties, and the strategy of lowering is not available in Chinese:

(14) *yi-ge ren zou-le.
 one-CL person leave-Prf
 A person left.

(15) a. you yi-ge ren zou-le.
 have one-CL person leave-Prf
 There is a person who left.

b. na-ge   ren   zou-le.
that-CL person leave-Prf
That person left.

Specifically, (14) is ruled out because it contains an unbound variable introduced by *yi-ge ren* 'a person', which is outside the VP and hence beyond the reach of ∃-closure. On the other hand, the variable in question is licensed by the existential predicate *you* 'have' in (15a), and by the demonstrative *na* 'that' in (15b).[6] Now consider the following sentence:

(16) * [IP Akiu [VP shuo [IP yi-ge   ren   [VP zou-le]]]].
        Akiu   say   one-CL person   leave-Prf
Akiu said that a person left.

Recall that, unlike English, there is no way to restore the embedded subject *yi-ge ren* to the lower VP Spec. Neither is the so-called presuppositional reading available, since Chinese indefinites are [-quantificational force] in Diesing's sense. If the mapping algorithm works in a top-down manner, the embedded subject should get licensing from ∃-closure on the matrix VP. This prediction, however, is falsified by the deviance of (16), which is parallel to that of (14).

Another possibility is to map VP_1 and VP_2 simultaneously. As noted by Irene Heim (p.c.), this move inherits the same problem as the top-down approach. Namely, we wrongly predict that the embedded subjects in (13) and (16) can be licensed by ∃-closure on the matrix VP.

The only option left is to implement the mapping cyclically, which, in my opinion, is the correct one. Let's start with (14). Bottom-up-wise, the first IP-VP pair is mapped to (17) according to (1):

(17) ... [IP firemen [VP are admirable]]

   → Gen_x [x is a fireman]   x is admirable

The variable introduced by *firemen* is bound by a generic operator triggered by the generic tense (cf. Wilkinson 1986), and the indefinite itself is mapped into the restrictive clause. On the other hand, since *admirable* counts as an individual-level predicate, whose subject cannot be restored to the VP Spec in Syntax, the following mapping is blocked:

(18) ... [IP firemen [VP ∃ [VP are admirable]]]

—x→ ∃_x x is a fireman ∧ x is admirable

Since the mapping is done in a local manner, ∃-closure due on the next cycle cannot affect the scope interpretation of *firemen*. This move thus correctly predicts the lack of the cardinal reading in (14). Similar situations obtain for (16), as illustrated below:

(19) ... [IP yi-ge ren   [VP ∃ [VP zou-le]]]
         one person   left

→ ∃_x x is a person ∧ x left

(20) ... [IP yi-ge ren   [VP ∃ [VP zou-le]]]
         one person   left

→ * [x is a person] ∃_x x left

As shown by (19), the subject *yi-ge ren* cannot be mapped into the nuclear scope, and therefore is not eligible for licensing from ∃-closure. When *yi-ge ren* does get mapped to the restrictive clause, as in (20), a variable is introduced, but no quantifier is available. Since the operation observes cyclicity (and applies derivationally; see below), nothing from the next cycle may rescue the violation. (16) is then ruled out in the same way as (15a).

A more interesting case comes from topic constructions containing an indefinite subject, as exemplified by (21a,b):

(21) a.* [CP Akiu, [IP Op_i [IP yi-ge nühai   [VP hen xihuan   e_i]]]].
          Akiu   one-CL girl   very like
      ?Akiu, a girl likes.

    b. [CP Akiu, [IP Op_i [IP you yi-ge nühai [VP hen xihuan e_i]]]].
        Akiu   have one-CL girl   very like
       Akiu, there is a girl who likes (him).

As a working hypothesis, we add (9) into the inventory of mapping principles, and tentatively assume that ∃-closure is associated with the nuclear scope rather than VP. Let's start with the lowest cycle of (21a) according to (1):

(22) ... [$_{IP}$ Op$_i$ [$_{IP}$ yi-ge nühai [$_{VP}$ hen xihuan e$_i$]]]
            one girl   very like
→ *λ_x [y is a girl] ∃$_y$ y likes x

Again, an unbound variable is created in the restrictive clause. Now even if the mapping proceeds to the next cycle according to (9), ∃-closure on the relevant nuclear scope (corresponding to IP) cannot license the offending variable, as indicated by the deviance of (21a). In other words, the following mappings should in principle be ruled out:

(23) [$_{CP}$ Akiu, [$_{IP}$ Op$_i$ [$_{IP}$ yi-ge nühai [$_{VP}$ hen xihuan e$_i$]]]]
          Akiu   one   girl   very like
→ Akiu, λ_x (∃$_y$ [y is a girl] y likes x) or
   Akiu, λ_x (∃$_y$ [y is a girl] ∃$_y$ (y likes x))

To achieve this, we have to implement the mapping cyclically, and decide its legitimacy in "real time", i.e., derivationally rather than representationally. On the other hand, since (21b) contains the existential predicate *you* 'have', which contributes quantificational force to the indefinite subject, the variable in question is licensed, and no ∃-closure applies in either cycle:

(24) [$_{CP}$ Akiu, [$_{IP}$ Op$_i$ [$_{IP}$ you yi-ge nühai [$_{VP}$ hen xihuan e$_i$]]]]
          Akiu   have one   girl   very like
→ Akiu, λ_x (∃$_y$ [y is a girl] y likes x)

As a matter of fact, this derivational view of mapping also entails a bottom-up-style composition. As we take a piece of syntactic structure into the machinery, the resulting representation automatically becomes the building block for another cycle of composition. When mapping succeeds, composition is also accomplished. The problem is how big a chunk we should take for a cycle of mapping-composition. The answer, in our opinion, lies in the notion of a syntactic predicate (in contrast to a modifier/restrictor), which, as an unsaturated function in Frege's sense, is ready to play the argument-taking role in composition. We may therefore define a mapping cycle as a domain containing a syntactic predicate and its subject (or whatever it predicates upon), of which the IP in (1) and the CP in (9) are only two outstanding examples. The nuclear scope, accordingly, is the domain of a syntactic predicate, as the VP in (1) and the IP in (9) represents. In section 2.1, we will show how the proposal fits into our characterization of $\exists$-closure, which in turn leads to our formulation of (11).

1.2. The Mapping Geometry of Topics

A fair comment on the theory presented so far concerns that, although it seems justified to say that the mapping mechanism (1) should apply cyclically, extending the same analysis to topic-comment constructions may push things too far. As Hubert Truckenbrodt and Orin Percus (p.c.) points out, a topic and a raised subject have the same status in regard to the mapping geometry. Namely, since both of them are located higher than VP, it is expected that they should be mapped into their respective restrictive clauses, manifesting similar specificity/definiteness effects. If topicalization is an instance of IP-adjunction (Baltin 1982, Lasnik & Saito 1992), (1) correctly predicts the parallel between subject-predicate and topic-comment constructions without resorting to the seemingly redundant statement (9).

However, there is a catch in this picture: it focuses on the similarity shared by topics and subjects, while a crucial distinction between them is missed. That is, a (discourse) topic can never be interpreted as cardinal, but a subject may or may not, depending on its ability to be restored to the VP Spec. From this point of view, the base-generation/non-movement hypothesis (8) is preferred to the adjunction hypothesis. As shown by (25), the base-generation hypothesis in principle rules out the cardinal reading (i.e. the possibility of being quantified by $\exists$-closure), since there is no way to restore the "topic-in-situ" back into VP:

(25)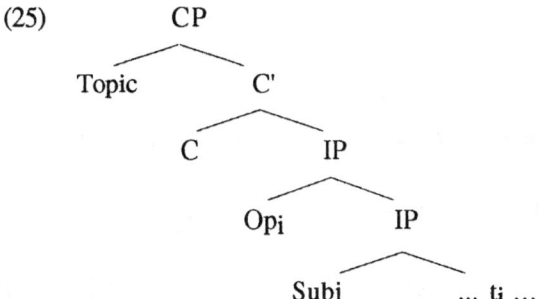

On the other hand, some stipulation has to be made for the adjunction hypothesis to prevent a topic from lowering (Diesing 1992a) or leaving a copy (Chomsky 1993). It is instructive to note that our observation does not necessarily go against the adjunction/movement analysis. In the first place, all the so-called topic island effects observed by Lasnik & Saito (1992) can be attributed to the operator adjunction in (25), as exemplified by (26a-d):

(26) a. * Where$_i$ did, that book, [$_{IP}$ Op$_j$ [$_{IP}$ you put t$_j$ t$_i$]]?

b. * he wonders where$_i$, that book, [$_{IP}$ Op$_j$ [$_{IP}$ you put t$_j$ t$_i$]].

c. * I cleaned the place where$_i$, that book, [$_{IP}$ Op$_j$ [$_{IP}$ you put t$_j$ t$_i$]].

d. * On the table$_i$, that book, [$_{IP}$ Op$_j$ [$_{IP}$ you put t$_j$ t$_i$]].

Besides, there is certainly no point to reconstruct an empty operator, just as we expect of the interpretation of topics. In the second place, it is widely noted that there are two types of topic (cf. Gundel 1974, Kitagawa 1982, Culicover 1991). One is the "discourse" topic, typically associated with the specificity/definiteness effects under discussion here. The other is often called the "contrastive" or "focus" topic. It has been proposed by Culicover (1991) that there are two distinct landing sites for them: the IP adjunction site for a discourse topic, and the Spec of Pol(arity)P for a focus topic. The topic island effects mentioned above are weakened when we stress the topics and eliminate the pauses:

(27) a. ?? She wonders where$_i$ THAT BOOK$_j$ you put t$_j$ t$_i$.

b. ?? I cleaned the place where$_i$ THAT BOOK$_j$ you put t$_j$ t$_i$.

c. ?? On the table$_i$ THAT BOOK$_j$ you put t$_j$ t$_i$.

Since it is substitution (i.e., raising to the PolP Spec) rather than adjunction that applies to the topic in question, A'-movement is not blocked in (27a-c). Another important distinction comes from the fact that a focus topic induces weak crossover effects (cf. Lasnik & Stowell 1991, among others), while a discourse topic does not, as shown by the following contrast (data from Culicover 1991):

(28) a. Robin$_i$, [$_{IP}$ Op$_i$ [$_{IP}$ his$_i$ mother really appreciates t$_i$]].

b. * OBIN$_i$ his$_i$ mother really appreciates t$_i$.

The absence of weak crossover effect in (28a) follows from our account straightforwardly: Since an empty operator does not bear referential dependency, whose major role is to mediate the identification of its trace (Chomsky 1986), no weak crossover configuration is formed. On the other hand, a focus does involve quantification of some sort (Chomsky 1977, Rooth 1985), and hence the weak crossover violation of (28b).

It is also possible to tease them apart in terms of indefinite interpretations. For example, one can say something like (29) in a perfectly good sense, provided that a contrast is made in the discourse:

(29) ONE PAPER, I can handle. (But two papers, that's too much.)

The topic in (29) is construed as cardinal, most naturally under stress. This suggests that the contrastive topic is really a focus, which undergoes raising to the Spec of F(ocus)P (or PolP in Culicover's sense), as illustrated below:

(30)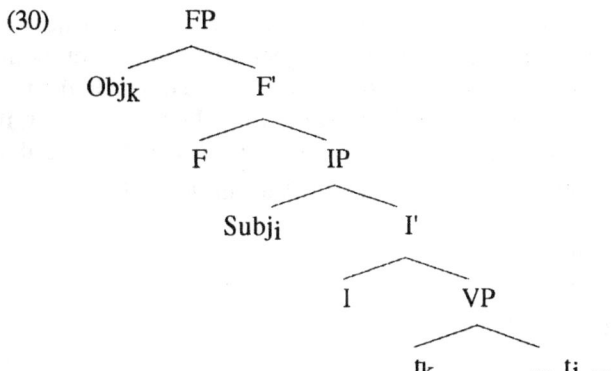

The discourse/focus distinction is even more clearly defined in Chinese. When a topic appears higher than a subject, both the discourse and contrastive construals are allowed, as shown by (31a) and (31b):

(31) a. zhe-pian/*yi-pian lunwen, wo hen xihuan.
 this-CL/one-CL paper I very like
 This paper/*a paper, I like very much.

  b. yi-pian lunwen, wo hai keyi yingfu. (liang-pian, na jiu
 one-CL paper I still can handle two-CL that then
 tai duo le.)
 too much Prt
 One paper, I still can handle. (Two papers, that's too much.)

On the other hand, when a topic appears lower than a subject, the contrastive construal is obligatory:

(32) a. wo zhe-pian lunwen xihuan, *(na-pian lunwen bu xihuan).
 I this-CL paper like that-CL paper not like
 This paper, I like, but that paper, I don't.

  b. wo yi-pian lunwen keyi yingfu, *(liang-pian jiu bu xing le).
 I one-CL paper can handle two-CL then not capable Prt
 One paper, I can handle, but two papers, I am not capable
 (of handling).

It is thus unlikely that the SOV order in (32a,b) is a consequence of double topicalization (i.e. with the subject and the object both topicalized). Otherwise we would expect the presence of an alternative discourse construal and the specificity effect shown by (31a). Rather, it is the object which undergoes focus movement, presumably into the Spec of an FP projection between IP and VP, as illustrated in (33):[8]

(33)

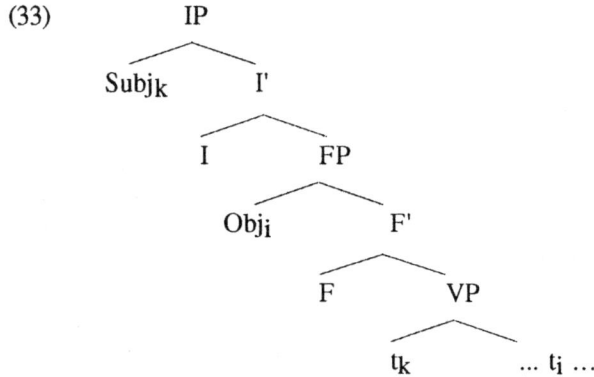

Our position is supported by the fact that a similar word order is also observed in focus constructions like *(lian) . . . ye* '(even) . . . also':

(34) a. Akiu (lian) zhe-dian   qian *(ye) yiao.
        Akiu even this-small-amount money also want
        Akiu even wants this (small) amount of money.

    b. Akiu (lian) yi-mao   qian *(ye) yiao.
        Akiu even one-penny money also want
        Akiu even wants one penny.

As shown by (34a,b), only in the presence of focus markers like *ye* 'also' is the object allowed to front, resulting in the SOV order.[9]

In sum, there seems to be a fundamental distinction between a discourse topic and a focus topic, not only in their syntactic behavior, but also in their mapping geometry. If our analysis is on the right track, then a discourse topic should not be included in the IP-VP cycle, but a focus topic should (here we regard FP as a "split" part of IP (Pollock 1989), whose head bears a V-feature in Chomsky's (1993) sense). Consequently, we correctly predict that focus topics do not display the specificity effects typically associated with discourse topics, since they are eligible for licensing from ∃-closure under reconstruction.

1.3. Summary

We have demonstrated that there are some merits to be gained if we conceive of the syntax/semantics mapping as a cyclic operation. Not only is the local nature of ∃-closure derived in a principled way, but the parallel between subject-predicate and topic-comment constructions also follows, provided that we associate ∃-closure with the nuclear scope instead of VP, and accordingly allow (9) to play along with (1) during mapping. This move, in turn, leads us to the conjecture that the mapping hypothesis has a wider range of application than previously thought. In the next section, we will address this issue, and present a general picture of where the mapping mechanism should apply.

2. ∃-closure as a Last Resort Operation

2.1. The Nature of ∃-closure

In Diesing's (1992a) original conception, the domain of VP and the nuclear scope appears to be synonymous with respect to the application of ∃-closure. In this chapter, we would like to contend that there are some differences between saying that ∃-closure closes off VP and saying that ∃-closure closes off the nuclear scope. Only with the latter is the addition of (9) possible. By claiming so, however, the role of ∃-closure is somewhat blurred. We are thus obliged to address the issue more closely.

The first notable property of ∃-closure is that it does not interact with other types of quantification. As demonstrated by Diesing, the following multiple-quantified sentence actually has three distinct logical representations:

(35) Every cellist played some variations.
 a. Every$_x$ [x is a cellist] Some$_y$ [y is a variation] x played y
 b. Some$_y$ [y is a variation] Every$_x$ [x is a cellist] x played y

c. Every$_x$ [x is a cellist] $\exists_y$ y is a variation $\wedge$ x played y

In the first two interpretations, the object is quantificational. Namely, it undergoes QR (quantifier raising), and interacts with the subject, resulting in the scope ambiguity: *every cellist* takes scope over *some variations* in (35a), while *some variations* takes scope over *every cellist* in (35b). Both interpretations presuppose the existence of a set of variations: (35a) should be read as 'Every cellist played some of the variations'; (35b) should be read as 'There are some variations which every cellist played'. These are so-called presuppositional readings for *some*. In contrast, the object is not quantificational in (35c), whose quantificational force is contributed by $\exists$-closure. Accordingly, *some* is read as cardinal, and there is no pre-established set of variations. The fact that (35) can not be construed as (36), which is roughly a logical equivalent of (35b) without the presupposition, indicates that the existential quantifier introduced by $\exists$-closure can never be QRed:

(36) $\exists_y$ Every$_x$ [x is a cellist] y is a variation $\wedge$ x played y   or
    $\exists_F$ Every$_x$ [x is a cellist] F(variation) $\wedge$ x played F

$\exists$-closure thus has a "last resort" quality, applying only in default of other types of quantification, as the term "closure" implies. Though associating $\exists$-closure with VP does characterize its narrow-scope-taking behavior, the stipulation itself does not dictate the peculiar property mentioned above. On the other hand, if we associate $\exists$-closure with the nuclear scope, as originally proposed by Heim (1982), then it applies dynamically in correspondence with the domain of a syntactic predicate. Under this view, $\exists$-closure applies to eliminate unwarranted variables within a mapping cycle, ensuring that the syntax-semantics mapping in question eventually converges. This move has an interesting implication: Economy is observed in Semantics as well. It is more so because existential closure actually involves LF insertion of an existential operator, a costly operation at any rate.

Second, $\exists$-closure does not induce relativized minimality effects. This point can be illustrated by the dual readings of Chinese wh's-in-situ, i.e., indefinite vs. interrogative. As noted by Cheng (1991) and Li (1992a), among others, Chinese *wh's-in-situ*, in parallel to Chinese indefinites, do not possess inherent quantificational force (see also M.

Hsieh 1994, and Liu 1994 for some peculiar properties of Chinese indefinite *wh's*). First compare (37a) and (37b,c,d):

(37) a. Akiu chi-le shenme (ne)?
Akiu eat-Prf what Q
What did Akiu eat?

b. Akiu mei chi shenme.
Akiu have-not eat what
Akiu didn't eat anything.

c. Akiu dagai/keneng chi-le shenme.
Akiu probably/possibly eat-Prf what
Akiu probably/possibly ate something.

d. Akiu shenme-dou chi.
Akiu what-all eat
Akiu eats everything.

While *shenme* 'what' gets the expected interrogative reading in (37a), it behaves like a negative polarity item in (37b), and is existentially quantified in (37c) and universally quantified in (37d). To take a closer look, we will start with Cheng's proposal, where *shenme* 'what' is treated as a polarity item in all four cases. In (37a), the optional *wh*-question marker *ne* and its empty counterpart are both triggers and binders, so is *dou* 'all' in (37d). On the other hand, negation and modality operators are triggers in (37b,c) respectively, while $\exists$-closure provides binders in both cases.[10] We may thus present the logical representations of (38a-d) as follows:

(38) a. $?_x$ [x is a thing] Akiu ate x
b. $\neg \exists_x$ x is a thing $\wedge$ Akiu ate x
c. $\lozenge \exists_x$ x is a thing $\wedge$ Akiu ate x
d. $\forall_x$ [x is a thing] Akiu eats x

Now let's consider a curious fact: (38b) is not the only reading of (37b), which can also be construed as a *wh*-question, as evidenced by the presence of the Q-marker *ne* in (39). The same observation applies to (37c), as in (40):

(39) Akiu mei chi shenme (ne)?
  Akiu have-not eat what Q
  What did Akiu not eat?

(40) Akiu dagai/keneng chi-le shenme (ne)?
  Akiu probably/possibly eat-Prf what Q
  What did Akiu probably/possibly eat?

In contrast, *shenme* 'what' cannot be construed as existentially quantified in (37a), or as interrogative in (37d), as illustrated by (41) and (42) respectively:[11]

(41) * Akiu chi-le shenme.
  Akiu eat-Prf what
  Akiu ate something.

(42) * Akiu shenme-dou chi (ne)?
  Akiu what-all eat Q
  What did Akiu eat all (the time)?

Since wh's-in-situ are treated as polarity items under Cheng's approach, they differ from indefinites in that ∃-closure is available for the former only when triggered by negation and modality operators, but no such trigger is required for the latter. This accounts for the deviance of (41), since there is neither a trigger for ∃-closure nor a trigger-binder such as *ne* or *dou*.

A question comes to mind at this stage: Why doesn't ∃-closure block the interrogative construals in (39) and (40), just as *dou* 'all' does in (42)? There is no *a priori* reason to discriminate between universal and existential quantifiers in regard to relativized minimality, and saying that ∃-closure is optionally triggered only trivializes the original insight. A more promising answer, it seems, lies in the timing of ∃-closure. That is, if the relevant existential quantifier is introduced along Syntax-Semantics mapping, then it is natural that it does not induce minimality effects either in Rizzi's (1990) sense or in Aoun & Li's (1989) sense. If there is no unbound variable in a logical representation after mapping, as in the case of (39) and (40), ∃-closure simply does not apply.

Alternatively, we may also hypothesize that negative operators such as *mei* 'have-not' and probability operators such as *dagai* 'probably' can be either strong or weak.[11] When they count as strong operators, interrogative construals from higher scope positions are in principle blocked, i.e., inducing so-called inner island effects. Furthermore, since *mei* and *dagai* cannot by themselves serve as binders of indefinites, ∃-closure must apply to license the *wh's-in-situ* in question. ∃-closure thus comes out as a last resort. In case that *mei* and *dagai* do count as weak, the interrogative construal from the Q morpheme becomes possible, as in (39) and (40), and ∃-closure remains as a last resort when there is no other potential binder.

The latter approach raises an interesting conceptual problem within the minimalist framework (Chomsky 1993): The crucial function of ∃-closure is to license unbound variables within the nuclear scope. Namely, it is not self-serving, which goes against the grain of the Greed principle.[13] The conclusion, however, is not forced if we reinterpret ∃-closure's role in mapping theoretical terms. Recall that we generalize the IP-VP split as formulated in (1) to a subject-predicate split in section 1.1. The intuition which we pursue here is that ∃-closure is a disambiguation device guaranteeing that there is only one open place per predication. It has been well established that the external q-role, if any, is unique to a syntactic predicate (i.e., a predicate which triggers predication rather than modification or restriction). A related observation is also made by Napoli (1989), according to whom a predicate can have only one subject role player. It follows that predication (in contrast to θ-role assignment) should in principle involve one-place predicates, in particular, one-place complex predicates. ∃-closure certainly works well to serve this purpose:

(43) a. [IP Subj$(x)_i$ [VP t_i ... Obj (y) ...]]
    → QP$_x$ [Subj(x)] λ_x $\exists_y$ (x ... Obj(y) ...)

b. [CP Topic, [IP Op$_i$ [IP ... t_i ...]]]
    → QP$_x$ [Topic(x)] λ_x ($\exists$) (... x ...)

As illustrated by (43a), there are two potential open places within VP: one is the trace left by subject raising; the other is the variable to be introduced by the indefinite object. As mapping proceeds, the object variable is "sealed off" by ∃-closure, while the subject trace, already indexed, triggers the predication on the raised subject. As for the topic-comment construction (43b), there is a one-to-one correspondence between the empty operator and the lambda operator. Since variable-licensing is settled on the previous cycle (i.e., within the domain of IP, cf. section 1.1), any variable beyond IP has to be licensed in a marked way. Hence the specificity /definiteness effects on topics.

Along this line, we may unify (1) and (9) in terms of (11b) and (11c), based on the assumption that (11a) and (11d) play a major role in the syntax-semantics interface:

(11) *Extended Mapping Hypothesis (EMH):*
    a. Mapping applies cyclically, and vacuous quantification is checked derivationally.
    b. Material from a syntactic predicate is mapped into the nuclear scope of a mapping cycle.
    c. Material from XP immediately dominating the subject chain of a syntactic predicate (excluding that predicate) is mapped outside the nuclear scope of a mapping cycle. A subject chain is an A-chain containing a subject (nominative case-marked) position.
    d. Existential Closure applies to the nuclear scope of a mapping cycle, and should be employed only as a last resort.

So far we have limited our discussion to the conceptual plausibility of the EMH. The next step, therefore, is to examine its empirical consequences, to see if the same analysis can be extended to other types of syntactic predicates. This will be our main task for the following sections.

2.2. Non-restrictive Relative Clauses

A ready candidate for our inspection comes from non-restrictive relativization, which shares a cluster of properties with topicalization. First, non-restrictive relativization does not display weak crossover effects, as evidenced by (44) and its Chinese counterpart (45):[14]

(44) [DP The students], [CP who_i [IP their_i teachers like t_i very much]], ...

(45) [DP naxie [CP Op_i [IP tamen_i (-de) laoshi hen xihuan t_i]] de xuesheng]
those   their   teacher very like
PNM student

Second, the paired reading shown by the *wh*-question (46a) is not available for relativization in (46b) and topicalization in (46c):

(46) a. Who likes whom?
     b. * The couple [who likes whom]
     c. * The couple, he likes her.

The contrast suggests that relative *wh's* and empty operators are not subject to scope absorption in the sense of Higginbotham & May (1981). In other words, they can not be "paired" in a particular CP domain. Third, neither non-restrictive relativization nor topicalization display scope interaction effects. As noted by May (1985), the following *wh*-question is ambiguous:

(47) What did everyone buy for Max?
     a. What is x, x a thing, such that for every y, y a person, y bought x for Max?
     b. For every y, y a person, what is x, x a thing, such that y bought x for Max?

(47a) is the so-called collective reading, with *what* taking scope over *everyone*. (47b) is the so-called distributive reading, with *everyone* taking wide scope. The same type of scope interaction, however, cannot be found in non-restrictive relative clauses and topic-comment structures, as shown by (48) and (49) respectively:

(48) [DP The present], [which_i [everyone bought t_i for Max]], ...

(49) [Top The present], [Op_i [everyone bought t_i for Max]].

In both (48) and (49), *everyone* can only be construed as collective, and no ambiguity is detected.[15] We thus conclude that the operators involved in non-restrictive relativization and topicalization are not quantifiers. Rather, we may call them "predicate markers", whose function is to define the domain of a complex predicate. This functional account, nevertheless, should be understood as a rationale behind relativization and topicalization. The mechanical execution of the operator movement, we believe, is achieved by morphological checking in Chomsky's (1993) sense. In other words, the empty operator in (48) and (49) should be treated like a relative *wh*, i.e., [+wh] but [-Q]. By checking its features on a functional projection, say, the CP Spec, the operator is in a c-commanding position to define the domain of a predicate, i.e., the relative clause in (48) or the comment clause in (49).

Here an important question emerges: What is the semantic distinction between (48) and (49) if both the non-restrictive relative clause and the comment clause are to be treated as predicates? Intuitively speaking, the semantic type of (48) should remain the same as that of its head after composition, i.e., an entity, whereas the composition of (49) should produce a truth value. Therefore, they cannot both involve predication. As a matter of fact, the relative clause in (48) behaves rather like an adjective associated with modification, which in principle does not change the semantic type of its "subject" (cf. Kamp 1975). The distinction, therefore, falls under the dichotomy between modification and predication, as the classic discussion of the difference between (50a,b) has already revealed:

(50) a. That is a big butterfly.

b. That butterfly is big.

As noted by Higginbotham (1985), the grading of bigness in (50a) is relative to the average size of a butterfly, while the grading is rather open-ended in (50b). Since a big butterfly could be small in comparison with other creatures, (50a) could hold true for an object for which (50b) counts as false. (50a) may be paraphrased as (51a) with the modifier *big* being treated as a conjunct, and (50b) as (51b):

(51) a. That is a butterfly, and it is big (for a butterfly).

b. That butterfly is big (for an x).

Toward LF Interface

As a comparison, Higginbotham further points out that there is another type of adjectival usage which does not induce restriction, as in "Look at the little butterfly". Since no assertion is made about the littleness relative to the average size of a butterfly, *little* can be treated as an ordinary conjunct, as paraphrased below:

(52) Look at the butterfly, and it is little.

What is involved here seems to be descriptive (based upon our world knowledge that butterflies are little things) rather than restrictive, a quality closer to (51b) than to (51a).

In parallel to the non-restrictive usage of adjectives, we also find a class of relatives which induce no restriction on head nouns. They are traditionally called non-restrictive or appositive relatives, often characterized by the tendency to form an isolated intonation group, as exemplified by (54):

(53) The man who has a big head got stuck in the manhole.

(54) The man, who has a big head, got stuck in the manhole.

Although restrictive and non-restrictive relatives almost have the same syntactic configuration as far as their internal structures are concerned, they do have different status in regard to the mapping geometry. That is, the restrictive relative in (53) should be mapped into a restrictive clause, while its non-restrictive counterpart in (54) should be mapped into the nuclear scope, as illustrated by (55a,b) respectively:

(55) a. The$_x$ [x is a man ∧ x has a big head] x got stuck in the manhole

b. The$_x$ [x is a man] x has a big head ∧ x got stuck in the manhole

It thus seems plausible to generalize the modification-predication dichotomy further to the distinction between restrictive and non-restrictive relatives. As a matter of fact, the same intuition has been pursued intensively in the literature. For example, Jackendoff (1977) distinguishes an appositive from a restrictive modifier by claiming that the former is a sisters of N", whereas the latter is a sister of N'. Following Emonds (1979), Napoli (1989) treats appositives as adjuncts under the I' node, which directly denies non-restrictive relatives their modifierhood. Safir (1986), on the other hand, proposes that non-restrictive relatives will not be attached to N" until a level after LF, i.e., LF', based on a set of binding puzzles typically associated with them (also cf. McCawley 1982). For the purpose of this chapter, we may tentatively treat a non-restrictive relative as a conjunct of the main predicate. As a result, (53b) has the following structure:

(56) The man$_i$, [$_{CP}$ who$_j$ [$_{IP}$ t$_i$ has a big head]] and [$_{VP}$ t$_i$ got stuck in the manhole]

An outstanding prediction of the EMH in this respect is that an indefinite subject cannot be construed as cardinal in the configuration of (56), since there is no way to restore it into only one of the conjuncts (namely, the main predicate) due to the across-the-board constraint. The other conjunct, i.e., the non-restrictive relative, behaves exactly like a comment clause in topicalization, allowing no reconstruction (cf. section 1.2). This prediction is borne out, as evidenced by the contrast between (57a,b) with SOME standing for strongly quantified (presuppositional) *some*, and Sm its weakly quantified (cardinal) counterpart (cf. Milsark 1974, Ioup 1975, Barwise & Cooper 1981, Reuland 1983, De Jong & Verkuyl 1985, Higginbotham 1987, Reinhart 1987, Partee 1988, and Diesing 1992a, among others):

(57) a. SOME/Sm fool who has a big head got stuck in the manhole.

b. SOME/*Sm fool, who has a big head, got stuck in the manhole.

The specificity effect associated with non-restrictive relatives is also found in the case of indefinite objects, as shown by the following contrast:

(58) a. The gas company will fire SOME/Sm fool who has a big head.

b. The gas company will fire SOME/*Sm fool, who has a big head.

The non-restrictive relative in (58b) behaves rather like a secondary predicate (cf. Rothstein 1983), and can be paraphrased as a separate conjunct:

(58') The gas company will fire some fool, and (s)he have a big head.

As the paraphrase indicates, the subject of non-restrictive relativization has to be specific (or familiar in the sense of Heim 1982 and Enç 1991). This is exactly the property which presuppositional *some* contributes to the object *fools* in (58b). The strong quantified object (i.e., *SOME fool*) is therefore preferred to the weakly quantified one (i.e., *Sm fool*). Here the EMH again makes the right prediction: Since only the non-restrictive relative in (58b) counts as a syntactic predicate, it takes *some fool* as the subject, and together they form a mapping cycle, as sketched below:

(59)

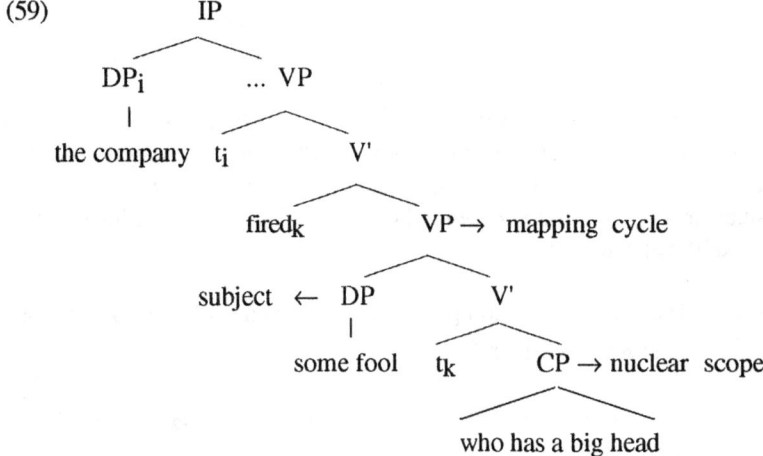

The non-restrictive relative is located in an inner adjunct position within the lower VP shell, serving as a complex predicate (cf. Larson 1988, Huang 1989b, Hale & Keyser 1991). The effect of ∃-closure thus shows up on the subject of predication in the relevant cycle (i.e., the lower VP node). It should be further pointed out that the object *some fool* will not be exactly in the lower VP Spec at LF either if we follow Diesing in claiming that presuppositional indefinites obligatorily undergoes QR, or if we adopt Chomsky's proposal that object NPs move covertly to the Spec of AGR_O under morphological checking. As a result, we are bound to consider a Chain an LF object (Chomsky 1991), and treat it accordingly in mapping theoretical terms.

The next step of mapping then applies where the main predicate discharge its external q-role, i.e., the Spec of IP. In other words, IP is the next mapping cycle, and I', the sister node of the subject *company*, is mapped into the nuclear scope, as illustrated below:

(59')

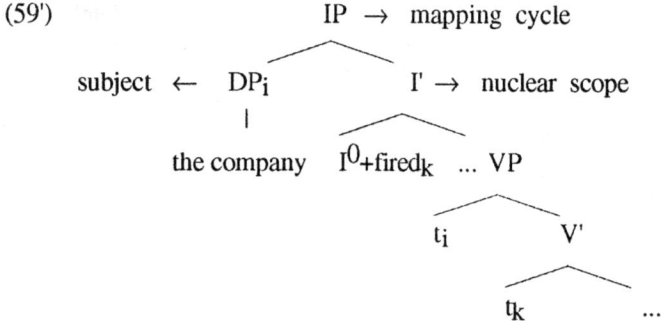

The restrictive relative in (58a), on the other hand, serves as a modifier in DP projections. Consequently, it is mapped into the restrictive clause in the case of presuppositional *some*, and stays in the nuclear scope when *some fool* is licensed by ∃-closure, as illustrated by (60a,b) respectively:

(60) a. The$_x$ [x is a gas company] some$_y$ [y is a fool ∧ ∃$_z$ (z is a big head ∧ y has z)]   x fired y

b. The$_x$ [x is a gas company] ∃$_y$ y is a fool ∧ ∃$_z$ (z is a big head ∧ y has z) ∧ x fired y

It is also instructive to note that, within the relative clauses, there is another cycle of mapping triggered by the predicate *has a big head*, during which ∃-closure applies to license the cardinal reading of *a big head*.

On empirical grounds, this "dynamic" version of mapping hypothesis is further supported by Percus's (1994) observation that, in addition to unergative subject indefinites, certain non-subject experiencer arguments also receive obligatory quantificational readings.

He correlates this peculiarity to a unique thematic role of object experiencer predicates, which may well counts as external and triggers predication on the experiencer argument in question. Since no raising is involved (at least in the immediate mapping geometry), the obligatory presence of specificity is expected under the EMH.

Moreover, Jonas & Bobaljik (1993) observes that a (non-specific) indefinite subject always precedes a (overtly) shifted direct object in Icelandic, which should be impossible under Diesing's approach. Bobaljik (1994) points out further that this paradox calls for a more dynamic splitting similar to the one dictated by the EMH.

If the above analysis is on the right track, then we should be able to find the same patterns in Chinese/Japanese-type languages, where NP projections are head-final, and relative clauses are uniformly located in prenominal positions. First consider the following Chinese examples:

(61) a. Akiu zai-xie [DP na-ben [CP Op$_i$ [dajia   dou hui xihuan e$_i$]]
     Akiu Prg-write   that-CL   people all will like
     de   shu].
     PNM book
     Akiu is writing that book which everybody will like.

  b. Akiu zai-xie [DP [CP Op$_i$ [dajia   dou hui xihuan e$_i$]] de
     Akiu Prg-write   people all will like   PNM
     na-ben   shu].
     that-CL book
     Akiu is writing that book, which everybody will like.

As shown by (61a), when a relative clause appears lower than a determiner, i.e., the definite specifier *na-ben*, the reading is restrictive. It could be the case that there are several books which *Akiu* is planning to write, and (61a) asserts that he is writing the would-be-popular one. In comparison, when a relative clause appears higher than a determiner, as in (61b), the reading is non-restrictive. What is asserted here is that *Akiu* is writing a book which is salient in the context, and the book will be popular.[16] Now we substitute *yi-ben* 'one-CL' for *na-ben* in (61a,b). The restrictive/non-restrictive asymmetry emerges (also cf. Tang 1975, Hou & Kitagawa 1987), as shown by the contrast between (62a,b):

(62) a. Akiu zai-xie [$_{DP}$ yi-ben [$_{CP}$ Op$_i$ [dajia dou hui xihuan e$_i$]]

    Akiu Prg-write   one-CL   people all will like
    de   shu].
    PNM book
    Akiu is writing a book which everybody will like.

  b. * Akiu zai-xie [$_{DP}$ [$_{CP}$ Op$_i$ [dajia dou hui xihuan e$_i$]]
    Akiu Prg-write   people all will like
    de   yi-ben   shu].
    PNM one-CL book
    Akiu is writing a book, which everybody will like.

The result follows straightforwardly from the EMH if we treat the nonrestrictive relative in (62b) as a syntactic predicate, and *yi-hen shu* 'a book' as its subject within the DP cycle.[17] Since the indefinite subject can be licensed neither by ∃-closure on the next cycle (cf. section 1.1) nor by $-closure on the current cycle through reconstruction (cf. section 1.2), the sentence is ruled out. In contrast, the restrictive relative in (62a), as a modifier, does not trigger predication. And no definiteness effect is detected, just as expected. The same observation holds for Japanese relative clauses, as exemplified below (data due to Hiroyuki Ura):

(63) a. ano [[e$_i$ ringo-o   katta] Op$_i$] hito
     that   apple-Acc bought   person
    The person who bought apples

  b. [[e$_i$ ringo-o   katta] Op$_i$] ano hito
           apple-Acc bought   that person
    The person, who bought apples

(64) a. san-ni-no   [[e$_i$ ringo-o   katta] Op$_i$] hito
    three-CL-Gen   apple-Acc bought   person
    Three persons who bought apples

  b. * [[e$_i$ ringo-o   katta] Op$_i$] san-ni-no   hito
        apple-Acc bought   three-CL-Gen person

Toward LF Interface *121*

Three persons, who bought apples

As Masa Koizumi and Hiro Ura (p.c.) point out, the restrictive/non-restrictive distinction between (a)- and (b)- clauses of (63) and (64) is parallel to that of Chinese relative clauses. The same pattern of contrasts once again emerges when non-restrictive relativization (and hence predication) is involved, as shown by the deviance of (64b).

As a first approximation, we may analyze the restrictive relative in (62a) as a sister of N', as illustrated in (65a), and the non-restrictive relative in (62b) as an adjunct of DP, as illustrated in (65b):

(65) a. restrictive relative:

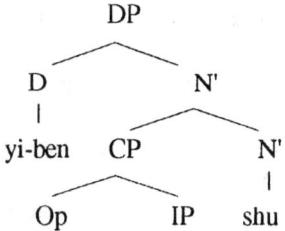

b. non-restrictive relative:

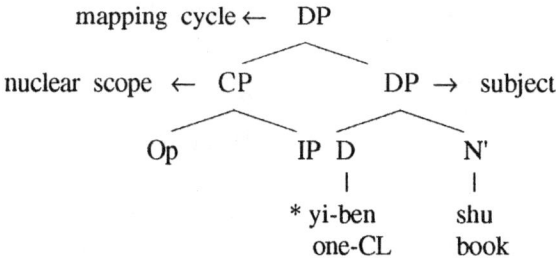

In (65a), the CP serves as a modifier, and no predication is involved. Therefore, there is no mapping cycle in the DP except a trivial one within the IP node. On the other hand, the CP in (65b) does trigger predication, and an independent mapping cycle is formed according to the EMH. The subject in question, i.e., *yi-ben shu* 'a book', cannot be restored back into the nuclear scope (the CP node). Nor can it get licensed from within the current cycle (the higher DP node). The mapping thus fails, and (62b) is correctly ruled out.

One thing has to be made clear before we leave this section. It is not easy to characterize Chinese non-restrictive relatives in such a way that we can get the desired semantics as in English: Since VP projections are essentially head-first in Chinese (vs. head-final in Japanese), there is no inner adjunct position to the left of head verbs. Consequently, while Japanese non-restrictive relativization can be treated as the mirror image of what happens in (60), its Chinese counterpart cannot. Something more, therefore, has to be said about either the mapping mechanism itself or the empirical status of Chinese non-restrictive relatives. We will delay the discussion till section 2.4.

2.3. Existential Constructions and Predication Licensing

2.3.1. Existential Predicates and (In)definiteness Restrictions

In our discussion of Chinese non-restrictive relativization, we tacitly avoided *use*-type verbs like *du* 'read' (vs. "creation" verbs like *xie* 'write') since they presuppose the existence of their objects (cf. Diesing 1992a). For example, the contrast between (62a,b) is blurred once we replace *zai-xie* 'is writing' with *du-guo* 'read (pst.)':

(66) a.   Akiu du-guo   [DP yi-ben [CP Op$_i$ [dajia dou hui xihuan e$_i$]]
      Akiu read-Exp   one-CL   people all will like
      de   shu].
      PNM book
      Akiu read a book which everybody will like.

    b. ? Akiu du-guo   [DP [CP Op$_i$ [dajia dou hui xihuan e$_i$]] de
      Akiu read-Exp   people all will like   PNM
      yi-ben shu].
      one-CL book
      Akiu read a book, which everybody will like.

To make a solid case out of the restrictive/non-restrictive asymmetry, we ought to find a construction where strongly quantified NPs are not allowed. Existential sentences with *you* 'have' are exactly what we need here:

(67) a. wo   you   yi-ge   erzi.
         I   have   one-CL   son
         I have a son.

   b. *wo   you   na-ge/mei(-yi)-ge/da-duo-shu-de erzi.
         I   have   that-CL/every(-one)-CL/most   son
       *I have the/every/most son(s).

You in (67a) expresses possession, and its subject is thematic. *You* may also express existence. As Huang (1987) observes, existential *you* only allows non-thematic subjects, which could be a locative nominal or simply an empty expletive, as shown by (68a) and (69a) respectively:

(68) a. fangjian-li   you   yi-ge   nühai.
         room-inside   have   one-CL   girl
         In the room, there is a girl.

   b. *fangjian-li   you   na-ge/mei(-yi)-ge/da-duo-shu-de nühai.
         room-inside   have   that-CL/every(-one)-CL/most   girl
       *In the room, there is/are the/every/most girl(s).

(69) a. e   you   yi-ge   nühai   zai   fangjian-li.
              have   one-CL   girl   at   room-inside
         There is a girl in the room.

   b. *e   you   na-ge/mei(-yi)-ge/da-duo-shu-de nühai   zai   fangjian-li.
              have   that-CL/every(-one)-CL/most   girl   at   room-inside
       *There is/are the/every/most girl(s) in the room.

Furthermore, as indicated by the deviance of (b) clauses of (67-69), both possessive *you* and existential *you* induce the (in)definiteness effects on their (structural) objects.[18] For one thing, although the existence of the object *erzi* 'son' in (67) is not directly asserted by possessive *you*, it is entailed by the semantics of possession. Besides, (67a) does not seem to have the literal meaning "I own a son". Rather, it should be read as "there is a son of mine". Consequently, if we replace *erzi* with a stereotype of possessions like *fangzi* 'house', the contrast is weakened:

(70) a. wo you yi-dong fangzi.
         I   have one-CL   house
         I have a house.

   b. ? wo you na-dong/mei(-yi)-dong/da-duo-shu-de fangzi.
        I   have that-CL/every(-one)-CL/most   house
        ? I have the/every/most house(s).

The deviance of (b) clauses is thus uniformly attributed to the incompatibility between existential assertion and definiteness (cf. Barwise & Cooper 1981, Huang 1987, among others), with the weakest violation when possession is involved.[19] If our analysis is on the right track, non-restrictive relatives should in principle be ruled out in *you*-sentences. This prediction is borne out, as evidenced by the following contrasts:

(71) a. wo you [$_{DP}$ yi-ge [$_{CP}$ Op$_i$ [e$_i$ xihuan nianshu]] de erzi].
         I   have one-CL   like studying PNM son
         I have a son who likes studying.

   b. * wo you [$_{DP}$ [$_{CP}$ Op$_i$ [e$_i$ xihuan nianshu]] de yi-ge erzi].
        I   have   like studying PNM one-CL son
        ?? I have a son, who likes studying.

(72) a. fangjian-li you [$_{DP}$ yi-ge [$_{CP}$ Op$_i$ [e$_i$ dai-zhe hong
         room-inside have   one-CL   wear-Dur red
         maodou]] de nühai].
         cloak   PNM girl
         In the room, there is a girl who wears a red cloak.

   b.* fangjian-li you [$_{DP}$ [$_{CP}$ Op$_i$ [e$_i$ dai-zhe   hong maodou]]
       room-inside have   wear-Dur red   cloak
       de yi-ge   nühai].
       PNM one-CL   girl
       ?? In the room, there is a girl, who wears a red cloak.

(73) a. e you [DP yi-ge [CP Op$_i$ [e$_i$ dai-zhe   hong maodou]]
         have   one-CL   wear-Dur red cloak
         de   nühai] zai fangjian-li.
         PNM   girl   at   room-inside
         There is a girl who wears a red cloak in the room.

   b.* e you [DP [CP Op$_i$ [e$_i$ dai-zhe   hong maodou]] de
       have   wear-Dur red cloak   PNM
       yi-ge   nühai] zai fangjian-li.
       one-CL girl   at   room-inside
     ?? There is a girl, who wears a red cloak, in the room.

As indicated by the deviance of (b) clauses of (71-73), non-restrictive relatives are not allowed to predicate on the indefinites in *you*-sentences. Restrictive relatives, on the other hand, are allowed to serve as their modifiers. The pattern of contrasts of (71-73) is therefore correlated to that of (67-69), just as the EMH predicts.

Another support of our conclusion comes from appearance /disappearance verbs like *lai* 'come', *qu* 'go', *fasheng* 'happen', and *si* 'die', which, as Huang puts it, assert "coming into existence" or "going out of existence". Syntactically, they also share the common property of being ergative. The (in)definiteness effects thus come out strong:

(74) a. e lai-le   liang-ge ren/*Lisi/*ta/*na-ge ren/*me-ge ren   le.
         come-Prf   two persons/Lisi/(s)he/that person/every person Prt
         (lit.) Came two persons/*Lisi/*(s)he/*the person/*everybody.

   b. e si-le   liang-ge ren/*Lisi/*ta/*na-ge ren/*me-ge ren   le.
       die-Prf   two persons/Lisi/(s)he/that person/every person Prt
       (lit.) Died two persons/*Lisi/*(s)he/*the person/*everybody.

The restrictive/non-restrictive asymmetry, as expected, shows up promptly when relativization is involved, as evidenced by the contrasts between (a) and (b) clauses of (75,76):

(75) a. e lai-le [DP liang-ge [CP Op$_i$ [Akiu yaoqing e$_i$]] de ren] le.
          come-Prf two-CL   Akiu invite   PNM person Prt
         (lit.) Came two persons who Akiu hates most.

b.* e lai-le [DP [CP Op$_i$ [Akiu yaoqing e$_i$]] de liang-ge ren] le.
   come-Prf   Akiu invite PNM two-CL person Prt
   (lit.) Came two persons, who Akiu hates most.

(76) a. e si-le[DP liang-ge [CP Op$_i$ [e$_i$ bu xi-zao]] de ren] le.
       die-Prf   two-CL   not take-bath PNM person Prt
       (lit.) Died two persons who don't take bathes.

   b.* e si-le[DP [CP Op$_i$ [e$_i$ bu xi-zao]] de liang-ge ren] le.
       die-Prf   not take-bath PNM two-CL person Prt
       (lit.) Died two persons, who don't take bathes.

So far we have shown that the definiteness effect induced by non-restrictive relativization and that displayed by topicalization are of the same nature. And they can be made to follow from the EMH given that predication is involved in both cases, an assumption warranted on both conceptual and empirical grounds.

2.3.2. Weak Existential Predicates and Secondary Predication

In addition to *you* 'have' and (dis)appearance verbs, Huang (1987) further point out two types of predicates which appear to be less existential in lexical-semantic terms. One concerns "location verbs", including intransitives like *zhu* 'live', *zuo* 'sit', *tang* 'lie', *you* 'swim', and transitives like *fang* 'put' and *gua* 'hang', *hua* 'paint'. They are characterized by their selection of locative arguments, and by their association with the durative aspect *-zhe*. (the perfective aspect *-le* is also possible with the transitives). In contrast to the first two types of existential predicates, the location verbs do not display the (in)definiteness effect as a rule, as shown below:

(77) a. pingguo-shu-xia zuo-zhe yi-ge kexuejia/na-ge kexuejia
       apple-tree-bottom sit-Dur one-CL scientist/that-CL scientist
       /Newton
       /Niudun.
       Under the apple tree sits a scientist/the scientist/Newton.

b. shui-li　　　you-zhe　　yi-tiao meirenyü/na-tiao meirenyü
water-inside　swim-Dur　one-CL mermaid/that-CL mermaid
/Zhubajie.
/Zhubajie
In the water swims a mermaid/the mermaid/Zhubajie.

c. qiang-shang hua-zhe/-le　yi-wei pusa/na-wei pusa
wall-top　　paint-Dur/Prf one-CL goddess/that-CL goddess
/Guanshiyin.
/Guanshiyin
On the wall is painted a goddess/the goddess/Guanshiyin.

The same observation holds for action verbs associated with the experiential aspect -*guo* and the perfective aspect -*le* :

(78) a. ta　jiao-guo　yi-ge xuesheng/na-ge xuesheng/Aiyinsitan.
s/he teach-Exp one-CL student/that-CL student/Einstein
S/he has the experience of teaching a student/the student/Einstein.

b. wo　gu-le　　yi-ge zhentan/na-ge zhentan/Chen Chali.
I　　hire-Prf　one-CL detective/that-CL detective/Charlie Chen
I hired a detective/the detective/Charlie Chen.

However, as noted by Huang, when we add a clausal predicate in the sentence-final position, the (in)definiteness effect obtains without exception. First compare (79a-c) with (77a-c) respectively. We find that once the secondary predication is involved, location verbs behaves exactly like the typical existential predicates.[20] In other words, the (in)definiteness effects re-emerge:

(79) a. pingguo-shu-xia　zuo-zhe yi-ge kexuejia/$^{?}$*na-ge kexuejia
apple-tree-bottom sit-Dur　one-CL scientist/that-CL scientist
/$^{?}$*Niudun [CP Op$_i$ [e$_i$　hen　xihuan　chi pingguo]].
/Newton　　　　　　　　very　like　　eat apple
Under the apple tree sits a scientist/the scientist/Newton, who likes eating apples.

b. shui-li   you-zhe   yi-tiao meirenyü/$^{?}$*na-tiao meirenyü
   water-inside swim-Dur one-CL mermaid/that-CL mermaid
   /$^{?}$*Zhubajie [CP Op$_i$ [e$_i$ hen   piaoliang]].
   /Zhubajie   very   pretty
   In the water swims a mermaid/the mermaid/Zhubajie, who is
   very pretty.

c. qiang-shang hua-zhe/-le yi-wei pusa/$^{?}$*na-wei pusa
   wall-top   paint-Dur/Prf one-CL goddess/that-CL goddess
   /$^{?}$*Guanshiyin [CP Op$_i$ [e$_i$ jiaota   lianhua]].
   /Guanshiyin   step-on   water lily
   On the wall is painted a goddess/the goddess/Guanshiyin, who
   steps on a water lily.

Action verbs inflected by *-guo* and *-le* also display the same pattern of contrasts. This point can be illustrated by comparing (78a,b) with (80a,b) respectively:

(80) a. ta jiao-guo   yi-ge xuesheng/$^{?}$*na-ge xuesheng/$^{?}$*Aiyinsitan
        s/he teach-Exp one-CL student/that-CL student/Einstein
        [CP Op$_i$ [e$_i$ conglai bu jiao   zuoye]].
                            ever   not hand-in homework
        S/he has the experience of teaching a student/the
        student/Einstein, who never handed in homework.

   b. wo gu-le   yi-ge zhentan/$^{?}$*na-ge zhentan/$^{?}$*Chen Chali
      I hire-Prf one-CL detective/that-CL detective/Charlie Chen
      [CP Op$_i$ [Akiu hen   manyi e$_i$]].
                  Akiu very   satisfied
      I hired a detective/the detective/Charlie Chen, with whom Akiu
      is quite satisfied.

Note that, given the EMH, the presence of a definite object is supposed to license the secondary predication. The contrasts in (79) and (80), however, suggest the opposite. Take (80a) for example:

Toward LF Interface

(81)

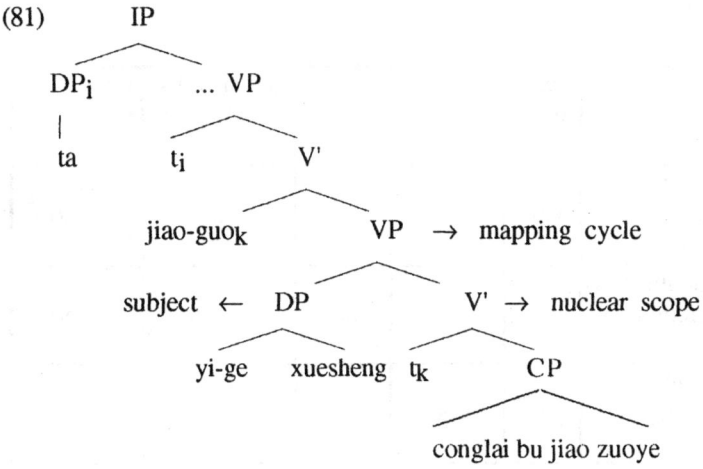

As illustrated by (81), the clausal predicate *conglai bu jiao zuoye* 'never handed in homework' may well stand as an inner adjunct in a Larsonian-style structure, triggering secondary predication on the object DP, just as a non-restrictive relative does in English. According to the EMH, this should induce specificity effects on the subject in the current mapping cycle (i.e. the object DP). On the contrary, the secondary predicate can only cooccur with indefinites such as *yi-ge xuesheng* 'a student' in (80a). The same observation applies to *yi-ge zhentan* 'a detective' in (80b). To get the complete picture, let's go through the following table first:

Table 1.

	you 'have'	*lai* 'come' & *si* 'die'	location verbs	action verbs plus Exp/Prf	non-existential predicates
existential assertion of object	yes	yes	no	no	no
(in)definiteness restriction on object	yes	yes	no	no	no
allowing secondary predication	yes	yes	yes	yes	no
(in)definiteness restriction in the presence of secondary predication	yes	yes	yes	yes	no

The first row shows that a location verb, unlike "strong" existential predicates such as *you* 'have' and *lai* 'come', conveys primarily the location of its object, and only secondarily its existence. The situation is thus very similar to that of possessive *you* when possession is its primary assertion (cf. the discussion around (70a,b)). In parallel, an action verb inflected by the experiential or perfective aspect denotes primarily an action, and secondarily the existence of an experience or event. The existence of its object, if any, appears to be an entailment of the secondary assertion. This pattern is directly related to the contrast in the second row: Only strong existential predicates impose the (in)definiteness restriction typically associated with *there*-constructions in English.

The generalization, however, is only superficial. While the secondary predication applies only when the existence of object NPs is either asserted or entailed, as in the third row, its presence reinforces the (in)definiteness restriction on the part of "weak" existential predicates such as *zuo* 'sit' and *jiao-guo* 'taught', as in the last row.

As Huang (1987) rightly points out, there are two factors playing around here: One concerns the (in)definiteness effects induced by existential predicates, which in turn are conditioned by the presence of secondary predication when the predicates are less existential; the other is a general condition on predication, as stated below:

(82) In sentences with a secondary clausal predicate in the sentence-final position, the NP in the object position must be specific.

The rationale behind (82), as provided by Huang (1987), is that the subject of continuative description has to be referential. This is exactly the intuition that we set to capture under the EMH.

As a result, if the (in)definiteness restriction and the predication requirement (82) apply at the same time, the object NP in question is bound to be a specific indefinite (i.e., a presuppositional indefinite in Diesing's terms). Following is the evidence cited by Huang to support this conclusion (with additions and modifications for ease of exposition):

(83) a. wo   jiao-guo   yi-ge   xuesheng.
         I   teach-Exp   one-CL   student
         I have taught a (certain) student.

    b. wo   jiao-guo   xuesheng.
        I   teach-Exp   student(s)
        I have taught (Sm) student(s).

(84) a. wo jiao-guo   yi-ge   xuesheng [$_{CP}$ Op$_i$ [e$_i$ hen
         I   teach-Exp one-CL   student   very
         congming]].
         clever
         I have taught a (certain) student, who is very clever.

    b. * wo jiao-guo   xuesheng [$_{CP}$ Op$_i$ [e$_i$ hen   congming]].
         I   teach-Exp student(s)   very clever
         ?? I have taught (Sm) student(s), who are very clever.

As shown by the contrast between (84a,b), while an indefinite with a numerical specifier (i.e. *yi-ge xuesheng* 'a (certain) student') allows an extra CP predicate, a bare indefinite with a non-generic reading (i.e., *xuesheng* '(Sm) student(s)') does not. When the secondary predication is not involved, the asymmetry disappears accordingly, as in (83a,b). The same observation applies to those predicates with even stronger existential assertions, as illustrated by the contrast between (85a,b), as well as that between (86a,b):

(85) a. fangjian-li you yi-ge nühai [$_{CP}$ Op$_i$ [e$_i$ hen
   room-inside have one-CL girl   very
   piaoliang]].
   pretty
   In the room, there is a (certain) girl, who is very pretty.

   b.* fangjian-li you nühai [$_{CP}$ Op$_i$ [e$_i$ hen piaoliang]].
   room-inside have girl(s)   very pretty
   ?? In the room, there is/are (Sm) girl(s), who is/are very pretty.

(86) a. e si-le yi-ge ren [$_{CP}$ Op$_i$ [e$_i$ mei   dai
   die-Prf one-CL person   have-not wear
   fangdumianjü]].
   gas mask
   (lit.) Died a (certain) person, who did not wear a gas mask.

   b.* e si-le ren [$_{CP}$ Op$_i$ [e$_i$ mei   dai   fangdumianjü]].
   die-Prf person(s)   have-not wear gas mask
   (lit.) Died (Sm) person(s), who did not wear a gas mask.

As a result, the definiteness effects displayed by (79) and (80) does not constitute counterexamples to the EMH: On the one hand, names and *that*-NPs are ruled out due to the incompatibility between existential assertions and definite expressions. On the other, specific indefinites are still allowed in all four types of existential constructions. This guarantees the success of the secondary predication since the restriction imposed by ∃-closure has been met (cf. section 2.1).

What is left unsolved, as noted by Huang in his conclusion, is the exact relationship between the (in)definiteness restriction and the predication requirement (82). In other words, problems still arise as to how ∃-closure and secondary predication conspire to reinforce the (in)definiteness restriction, as in (79) and (80), which are otherwise invisible, as in (77) and (78). It is in this respect that the VP-shell analysis really shines: As we have sketched in (81), the domain of the complex predicate (i.e., the secondary clausal predicate) may well be extended to the trace left by the main verb, and hence to the verb itself on the assumption that a Chain as a whole is an LF object (cf. Chomsky 1991).

Consequently, the existential entailment of *jiao-guo* 'teach-Exp' is spelled out and predicated of the subject of the current mapping cycle, along with whatever properties the secondary predicate denotes. The (in)definiteness restriction is thus reinforced. In contrast, when the clausal predicates are absent, as in the case of (77) and (78), the existential entailment remains unarticulated.

2.3.3. A Dilemma

Now we have an apparent dilemma at hand. As mentioned above, the object DP in (81) (i.e., the subject of secondary predication) has to be a specific indefinite due to the conspiracy between the (in)definiteness restriction and the EMH. However, the mere existence of specific indefinites casts doubt on Cheng's (1991) claim that Chinese indefinites are non-quantificational, as long as we follow Diesing (1992a) in identifying specificity with presuppositionality (which in turn triggers QR). Then what if we claim instead that Chinese indefinites are just like their English counterparts, i.e., being ambiguous between cardinal and presuppositional readings? This move, however, undermines Cheng's analysis of the specificity/definiteness effects associated with Chinese subjects (cf. section 1.1). Even if we confine the stipulation to indefinite objects, bare indefinites still remain uncommitted, as we have seen in (b) clauses of (84-86).

A possible way out is to say that the presence of specificity in the indefinites has something to do with existential sentences in general, based on the fact that the clausal predicates almost exclusively appear in existential constructions. This possibility is first pointed out by Huang, but then rejected on the ground that there are verbs which allow the secondary predication, but do not appear to have anything to do with existence (data from Huang 1987):

(87) a. wo hen xiang xuan yi-men ke [$_{CP}$ Op$_i$ [tamen shuo [e$_i$
    I very hope select one-CL class   they say
    hen   youqu]].
    very interesting
    I very much hope to select a course, which they say is very
    interesting.

  b. wo zheng   zai-kan   yi-ben shu [$_{CP}$ Op$_i$ [e$_i$ hen
     I right-now Prg-see one-CL book   very
     youyisi]].
     interesting
     Right now I am reading a book, which is very interesting.

As shown by (87a,b), verbs like *xuan* 'select' and *kan* 'read' do not make existential assertion. Still, they have no problem with the extra CP predicate. Nevertheless, they do make existential presuppositions, namely, presupposing the existence of their objects. In other words, they fall under the category of *use*-type verbs in Diesing's (1992) sense. Once we substitute creation verbs like *kai* 'open' and *xie* 'write', the sentences degrade:

(88) a. * wo hen xiang kai   yi-men ke   [Op$_i$ [tamen shuo [e$_i$
       I very hope   open   one-CL class   they say
       hen   youqu]].
       very interesting
       I very much hope to open a course, which they say is very
       interesting.

  b.$^?$*wo zheng   zai-xie yi-ben shu [Op$_i$ [e$_i$ hen youyisi]].
     I right-now Prg-write one-CL book   very interesting
     Right now I am writing a book, which is very interesting.

The secondary predication in (87a,b) is thus licensed in the same way as English non-restrictive relativization is licensed when presuppositional *some* is present (cf. (57b) and (58b)). Also note that If we twist (88a,b) a little bit further by supplying the experiential and perfective aspects, grammaticality improves:

Toward LF Interface 135

(89) a. wo kai-guo yi-men ke [Op$_i$ [tamen shuo [e$_i$ hen
　　　 I open-Exp one-CL class　　they say　　　very
　　　 youqu]].
　　　 interesting
　　　 I have the experience of opening a course, which they say is very interesting.

　　b. wo xie-le　 yi-ben　shu [Op$_i$ [e$_i$ hen　 youyisi]].
　　　 I write-Prf one-CL book　　　　very interesting
　　　 I wrote a book, which is very interesting.

The observation, however, cannot be taken to indicate that all the existential sentences make presuppositions. As a matter of fact, none of them (except, of course, those headed by *use*-type verbs) make presuppositions about the existence of their objects. This point can be illustrated by adding negation on the sentences containing specific indefinites (i.e., (a) clauses of (84-86)):

(90) a. * wo mei　 jiao-guo　yi-ge xuesheng [$_{CP}$ Op$_i$ [e$_i$ hen
　　　 I have-not teach-Exp one-CL student　　　　　　　very
　　　 congming]].
　　　 clever
　　　 * I have not taught a student, who is very clever.

　　b. * fangjian-li　mei-you yi-ge　　nühai [$_{CP}$ Op$_i$ [e$_i$ hen
　　　 room-inside　not-have one-CL　girl　　　　　　　　very
　　　 piaoliang]].
　　　 pretty
　　　 * In the room, there is no girl, who is very pretty.

　　c. * e mei　　si yi-ge　　ren [$_{CP}$ Op$_i$ [e$_i$ mei　 dai
　　　 have-not die one-CL person　　　　　　 have-not wear
　　　 fangdumianjü]].
　　　 gas mask
　　　 (lit.) Didn't die a person, who did not wear a gas mask.

As shown by (90a-c), the secondary predication fails in the presence of negation. This suggests that the specificity in question comes from existential assertions or their entailments, since presuppositions as a rule cannot be falsified by negation (see, for example, Chierchia and McConnell-Ginet 1990, Heim 1991). Our position is further backed up by the fact that when we take out the CP predicate, the sentences become acceptable only if the indefinites are construed as cardinal/existential, behaving rather like a negative polarity item under the scope of negation:

(91) a. wo   mei   jiao-guo   yi-ge   xuesheng.
       I have-not teach-Exp one-CL   student
       I have not taught any/* a certain student.

  b. fangjian-li   mei-you   yi-ge   nühai.
     room-inside   not-have   one-CL   girl
     In the room, there is no/* not a certain girl.

  c. e mei   si   yi-ge   ren.
     have-not die   one-CL   person
     (lit.) Didn't die any/* a certain person.

That is, the specific reading disappears when existential assertions/entailments are undone. As a result, the indefinites in (91a-c) can only get licensing from ∃-closure (also cf. Cheng 1991). But what role does the negative polarity reading play in regard to predication licensing? Why doesn't it license the predication clauses in (90a-c)? This again leads us back to the cyclicity of mapping. Let's take (90a) for example:

Toward LF Interface

(92)

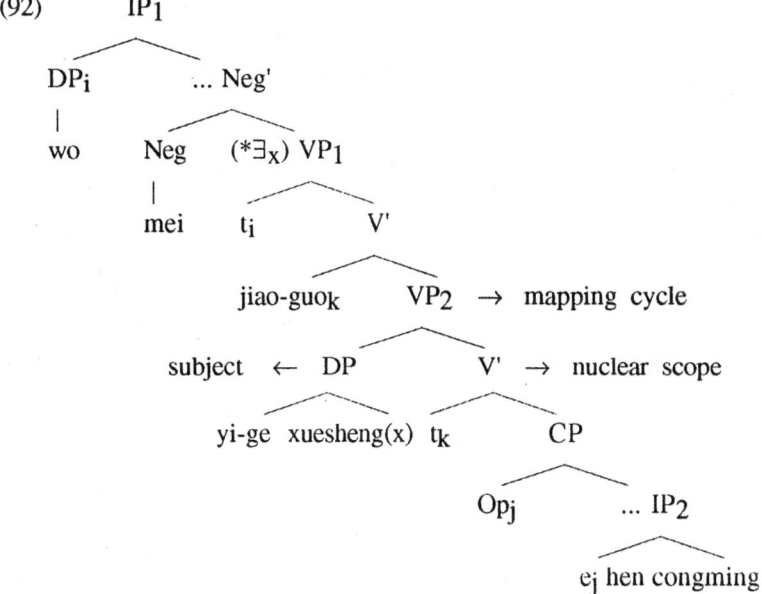

First let's put aside the trivial mapping cycle within the secondary CP predicate, and focus on the VP shells of the main clause. Bottom-up-wise, the first predicate encountered is the predication CP. Its immediate c-commanding XP is the lower VP shell (i.e., VP_2), which constitutes an independent mapping cycle according to the EMH (11). ∃-closure may apply on the nuclear scope corresponding to the CP node,[21] but does not apply since there is no unbound variable within the predicate.

On the other hand, a variable is introduced by *yi-ge xuesheng* 'a student' (i.e., the subject of secondary predication) in (92), which is left unbound at the end of this mapping cycle: It cannot be licensed by ∃-closure on the next cycle (cf. section 1.1), nor can it get licensing from the experiential aspect *-guo*, since negation undoes the assertion of the existence of the student-teaching action/event, as well as the entailment concerning the existence of the object *xuesheng* 'student'. As a result, (90a) is correctly ruled out in mapping theoretical terms. As for (91a), where the predication CP does not occur, there is only one mapping cycle (i.e., IP_1). The variable in question is thus bound by ∃-closure, resulting in the negative polarity (cardinal) reading.

The conclusion, therefore, appears to be that presuppositionality cannot be equated to specificity, as far as the predication requirement (82) is concerned. Rather, presuppositional indefinites should be treated as a proper subset of specific indefinites. If our observation is on the right track, then the specific reading of indefinites does not necessarily result from inherent quantificational force, nor does in-situ licensing of indefinites involve $\exists$-closure as a rule. Rather, evidence strongly suggests that the existential entailment of experiential and perfective aspects has its share in licensing object indefinites.

As a result, there is no conflict between (82) and Cheng's claim that Chinese indefinites are non-quantificational, and her analysis of the specificity/definiteness effects on Chinese subjects is also maintained.

2.3.4. Bare Indefinites

A notable drawback under our approach concerns the bare indefinites in (b) clauses of (84-86). That is, if it turns out to be true that the specific readings of (84a-86a) are contributed by secondary predication, it is still unclear why (84b-86b) with bare indefinites do not benefit from the same application. Here our hunch is that the licensing between indefinites and existential predicates is mutual: An indefinite with a numerical determiner like *yi-ge* 'one-CL' is intuitively more specific than a bare indefinite, and thus more likely to get licensing from the existential entailment spelled out by the secondary predication (cf. section 2.3.2). As a matter of fact, the above intuition conforms to Carlson's (1977a) observation that there are a number of asymmetries between English bare plurals (e.g., *policemen*) and ordinary indefinites (e.g., *a policeman*). One of them concerns the lack of specific readings on the part of bare plurals, as shown by the following contrast:

(93) Miles wants to meet a policeman.
    a. $\exists_x$ x is a policeman $\wedge$ Miles wants to meet x
    b. Miles wants ($\$_x$ x is a policeman $\wedge$ Miles meet x)

(94) Miles wants to meet policemen.
    a. $^\#\exists_x$ x is a policeman $\wedge$ Miles wants to meet x

b. Miles wants ($\exists_x$ x is a policeman ∧ Miles meet x)

(93a) is the "transparent" reading in Quine's sense, which can be paraphrased roughly as 'There is a (particular) policeman that Miles wants to meet'. (93b), on the other hand, does not refer to any specific policeman, and the indefinite in question takes the narrow scope. This ambiguity, as Carlson points out, does not hold for the bare plural *policemen* in (94). Namely, the transparent/specific reading is missing.

The same thing can be said about Chinese bare indefinites, which can be either plural or singular:

(95) Akiu xiang zhao yi-ge jingcha.
     Akiu want send-for one-CL policeman
    a. $\exists_x$ x is a policeman ∧ Akiu wants to send for x
    b. Akiu wants $\exists_x$ (x is a policeman ∧ Akiu sends for x)

(96) Akiu xiang zhao jingcha.
     Akiu want send-for policeman/policemen
    a. $^\#$ $\exists_x$ x is a policeman ∧ Akiu wants to send for x
    b. Akiu wants $\exists_x$ (x is a policeman ∧ Akiu sends for x)

As shown by the above contrast, the bare indefinite *jingcha* 'policeman/policemen' in (96) cannot refer to a particular policeman, whereas its more "specified" counterpart in (95) can. At the other end of the scale, *jingcha* may also refer to a kind, serving as a proper name, just as its English counterpart (cf. Carlson 1977a):

(97) Akiu jian-guo jingcha.
     Akiu meet-Exp policeman/policemen
    Akiu met policemen (this kind of people) before.

Nonetheless, differences do exist. Chinese bare indefinites allow a curious kind of construal which is best described as "diectic" or "demonstrative", as shown by (98):

(98) ren lai-le.
     person(s) come-Inc
    That/Those person(s) is/are just coming.

The closest paraphrase of (98) is literally *ta lai-le* '(S)he is just coming' or *tamen lai-le* 'They are just coming'. This usage is also found in the object position, typically in alternation with non-specific construals such as (99b):[22]

(99) Akiu zhao-dao ren   le.
     Akiu find-reach person(s) Inc
     a. Akiu has found that/those person(s).
     b. Akiu has found (Sm) person(s).

Again, (99) can be paraphrased as *Akiu zhao-dao ta(men) le* 'Akiu has found her/him/them'. For our purpose here, it suffices to recognize that the deictic reading may well correlate to the fact that Chinese is a pro-drop language, where *ren* 'person' can be headed an empty demonstrative.

The generalization then seems to be that the resistance of specificity construals is an attribute shared by bare (in)definites across languages. In other word, these "bare DPs" can be either definite (i.e., the deictic and kind readings), or non-specific (i.e., the generic and existential readings), but never in between. The deviance of (84b-86b) thus falls under our account: On the one hand, the definite readings are blocked by the (in)definiteness restriction imposed by existential predicates. The existential reading, on the other, is blocked because $\exists$-closure is not available in the mapping cycle of the secondary predicates, and because bare indefinites are, in a sense, defective in receiving the specific interpretation made available by the existential predicates. As a result, bare indefinites are disallowed wherever the conspiracy between the (in)definiteness restriction and the EMH takes effect.

2.4. A Refinement

As a reflection, one may wonder, if our conception of the EMH is correct, why non-restrictive relativization fails where secondary predication is allowed, as made clear by comparing (100a,b) with (101a,b) respectively ((72b), (76b), (85a), and (86a) repeated below):

(100) a. fangjian-li   you   yi-ge   nühai [CP Op$_i$ [e$_i$ hen
       room-inside have   one-CL   girl   very
       piaoliang]].
       pretty
       In the room, there is a (certain) girl, who is very pretty.

    b. e si-le   yi-ge   ren [CP Op$_i$ [e$_i$ mei   dai   fang
       die-Prf one-CL person   have-not wear gas
       dumianjü]].
       mask
       (lit.) Died a (certain) person, who did not wear a gas mask.

(101) a. * fangjian-li you [DP [CP Op$_i$ [e$_i$ dai-zhe hong maodou]] de
        room-inside have   wear-Dur red cloak PNM
        yi-ge nühai].
        one-CL girl
     ?? In the room, there is a girl, who wears a red cloak.

    b.* e si-le [DP [CP Op$_i$ [e$_i$ bu   xi-zao]] de liang-ge ren]   le.
        die-Prf   not take-bath PNM two-CL person Prt
        (lit.) Died two persons, who don't take bathes.

To put the question in a different way, on what grounds do existential predicates such as *you* 'have' and (dis)appearance verbs such as *si* 'die' discriminate between non-restrictive relatives and secondary predicates in regard to predication licensing?

    An immediate answer comes from their distinct mapping geometries: While existential assertions can be made available to indefinite objects by extending the domain of secondary predicates to verb traces (and hence to the whole V^0-Chain in (102a)), the same access is denied to the subjects of non-restrictive relativization (i.e., the head nouns in (101a,b)), because the relevant mapping cycle is the higher DP node in (102b), and there is no way to relate existential predicates to non-restrictive relatives:

(102) a.

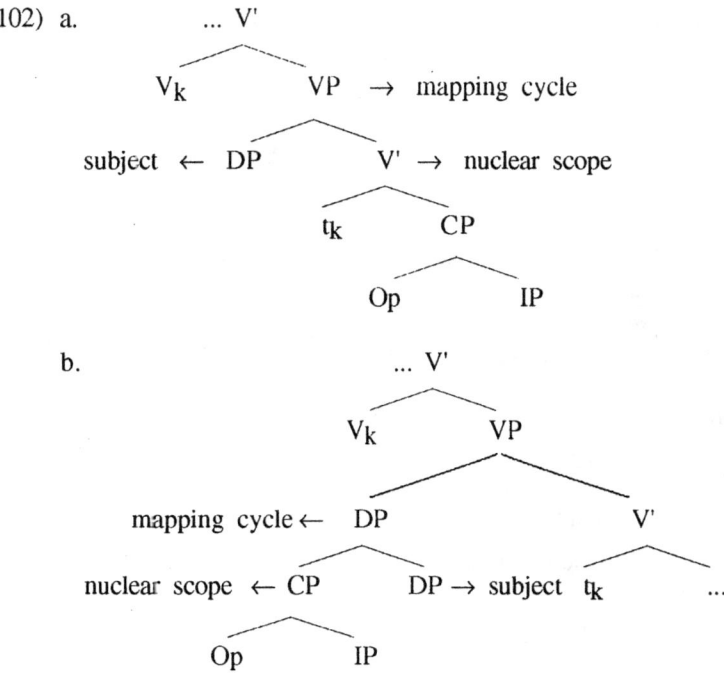

b.

The same observation applies to weak existential predicates such as action verbs inflected by the experiential/perfective aspects, as illustrated by the contrasts between (103a-c) with (104a-c):

(103) a. wo jiao-guo yi-ge xuesheng [CP Op$_i$ [e$_i$ hen
 I teach-Exp one-CL student very
 congming]].
 clever
 I have taught a (certain) student, who is very clever.

b. wo kai-guo yi-men ke [CP Op$_i$ [tamen shuo [e$_i$hen
 I open-Exp one-CL class they say very
 youqu]].
 interesting
 I have the experience of opening a course, which they say is very interesting.

c. wo xie-le   yi-ben   shu [$_{CP}$ Op$_i$ [e$_i$ hen youyisi]].
   I write-Prf one-CL   book   very interesting
   I wrote a book, which is very interesting.

(104) a. * wo jiao-guo [$_{DP}$ [$_{CP}$ Op$_i$ [e$_i$ hen   congming]] de
         I teach-Exp   very   clever   PNM
         yi-ge   xuesheng].
         one-CL   student
         I have taught a (certain) student, who is very clever.

     b. * wo kai-guo [$_{DP}$ [$_{CP}$ Op$_i$ [tamen shuo [e$_i$ hen youqu]]
         I   open-Exp   they   say   very interesting
         de yi-men   ke].
         PNM one-CL   class
         I have the experience of opening a course, which they say is
         very interesting.

     c. * wo xie-le [$_{DP}$ [$_{CP}$ Op$_i$ [e$_i$ hen youyisi]] de yi-ben   shu].
         I write-Prf   very interesting PNM one-CL book
         I wrote a book, which is very interesting.

Although both (103) and (104) involve predication rather than modification, the configuration for predication licensing turns out quite differently due to their distinct mapping geometries, as we have seen in (102a,b). Once we put the relative clauses under the scope of numerical specifiers, the contrasts disappear, as evidenced below:

(105) a. wo   jiao-guo [$_{DP}$ yi-ge   [$_{CP}$ Op$_i$ [e$_i$ hen   congming]]
         I   teach-Exp   one-CL   very   clever
         de   xuesheng].
         PNM   student
         I have taught a (certain) student who is very clever.

     b. wo kai-guo [$_{DP}$ yi-men [$_{CP}$ Op$_i$ [tamen shuo [e$_i$ hen
         I open-Exp   one-CL   they   say   very
         youqu]] de ke].
         interesting PNM class
         I have the experience of opening a course which they say is

very interesting.

c. wo xie-le [$_{DP}$ yi-ben [$_{CP}$ Op$_i$ [e$_i$ hen youyisi]]
   I write-Prf   one-CL   very interesting
de   shu].
PNM book
I wrote a book which is very interesting.

This is because what is involved in (105a-c) is modification. Consequently, the restrictive relatives do not constitute independent mapping cycles. Rather, they are mapped into the relevant restrictive clauses. The EMH thus correctly predicts that the predication requirement (83) is irrelevant here.

A noticeable problem with the view presented so far is that, although the EMH makes the right prediction in the configuration (102b), the semantic type produced is wrong. As we point out in section 2.2, the higher DP node (i.e., the current mapping cycle) should correspond to an entity or individual rather than a proposition. A possible way out, as Noam Chomsky (p.c.) points out, is to claim that the one-to-one correspondence between syntactic structures and semantic representations simply cannot be maintained everywhere. For one thing, the non-restrictive usage of adjectives obviously needs independent treatments other than the EMH (cf. the discussion around (52)).

Alternatively, we may reconsider the empirical status of non-restrictive relatives in Chinese. As a matter fact, Chao (1968) argues for a virtually opposite view of the restrictive/non-restrictive distinction. According to Chao, an "inner" relative is non-restrictive (or descriptive in his terms), whereas an "outer" relative is restrictive. He nevertheless points out that the former could also be restrictive when contrastively stressed. It should be admitted that at least some of the speakers consulted have difficulty in deciding whether the outer relative in (106) is restrictive or not:

(106) Akiu kaichu-le [$_{DP}$ [$_{CP}$ Op$_i$ [e$_i$ bu xizao]] dena-ge/*san-geren].
     Akiu fire-Prf   not bathe PNM that-CL/three-CL person
     Akiu fired those/three people(,) who do not take bath.

But they all agree that the contrast between *na-ge* 'that-CL' and *san-ge* 'three-CL' is clear-cut, and the most natural reading of the inner relative in (107) is restrictive:

(107) Akiu kaichu-le [$_{DP}$ na-ge/san-ge [$_{CP}$ Op$_i$ [e$_i$ bu xizao]] de ren].
Akiu fire-Prf that-CL/three-CL not bathe PNM person
Akiu fired those/three people(,) who do not take bath.

A classic argument for the non-restrictiveness of inner relatives comes from Huang (1982). He points out that an inner relative can appear in an appositive expression, as in (108a), while its outer counterpart cannot, as in (108b):

(108) a. niuyue, [$_{DP}$ zhe-ge [$_{CP}$ Op$_i$ [renren dou xiaode e$_i$]]
New York this-CL everyone all know
de chengshi].
PNM city
This city, New York, which everyone knows.

b. *niuyue, [$_{DP}$ [$_{CP}$ Op$_i$ [renren dou xiaode e$_i$]] de
New York everyone all know PNM
zhe-ge chengshi].
this-CL city

Our worry is that the relative clause in question is only a part of an appositive, not the appositive itself. In fact, we would translate (108a) as 'New York, the city which everyone knows' rather than the one given above. The deviance of (108b), on the other hand, does indicate that there is something wrong with our analysis sketched earlier. The real problem, therefore, still lies in the outer relatives.

As noted by Jim Huang (p.c.), there is a middle ground between the two opposite views. That is, we may entertain the possibility that all relative clauses are restrictive in Chinese, and the closest equivalents of English non-restrictive relatives are actually those secondary predicates in existential constructions. This move, however, renders the EMH irrelevant for the specificity displayed by (106). Namely, since the outer relative does not trigger predication, there is no mapping-theoretical account (such as that given in (102)) available for the asymmetry between "outer" relativization and secondary predication. Therefore, we have to find another way to characterize the relatives in question.

Carlson (1977b) provides a suggestive clue: He argues that there is a type of relatives which can neither be classified as restrictive nor as non-restrictive. One of the defining properties is that their head nouns can only take definite articles, universal quantifiers, and free-choice *any* as their determiners, as illustrated by the following contrasts:

(109) a.   The people [there were on the life-raft] died.

b.   Every person [there was on the life-raft] died.

(110) a. * Several people [there were on the life-raft] died.

b. * Each person [there was on the life-raft] died.

Carlson calls the type "amount relatives", since the constructions at issue typically involve cardinality of some sort, as is self-evident in the above *there-be* clauses (see also Heim 1987). He proposes that there is a cardinal expression associated the relativized NP in (109) and (110), which in turn induces (dis)matching effects on the matrix determiners. For instance, while *the forty men* and *every ten minutes* are well-formed, *several many ladies* and *each fifty minutes* are not. The same trait is also found in Chinese outer relative, as exemplified below:

(111) a. Akiu   kaichu-le [DP [CP Op$_i$ [e$_i$ bu xizao]] de mei-yi-geren].
      Akiu   fire-Prf   not bathe PNM every-one-CL person
      Akiu fired every person who do not take bath.

b.*Akiu kaichu-le [DP [CP Op$_i$ [e$_i$ bu xizao]] de xuduo(-de) ren].
   Akiu fire-Prf   not bathe PNM several person
   Akiu fired several persons who do not take bath.

It thus appears that the property of an English relative is determined by the type of constructions it contains, while that of a Chinese relative is determined by the type of constructions it modifies. It is quite possible that the outer relative in question is not an adjunct of DP, but an adjunct of so-called "measure phrase" (MP), a trio consisting of a determiner, a numeral, and a classifier (e.g., *mei-yi-ge* 'every-one-CL' in (111a); see also Huang 1982 and Tang 1990), as illustrated in (112b):

(112) a. inner relative:

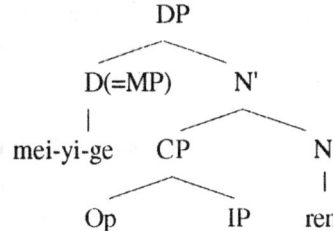

b. outer relative:

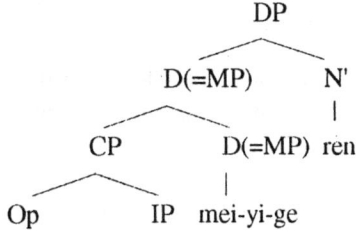

An inner relative, as in (112a), can never be a part of an MP due to its structural height. Hence the absence of (dis)matching effects in (107). On the other hand, the seeming specificity effect of (106), as well as that of (111), can be attributed to the amount construals of outer relatives.

Furthermore, our analysis is also consistent with the well-known scope interaction between MPs and other prenominal modifiers (cf. Huang 1982). For example, (113a) and (113b) have exactly the same lexical items. But with a switch of the word order between the MP and the relative clause, different interpretations emerge:

(113) a. Akiu kaichu-le [$_{DP}$ na-san-ge [$_{CP}$ Op$_i$ [e$_i$ bu xizao]] de ren].
    Akiu fire-Prf   that-three-CL   not bathe PNM person
    Akiu fired those three people who do not take bath.

  b. Akiu kaichu-le [$_{DP}$ [$_{CP}$ Op$_i$ [e$_i$ bu xizao]] de na-san-geren].
    Akiu fire-Prf   not bathe PNM that-three-CL person
    Akiu fired that group of three people who do not take bath.

(113a) sports a scenario where there is a group of people who do not bathe, and Akiu specifically picked up those three and fired them. (113b), on the other hand, asserts that there are groups of three people, and Akiu picked up the group characterized by not taking bath and fired its members. This point can be further illustrated by contrasting the outer relative:

(114) Akiu kaichu-le [DP [CP Op_i [e_i bu xizao]] de na-san-geren],
 Akiu fire-Prf   not bathe PNM that-three-CL person
 bu shi [DP [CP Op_i [e_i bu chuan yifu]] de na-san-ge   ren]
 not be   not wear clothes PNM that-three-CL person
 Akiu fired that group of three people who do not bathe, not that
 group of three who do not dress.

Moreover, it is impossible to contrast the MP in (113b), either by setting the determiner *zhe* 'this' against *na* 'that', or by setting the numeral *wu* 'five' against *san* 'three':

(115) *Akiu kaichu-le [DP [CP Op_i [e_i bu xizao]] de na-san-ge ren],
 Akiu fire-Prf   not bathe PNM that-three-CL person
 bu shi [DP [CP Op_i [e_i bu xizao]] de zhe-san-ge/na-wu-ge ren]
 not be   not bathe PNM this-three-CL/that-five-CL person
 Akiu fired that group of three people who do not take bath, not
 this group of three/that group of five.

By assuming that the outer relative restricts the MP, as sketched in (112b), we correctly predicts the group-firing reading of (113b) (vs. the individual-firing reading of (113a)). As for (113a), the pattern of contrasting is the other way around. Namely, only the MP, but not the inner relative, can be contrasted, as shown below:

(116) a. Akiu kaichu-le [DP na-san-ge [CP Op_i [e_i bu xizao]] de ren],
   Akiu fire-Prf   that-three-CL   not bathe PNM person
  bu shi [DP zhe-san-ge/$^?$na-wu-ge [CP Op_i [e_i bu xizao]]de ren].
  not be   this-three-CL/that-five-CL   not bathe PNM person
  Akiu fired that group of three people who do not take bath, not
  this group of three/that group of five.

b.*Akiu kaichu-le [$_{DP}$ na-san-ge [$_{CP}$ Op$_i$ [e$_i$ bu xizao]] de ren],
Akiu fire-Prf   that-three-CL   not bathe PNM person
bu shi [$_{DP}$ na-san-ge [$_{CP}$ Op$_i$ [e$_i$ bu chuan yifu]] de ren].
not be   that-three-CL   not wear clothes PNM person
Akiu fired that group of three people who do not bathe, not
that group of three who do not dress.

This in turn suggests that, given the structural distinction between (112a,b), Chao's (1968) contrasting criterion for the restrictiveness of relatives is actually a criterion for their scopal height. That is, only the topmost restrictor can be contrasted in neutral stress environment. Therefore, the inner relative cannot be contrasted not because it is non-restrictive, but because it can not take scope over the MP.

In sum, we have demonstrated that the asymmetry between outer relativization and secondary predication can be captured even if the original mapping theoretical account does not hold (cf. (102)). The key lies in the notion "amount relative", and the fact that the MP trio is unusually productive in Chinese. Although it remains to be seen how the (dis)matching mechanism can be formulated in a proper way, our solution appears to point to the right direction.

2.5. Not Unlikely Extensions

2.5.1. Small clauses

Given our analysis of secondary predicates in Chinese existential constructions, the most natural question to ask is whether predication in small clauses also fall under the general scheme of the EMH. The answer appears to be positive. First let's consider the following contrast:

(117) Akiu ate apples.
    a. Akiu ate Sm apples.
    b. Akiu ate the kind "apple".

(118) Akiu ate [$_{SC}$ apples unpeeled].
    a. # Akiu ate Sm apples unpeeled.

b. Akiu ate the kind "apple" unpeeled.

The bare plural *apples* in (117) is ambiguous between the existential reading contributed by ∃-closure, as paraphrased as (117a), and the kind reading in Carlson's (1977a) sense, as paraphrased as (117b), where *apples* is a proper name of a species or a kind. As pointed out by Irene Heim (p.c.), the (b) readings may result from habitual construals. Namely, the bare plural in question can be licensed by a generic operator associated with past tense. Since both alternatives are compatible with our analysis, we will leave the choice open here.

This ambiguity, however, disappear when the bare plural in question is predicated by a secondary predicate such as *unpeeled*, as shown by the contrast between (118a,b). The reason is transparent from the viewpoint of the EMH: As *unpeeled* triggers predication in (118), it is mapped into the nuclear scope, and the SC node by definition constitutes an independent mapping cycle, as sketched below:

(119)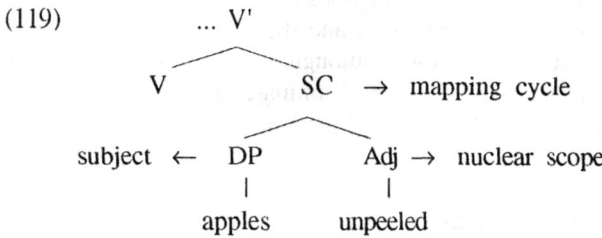

As a result, the subject of the current cycle cannot be licensed by ∃-closure due on the next cycle, and the existential reading is ruled out. In contrast, when *apples* refers to a kind, it is in itself definite. The kind reading thus survives.

The same observation applies to singular indefinites such as *an apple* in (120). Here the ambiguity is between the existential reading of (120a) and the specific reading of (120b):

(120) Akiu ate an apple.
     a. Akiu ate Sm apple.
     b. Akiu ate a certain apple.

Toward LF Interface

In a way strikingly similar to its bare plural counterpart, the existential reading of *an apple* is disallowed when secondary predication applies, as evidenced by the contrast between (121a,b):

(121) Akiu ate [SC an apple unpeeled].
    a. #Akiu ate Sm apple unpeeled.
    b. Akiu ate a certain apple unpeeled.

Given that (121) also assumes the small clause configuration in (119), the specificity follows straightforwardly. That is, the local subject must be headed by a strong determiner, as in (122), where only specific *a(n)* can serve this purpose:

(122)
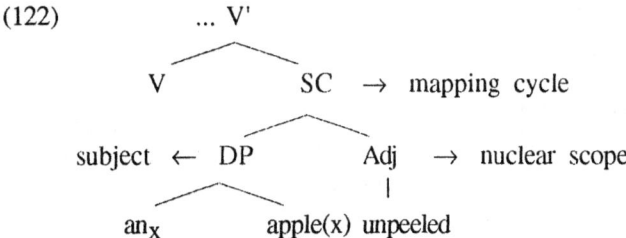

Otherwise, the mapping crashes, since the variable introduced by *apple* is unbound within the SC node.

2.5.2. Secondary temporal predicates

Another relevant fact comes from some peculiar interaction between object indefinites and secondary temporal predicates: Frequency adverbials such as *twice* and duration adverbials such as *two years* often have curious effects on the interpretation of indefinites (cf. Dowty 1972, Carlson 1977a). As shown by the now familiar contrast between the kind and existential readings of (123) and (124), *twice* and *for two years* seem to have the same theoretical status as a secondary predicate in small clauses (cf. (118)):

(123) Akiu ate apples twice.
    a. # Akiu ate Sm apples twice.

b. Akiu ate the kind "apple" twice.

(124) Akiu ate apples for two years.
    a. #Akiu ate Sm apples for two years.
    b. Akiu ate the kind "apple" for two years.

As one might expect, a similar pattern is found in singular indefinites, as evidenced by (125) and (126). Also note that the situation depicted in (b) readings is a little odd, but not impossible in appropriate contexts.[23]

(125) Akiu ate an apple twice.
    a. #Akiu ate Sm fish twice.
    b. ?Akiu ate a certain apple twice.

(126) Akiu ate an apple for two years.
    a. #Akiu ate Sm apple for two years.
    b. ?Akiu ate a certain apple for two years.

As noted by Irene Heim (p.c.), examples such as (123-126) are likely candidates for mapping-theoretic accounts: It is generally assumed that *twice* and *for two years* are predicates of implicit event arguments (cf. Kratzer 1989). The problem is that it is unclear how to characterize the relationship such that the relevant mapping geometry involves object indefinites.

For one thing, the usual postulated positions for temporal arguments (e.g., the Spec of TP) are too high for our purpose here. A plainly syntactic account of tense structures from Stowell (1993) nonetheless provides us important clues. Loosely adopting Higginbotham (1985), Stowell proposes that N is predicative in nature and accordingly generated with an external argument (or an index in Higginbotham's terms), which in turn can be saturated by binding from determiners like *the* and *every*:

Toward LF Interface 153

(127)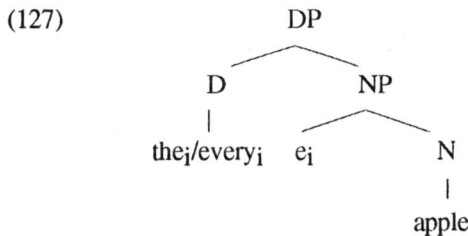

Since the external argument in question could be temporal-spatial, as in *yesterday's papers* and *mountain gorilla*, a natural extension along our line is to claim that what *twice* and *for two years* actually predicate upon in (123) and (124) is the temporal argument associated with the bare plural *apples*, as sketched below:

(128)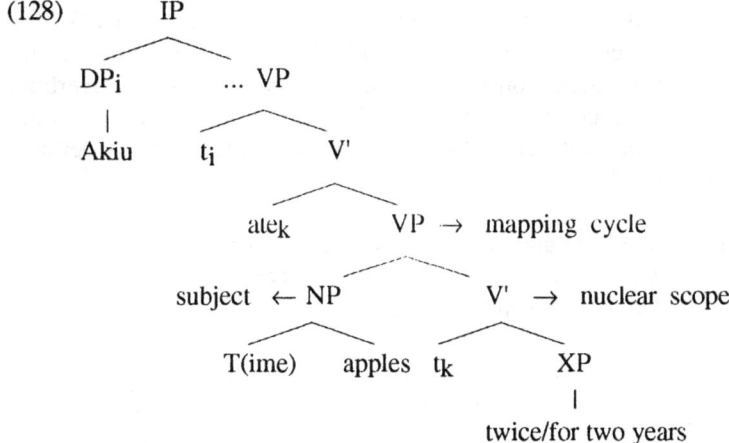

The same analysis carries over to (125) and (126), except that *an apple* does have a determiner (i.e., the indefinite article), though not strong enough to act as a binder when construed as non-specific (i.e., the Sm reading).

This approach, though tentative in nature, appears to be a productive way to look at a number of mysteries around the relation between object indefinites and temporal predicates. For instance, as observed by Huang (1991) and Tang (1991), Chinese bare indefinites are also incompatible with postverbal duration and frequency phrases:

(129) Akiu chi-guo pingguo liang-ci.
Akiu eat-Exp apple two-time
  a. # Akiu ate that/those apple(s) twice.
  b. # Akiu ate Sm apple(s) twice.
  c. ?? Akiu ate the kind "apple" twice.

(130) Akiu zhao-le ren yi-ge xiawu.
Akiu look-for-Prf person one-CL afternoon
  a. # Akiu has looked for that/those person(s) for the whole afternoon.
  b. # Akiu has looked for Sm person(s) for the whole afternoon.
  c. ?? Akiu has looked for the humankind for the whole afternoon.

First note that the deictic readings mentioned in section 2.3.4 are inadequate here, as in (129a) and (130a), probably because they are discourse-oriented construals, and incompatible with adverbials expressing frequency and duration. This point can be further illustrated by the fact the sentences improve considerably when ordinary definites are substituted:

(131) a. Akiu chi-guo na-zhong pingguo liang-ci.
      Akiu eat-Exp that-kind apple two-time
      Akiu ate the kind of apple twice.

     b. Akiu zhao-le na-ge ren yi-ge xiawu.
      Akiu look-for-Prf that-CL person one-CL afternoon
      Akiu has looked for the person for the whole afternoon.

The existential readings of (129b) and (130b) are also disallowed, in parallel with their English counterparts in (123a) and (124a). This parallel is predicted by the EMH, given that Larsonian structures in the genre of (128) are assigned to (129) and (130) as well:

(132)

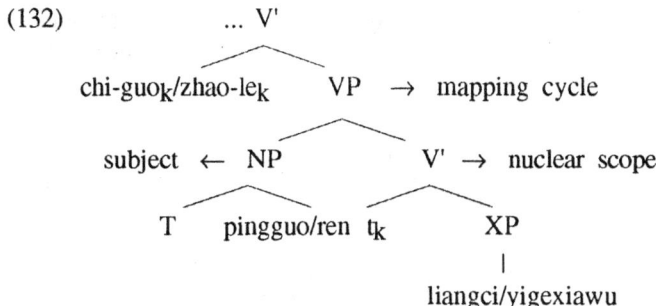

One way to improve the existential construal is to reverse the word order between object indefinites and frequency/duration phrases, as exemplified by (133a,b):

(133) a. Akiu chi-guo liang-ci (de) pingguo.
Akiu eat-Exp two-time PNM apple
Akiu ate Sm apple(s) twice.

b. Akiu zhao-le yi-ge xiawu (de) ren.
Akiu look-for-Prf one-CL afternoon PNM person
Akiu has looked for Sm person(s) for the whole afternoon.

This phenomenon is significant in two ways. First, the reverse of word order means the change of structural hierarchy. It is highly possible that *liang-ci* 'twice' and *yi-ge xiawu* 'for the whole afternoon' are no longer in a position to serve as secondary predicates in (133a,b). In other words, they are out of the c-command domain of *pingguo* 'apple' and *ren* 'person' (cf. Rothstein 1983). Consequently, no predication occurs in the lower VP shell, and hence the lack of specificity effects on the object indefinites. This in turn lends further support to our predication story for (129) and (130).

Second, in the reverse order, a prenominal modifier marker *-de* can be attached to the frequency/duration phrases, as if they are part of the object indefinites. This "syntax-semantics mismatch" in Huang's (1993b) sense indicates that there must be some subtle connection between the bare indefinites and the pseudo-specifiers which enables the reanalysis (or incorporation the same effect). Since liang-*ci* 'twice' and *yi-ge xiawu* 'for the whole afternoon' are by no means determiners of ordinary breed (i.e., they are MPs of verbs, in a way of speaking), it would make much more sense to say that they actually quantify over the proposed temporal argument rather than the head noun itself, as sketched in (134):

(134)

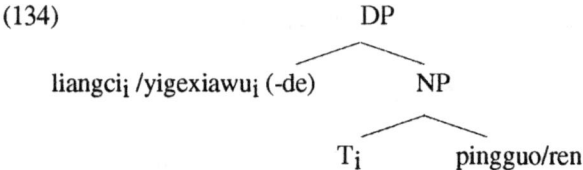

Our analysis is thus compatible with both Tang's (1990) position that the frequency/duration phrases are actually MPs (or classifier phrases), and Huang's view that the DP in question is an event-denoting gerundive ($IP_{[+N]}$ in his terms), selected by a empty verb meaning 'do'.

As a result, (133a,b) not only reinforces our argument for the EMH, but also demonstrates that the view presented in (128) and (132) is more than sheer speculation.

The kind readings of (129c) and (130c), on the other hand, are possible if forced, provided that *Akiu* is, say, a Martian, who rarely ate apples or met human before. This type of construal is most natural when we topicalize the bare indefinites:

(135) a. pingguo   (a),   Akiu   chi-guo   liang-ci.
         apple   (Top)   Akiu   eat-Exp   two-time
         Apples, Akiu ate twice.

      b. ren   (a), Akiu zhao-le   yi-ge   xiawu.
         person (Top) Akiu   look-for-Prf one-CL   afternoon
         The humankind, Akiu has searched for the whole afternoon.

As in English, Chinese singular indefinites disallow existential readings when predicated by frequency/duration phrases:

(136) Akiu   chi-guo   yi-ge   pingguo   liang-ci.
      Akiu   eat-Exp   one-CL   apple   two-time

   a. #Akiu ate Sm apple twice.

   b. ?Akiu ate a certain apple twice.

(137) Akiu zhao-le   yi-ge   ren   yi-ge   xiawu.
      Akiu look-for-Prf one-CL person one-CL afternoon

   a. #Akiu has looked for Sm person for the whole afternoon.

   b. ?Akiu has looked for a certain person for the whole afternoon.

Despite the claim that Chinese indefinites are non-quantificational, the sentences are more than marginal if *yi-ge pingguo* 'an apple' and *yi-ge ren* 'a person' are interpreted as specific, as (136b) and (137b). This is reminiscent of the dilemma we encountered in section 2.3.3. The solution offered there also carries over in a straightforward manner, since, just like secondary clausal predicates, frequency/duration phrases co-occur only with experiential and perfective aspects:

(138) a.   Akiu na-zhe   yi-ge   pingguo.
           Akiu take-Dur one-CL apple
           Akiu holds an apple.

      b. * Akiu na-zhe   yi-ge   pingguo liang-ci.
           Akiu take-Dur one-CL apple   two-time
         * Akiu holds an apple twice.

(139) a.   Akiu zai-zhao   yi-ge   ren.
           Akiu Prg-look-for one-CL person
           Akiu is looking for a person.

      b. * Akiu zai-zhao   yi-ge   ren   yi-ge   xiawu.
           Akiu Prg-look-for one-CL person one-CL afternoon
         * Akiu is looking for a person for the whole afternoon.

(138) and (139) shows that durative and progressive aspects, unlike their experiential and perfective counterparts, are not compatible with secondary temporal predicates. Consequently, the EMH makes the correct prediction that (136a) and (137a) are ruled out due to the typical specificity effect induced by secondary predication:

(140)

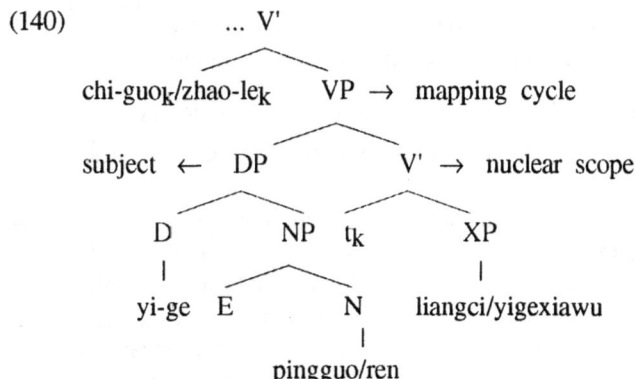

(136b) and (137b), on the other hand, are ruled in due to the existential entailment associated with experiential and perfective aspects, spelled out as part of the property of the complex predicate V', as illustrated above. This parallel again confirms our working hypothesis that a frequency/duration phrase are nothing less than a syntactic predicate in mapping-theoretic terms.

2.5.3. Resultative Complements

In addition to frequency/duration phrases, Chinese resultative complements (RCs) also display traits of secondary predicates. As Huang (1988, 1992) observes, a resultative complement can be treated as an open sentence with a subject pro, as shown by the following examples :

(141) a. Akiu da-de [na-ge ren]$_i$ [RC pro$_i$ zhan-bu-qilai].
       Akiu beat-Res that-CL person   stand-not-up
       Akiu beat that person to the extent that (s)he cannot stand up.

   b. Akiu ba [na-ge ren]$_i$ da-de [RC pro$_i$ zhan-bu-qilai].
        Akiu BA that-CL person beat-Res   stand-not-up
        Akiu beat that person so much as to make her/him unable to stand up.

Toward LF Interface 159

In the spirit of Larson (1988), the RCs of (141a,b) can be placed in the inner adjunct position, predicating upon the object *na-ge ren* 'that person' in the Spec of the lower VP shell, as illustrated below:

(142)

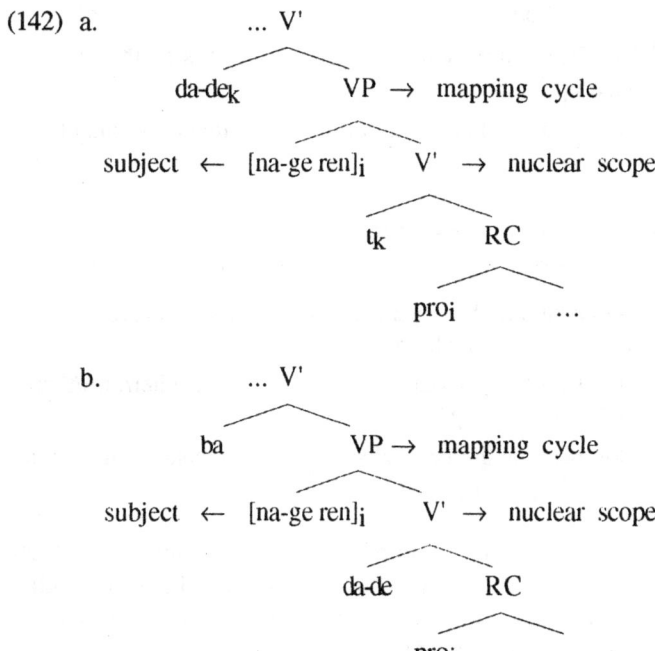

The only difference is that the primary predicate *da-de* 'beat-Res' undergoes V-to-V movement in (141a), as in (142a), while it remains in-situ in (141b), with the upper V node filled by *ba*, which serves as a place holder for subsequent LF head movement of *da-de*, as in (142b) (also cf. Tsai 1995). Alternatively, *ba* can also be analyzed as a light verb of some sort, expressing "affectedness". In either case, secondary predication applies, assigning an extra PATIENT role to the object according to Huang (1992). This adds to the default "extent" reading a "victimizing" touch, which is particularly explicit in the presence of *ba*.

When we substitute bare indefinites for the definte objects in (141a,b), the familiar pattern emerges: The existential reading is blocked as a rule, as in (143b) and (144b):

(143) Akiu da-de ren$_i$ [RC pro$_i$ zhan-bu-qilai].
      Akiu beat-Res person   stand-not-up

   a. $^?$ Akiu beat that/those person(s) to the extent that (s)he/they
        cannot stand up.
   b. $^\#$ Akiu beat Sm person(s) to the extent that (s)he/they cannot
        stand up.
   c. $^\#$ Akiu beat the humankind to the extent that they cannot
        stand up.

(144) Akiu ba ren$_i$ da-de [RC pro$_i$ zhan-bu-qilai].
      Akiu BA person   beat-Res   stand-not-up

   a. Akiu beat that/those person(s) so much as to make
        her/him/them unable to stand up.
   b. $^\#$ Akiu beat Sm person(s) so much as to make her/him/them
        unable to stand up.
   c. $^\#$ Akiu beat the humankind so much as to make them unable
        to stand up.

The deictic construal somehow improves over its counterpart in (129)
and (130), as in (143a) and (144a). In contrast, the kind reading
degrades, probably because even the Martian scenario falls short in
making sense out of (143c) and (144c).

Resultative constructions with singular object indefinites also
behave slightly different, as shown below:

(145) Akiu da-de   [yi-ge ren]$_i$ [RC pro$_i$ zhan-bu-qilai].
      Akiu beat-Res one-CL person   stand-not-up

   a. $^\#$ Akiu beat Sm person to the extent that (s)he cannot stand
        up.
   b.$^\#$ Akiu beat a certain person to the extent that (s)he cannot
        stand up.

(146) Akiu ba [yi-ge   ren]$_i$ da-de [RC pro$_i$ zhan-bu-qilai].
      Akiu BA one-CL person beat-Res   stand-not-up

a. # Akiu beat Sm person so much as to make her/him unable to stand up.
b.# Akiu beat a certain person so much as to make her/him unable to stand up.

The specific reading, as well as the existential reading, is blocked. This is because there is no experiential or perfective aspect in this case, and the connotation of the resultative maker -*de*, if any, remains obscure. As a result, no existential assertion/entailment is available for licensing the object indefinite. Our position is further strengthened by the fact that, unlike secondary clausal predicates in existential constructions, RCs do not impose (in)definiteness restriction, as we have seen in (141a,b).

2.5.4. *A preverbal-postverbal asymmetry of temporal adjuncts*

A significant implication of the original IP-VP split is that not only arguments but also adjuncts have to observe specificity, as long as they are nominals and outside VP. This prediction, interestingly enough, turns out to be true in Chinese, as evidenced by the contrasts of (147) and (148):

(147) Akiu zhe-liang-nian/you-liang-nian/*liang-nian qu-le meiguo.
 Akiu this-two-year/have-two-year/two-year go-Prf America
 Akiu went to America these two years/for two specific years/for two years.

(148) Akiu zhe-liang-ci/you-liang-nian/*liang-ci zhu lüguan.
 Akiu this-two-time/have-two-time/two-time stay hotel
 Akiu stayed in hotel these two times/two specific times/twice.

As shown above, frequency/duration phrases like *liang-nian* 'two years' and *liang-ci* 'twice' do not occur preverbally without being headed by strong determiners such as *zhe* 'this' and *you* 'have'. As noted by Li & Thompson (1981), among others, the descriptive generalization appears to be that preverbal expressions tend to be specific or definite, whereas postverbal expressions tend to be non-specific and indefinite.

The only problem with this picture in regard to the EMH, as pointed out by Ken Hale (p.c.) concerns the (non-)specificity restriction on postverbal adjuncts, as shown by the following examples:

(149) Akiu qu-le meiguo liang-nian/*you-liang-ci/*zhe-liang-nian.
Akiu go-Prf America two-year/have-two-time/this-two-year
Akiu went to America for two year/for two specific years/for these two years.

(150) Akiu zhu-guo lüguan liang-ci/*you-liang-ci /*zhe-liang-ci.
Akiu stay-Exp hotel two-time/have-two-time/this-two-time
Akiu stayed in hotel twice/two specific times/these two times.

Here the pattern of contrasts is reversed. Namely, frequency/duration phrases like *liang-nian* 'two years' and *liang-ci* 'twice' cannot occur postverbally when headed by strong determiners such as *zhe* 'this' and *you* 'have'. Neither the IP-VP split nor the EMH makes relevant prediction here, and the cause remains mysterious.

In the light of the discussion in section 2.5.2, however, we are able to address the issue in a more productive way. Given our proposal that *liang-nian* and *liang-ci* should be treated as syntactic predicates, they must contain some open position so as to qualify as an unsaturated function. Since *zhe* and *you* only serve to "seal" open positions by saturating unbound arguments (cf. Higginbotham 1985, Stowell 1989, 1993), it is just natural that they should be ruled out in this type of configuration.

3. Chain-formation as a Copying Operation

3.1. A Few Good Questions

Although the EMH works reasonably well in accounting for the specificity and (in)definiteness effects resulted from the interaction between predication and quantification, there are still a couple of puzzles when we reflect upon the issue more closely: One concerns the availability of lowering as a way to derive the ambiguity (i.e., specific/generic vs. existential/cardinal) of English subject indefinites.

The other has something to do with the unavailability of lowering as a way to salvage Chinese subject indefinites.

Let's consider them one by one. It is well-known that English singular indefinites are ambiguous, as exemplified below:

(151) A dog ran away.
 a. A certain dog ran away. (presuppositional/specific)
 b. Sm dog ran away. (existential/non-specific)

The reason, as provided by Diesing (1992a), is that the subject *a dog* can be lowered back to its original position, i.e., the VP Spec, given the VP-internal subject hypothesis, as illustrated by (152b):

(152) a. [$_{IP}$ A dog$_i$ ... (*∃) [$_{VP}$ t$_i$ [$_{V'}$ ran away]]].
 (presuppositional/specific)

 b. [$_{IP}$ ... ∃$_x$ [$_{VP}$ a dog(x) [$_{V'}$ ran away]]].
 (existential/non-specific)

While this type of "reconstruction" effect is very common for A'-chains created by QR, *wh*-movement, and VP-fronting, it has been widely observed that A-chains created by NP-movement do not seem to have the same property. This point can be illustrated by the contrast between (153a,b), as well as that between (154a,b) (data from Huang 1993a):

(153) a. * It seems to him$_i$ that [$_{DP}$ the claim that John$_i$ overslept] is false.

 b. [$_{DP}$ the claim that John$_i$ overslept]$_k$ seems to him$_i$ [t$_k$ to be false].

(154) a. The pictures of John$_i$ surprises him$_i$.

 b. * He$_i$ is surprised t$_i$ by the pictures of John$_i$.

If the "heavy" DP in (153b) reconstructs to its initial trace, the sentence should be as bad as (153a) due to Binding Principle C violation. On the other hand, if the subject pronoun *he* in (154b) reconstructs to its base position, the sentence should be as good as (154a). These predictions, however, are not borne out. We are thus bound to question the nature of the lowering mechanism.

The third issue concerns the fact that Chinese cardinal NPs do not appear in the IP Spec without "marked" licensing (also cf. section 1.1):

(155) a. * yi-zhi   gou pao-le.
         one-CL dog run-Prf
         A dog ran away.

   b. yi-zhi   gou *(neng) pao duo   kuai?
      one-CL dog   can   run how fast
      How fast can a dog run?

   c. you yi-zhi   gou pao-le.
      have one-CL dog run-Prf
      There is a dog that ran away.

   d. na-yi-zhi   gou pao-le.
      that-one-CL dog run-Prf
      That dog ran away.

The singular indefinite *yi-zhi gou* 'a dog' is licensed by a modal in (155b), by a existential predicate in (155c), and by a demonstrative in (155d). Without the licensing, the sentence is simply ruled out, as in (155a). The same observation by and large holds for bare indefinites as well:

(156) gou pao-le.
      dog run-Prf
      a. That/Those dog(s) ran away.
      b. # Sm dog(s) ran away.

(157) gou yao   weiba
      dog swing tail
      a. Dogs, in general, swing tails.
      b. # Sm dogs swing tails.

(158) you-de   gou pao-le.
      have-PNM dog run-Prf

'Some of the dogs ran away.'

(159) na-xie gou pao-le.
those dog run-Prf
'Those dogs ran away.'

As shown by the contrast between (156a,b), the existential reading is ruled out, while the deictic reading survives. As for (157), only the generic reading is possible, presumably induced by the generic tense. (158) and (159) show patterns similar to (155c,d) respectively. As proposed by Cheng (1991), these facts will follow from the IP-VP split directly if we assume that Chinese indefinites, bare or not, are non-quantificational, and more importantly, that Chinese subjects do not undergo lowering. We thus appear to have got some hold of how the linguistic variation can be handled in mapping-theoretic terms. The problem is that we still do not know why the lowering mechanism should behave this way.

The solutions which we are going to offer are based on the copy theory developed by Chomsky (1993) and the notion of individual variable conceived in Heim (1987) and Frampton (1990). We will start with English indefinites first.

3.2. Lowering or Copying?

One of the revealing insights of Chomsky (1993) concerns the observation that the interpretation procedure known as "reconstruction" in the literature can be implemented in terms of "copying" instead of lowering. The crucial assumption is that Move-α leaves behind a copy rather than a trace. This copy deletes at PF, while providing reconstruction materials at LF, as exemplified below:

(160) PF: [Which book] did John read t ?
LF: [Which book] did John read [which book]?

a. [which book] John read t
→ Which$_x$ [x is a book] John read x
b. [which] John read [t book]
→ Which$_F$ (F(book) ∧ John read F)

Whereas the PF deletion applies under identicalness, its LF counterpart is further restricted by the need to avoid vacuous quantification. As a result, there are two converging derivations for the above sentence: First, if the whole copy deletes at LF, the trace count as a DP variable, as in (160a). The answer to the question could be either *the red one* or *War and Peace*. Second, if the head noun of the moved DP and the determiner of the remaining copy delete at LF, the trace count as a D variable (or a functional variable), as in (160b). The answer could be *that (book)*.

First note that there is no theory-internal reason why the copying mechanism should discriminate between A-chains and A'-chain.[24] To block reconstruction in sentences like (154b), we would like to claim that quantificational expressions are in general subject to copying, as implicitly assumed in Chomsky (1993), while referential expressions are not. Alternatively, we may assume that Move-a always leaves copies, and that in a chain bearing referential dependency, LF deletion must apply downward due to the recoverability condition, as illustrated in (161b):

(161) LF: He$_i$ is surprised he$_i$ by the pictures of John$_i$.
    a. * He$_i$ is surprised t by the pictures of John$_i$
    b. * t is surprised he$_i$ by the pictures of John$_i$

When the copy does delete, as in (161a), the representation is ruled out according to Principle C. We will leave the choice open here.

The latter approach also provides us an explanation of the absence of reconstruction effects in (153b), as shown below:

(162) LF: [DP the claim [CP that John overslept]]$_k$ seems to him
    [[DP the claim [CP that John overslept]]$_k$ to be false].

    a. [DP the claim [CP that John$_i$ overslept]] seems to him$_i$
       [t to be false]
    b. * [DP the claim] seems to him [[DP t [CP that John overslept]] to be false]
    c. * [DP the] seems to him$_i$ [[DP t claim [CP that John$_i$ overslept]] to be false]

Toward LF Interface 167

There are a number of ways to implement the deletion besides deleting the whole copy as in (162a). For ease of exposition, let's pick only the major constituents, i.e., *the claim* and *that John overslept*, as illustrated in (162b,c). (162b) is ruled out because no operator-variable pair is formed. (162c), on the other hand, violates Principle C. Consequently, there is no other way to converge the derivation except deleting the whole copy. The possibility of reconstruction is therefore blocked.

The next step is to examine how copying works for English indefinites. Deriving the specific reading for *a dog* in (151) is quite straightforward, as shown by (163a):

(163) LF: [$_{IP}$ a dog$_k$ [$_{VP}$ a dog$_k$ ran away]].

    a. [$_{IP}$ a dog [$_{VP}$ t ran away]]
      → $\exists_x$ [x is a dog]   x ran away
    b. [$_{IP}$ [$_{VP}$ a dog ran away]]
      → $\exists_x$ (x is a dog ∧ x ran away)

For the non-specific reading, we do not have a proper operator-variable pair immediately after upward deletion. However, $\exists$-closure introduced by subsequent mapping salvages the derivation, as illustrated in (163b). The same observation applies to bare plural subjects, as shown below:

(164) LF: [$_{IP}$ dogs$_k$ [$_{VP}$ dogs$_k$ bark]].

    a. [$_{IP}$ dogs [$_{VP}$ t bark]]
      → Gen$_x$ [x is a dog]   x bark
    b. [$_{IP}$ [$_{VP}$ dogs bark]]
      → $\exists_x$ (x is a dog ∧ x bark)

An obvious advantage of the copy theory is that we no longer need to worry about an asymmetry between overt *wh*-extraction and LF quantification. That is, under the trace-leaving approach, something more has to be said about why representations such as (165) are allowed at LF, but not at PF:

(165) Which$_i$ did John read [t$_i$ book]?

Traditionally, this fact can be made to follow from the head-government requirement or the leftness condition in Ross's (1967) sense, but only at the cost of stipulating that these constraints apply only at S-structure or PF (e.g., WAHL's (1987) split ECP approach). Now by assuming that PF deletion applies under identicalness and in accordance with temporal sequence (i.e., rightward),[25] we may derive the asymmetry in a straightforward manner (cf. (160)).

3.3. An Individual Variable Account of Stage-Individual Asymmetries

At first glance, it might seem that we are simply reformulating the problem to avoid controversies around the lowering hypothesis. Below we will show that there is much more to the copy theory than just an alternative to derive reconstruction effects.

A natural extension of our view is that the VP-internal subject hypothesis should be maintained for both stage-level and individual-level predicates, and the difference is that the former allows a copy in the VP Spec, thus subject to reconstruction, whereas the latter do not. The problem, of course, is why this should be the case.

A suggestive clue comes from Frampton (1990). Based on Heim (1987), He points out that the referential/non-referential asymmetry of *wh*-extraction in Cinque's (1989) sense can be recast as an asymmetry between individual variables and amount/degree variables (also cf. Cresti 1994). The distinction roughly corresponds to that of DP and D variables drawn by Chomsky (1993) (see also Chomsky 1977, Cooper 1983, among others). For example, *how many books* can have two types of interpretation, depending on its logical representations, as illustrated below:

(166) How many books does Bill think that Mary read?
    a. (how_x) [x many books: y] Bill think that Mary read y
    b. (how_x) Bill think that Mary read (x many books)

(166a) represents the reading where a set of books is presupposed. The whole copy is deleted, and the object variable *y* has the standard interpretation for *wh*-traces, counting as an R-expression. As for (166b), no presupposition is made, and *x many books* is construed as a function variable (cf. Engdahl 1980, Reinhart 1992, 1993). In this case, the highest N' of the moved *wh*-phrase and the determiner of the in-situ copy are deleted.

This ambiguity, however, disappears when *wh*-island constructions are involved, as evidenced by the contrast between (167a,b):

(167) How many books does Bill wonder whether Mary read?
    a. (how$_x$) [x many books: y] Bill wonders whether Mary read y
    b.#(how$_x$) Bill wonders whether Mary read (x many books)

The reason, as offered by Frampton, is that the long-distance dependency in question can only be licensed by virtue of the variable it dwells upon, as formulated below:

(168) A trace of long movement must be interpreted as an individual variable.

If the variable refers to an individual, long *wh*-movement is allowed according to (168). In contrast, if the variable refers to an amount or a degree, *how many books* can only undergo successive cyclic movement, inducing the *wh*-island effect of (167b). In copy theoretic terms, this would mean that long movement always requires deletion of the entire copy.

Now compare the individual-amount asymmetry with the following contrast:

(169) How many people are available?
    a. (how$_x$) [x many people:y] y are available
    b. (how$_x$) (x many people) are available

(170) How many people are admirable/intelligent?
    a. (how$_x$) [x many people:y] y are admirable/intelligent
    b.#(how$_x$) (x many people) are available/intelligent

(169) contains a stage-level predicate, i.e., *available*, and allows both the individual and amount readings. (170), on the other hand, contains an individual-level predicate, i.e., *admirable*, and allows only the individual reading, where a group of people is presupposed. A working hypothesis thus can be sketched to capture this parallel:

(171) Individual-level predicates can only predicate upon individual variables.

An immediate question coming to mind is whether the terms "individual" from both parties refer to the same thing. According to Carlson (1977a), an (individual) object can be defined as a collection of a series of stages which roughly correspond to spatiotemporal slices in terms of intensional semantics. An individual-level predicate thus expresses properties consistent to all stages of its subject, or all members of its subject as a group. In the same vein, an individual variable refers to an individual group (or an individual kind in Carlson's terms). Furthermore, the amount/degree construal also appears to have similar semantics as the stage construal, at least in pure formal terms:

(172) a.

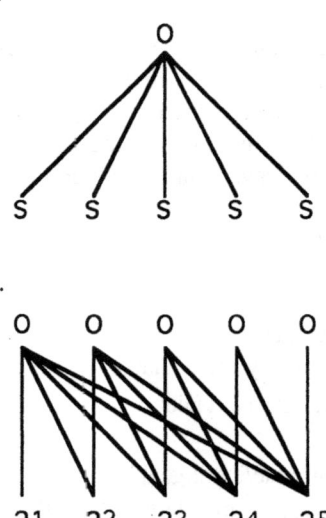

b.

As shown by (172a), the stage construal essentially slices an object according to some arbitrary spatiotemporal coordinates. In comparison, the amount/degree construal divides a group of objects according to the given criterion of measurement (e.g., *x many books*), as illustrated in (172b).

As a result, it follows from (171) that stative or individual-level predicates cannot predicate upon amounts or degrees, since they have the same theoretical status as stages. *There-be* constructions thus provides an ideal testing ground for our hypothesis, where the amount/degree construal is obligatory. This intuition has been formulated by Heim (1987) in the following terms:

(173) * *There be x*, where *x* is an individual variable.

In other words, (171) predicts that stative or individual-level predicates is incompatible with the structural object of *there-be* constructions. The prediction is borne out, as evidenced by the contrast between (174) and (175):

(174)   There are people available.

(175) * There are people admirable/intelligent.

Further support comes from DPs of artificial measurement like *how many pounds*. As observed by Cinque (1989,1990) and Rizzi (1990), long *wh*-movement is typically not available for these so-called non-referential DPs, which, translated in Heim-Frampton's terms, means that they can never leave individual variables. Here (171) again makes the right prediction: That is, stative or individual-level predicates cannot predicate upon nominals introducing amount variables, as evidenced by the contrasts between (175) and (176) on the one hand, and (177) and (178) on the other:

(176)   How many/1000 pounds exceeds the capability of this scale

(177)   How many/1000 pounds is beyond detection for this scale

(178) ?? How many/1000 pounds impresses a human being

(179) ?? How many/1000 pounds is beyond belief for a human being

Since *exceed* and *beyond detection* count as "amount-level" or "degree-level" predicates under our view, they are compatible with amount expressions such as *how many pounds* and *1000 pounds*, as in (176) and (177). In contrast, since there is no notion like "an individual group of pounds", individual-level predicates such as *impress* and *beyond belief* are ruled out in the presence of amount expressions, as in (178) and (179).

If our observation turns out to be on the right track, then there is a way to characterize the stage-individual (or state-action) asymmetries in copy theoretic terms, that is, in terms of their logical representations rather than their structural representations such as (155) and (156): A stative or individual-level predicate requires absolute deletion of the copy in the VP Spec because its subject can only be an individual variable, as illustrated by (180a):

(180) LF: [IP firemen$_k$ [VP firemen$_k$ are admirable]].

    a. [IP firemen [VP t are admirable]]
       → Gen$_x$ [x is a fireman] x are admirable
    b. * [IP [VP firemen are admirable]]
       → $\exists_F$ F(firemen) are admirable

If LF deletion applies upward, as in (180b), what is left behind is a function variable (or a D variable in Chomsky's terms). Though $\exists$-closure may undo this vacuous quantification during the subsequent mapping, the variable in question fails to satisfy the requirement imposed by *admirable*. We thus correctly predict that the existential reading is blocked for *firemen* in (180). In contrast, there is no such restriction associated with stage-level predicates such as *available*. Consequently, both the generic and existential readings are licensed in (181):

(181) LF: [IP firemen$_k$ [VP firemen$_k$ are available]].

    a. [IP firemen [VP t are available]]
       → Gen$_x$ [x is a fireman] x are available
    b. [IP [VP firemen are available]]
       → $\exists_F$ F(firemen) are available

In the light of the above discussion, a tentative account can also be sketched for objects of stative predicates. Following Chomsky (1993), we would like to assume that the English object *dogs* undergoes LF movement to the Spec of AGRo for Case-checking, as illustrated below:

(182)

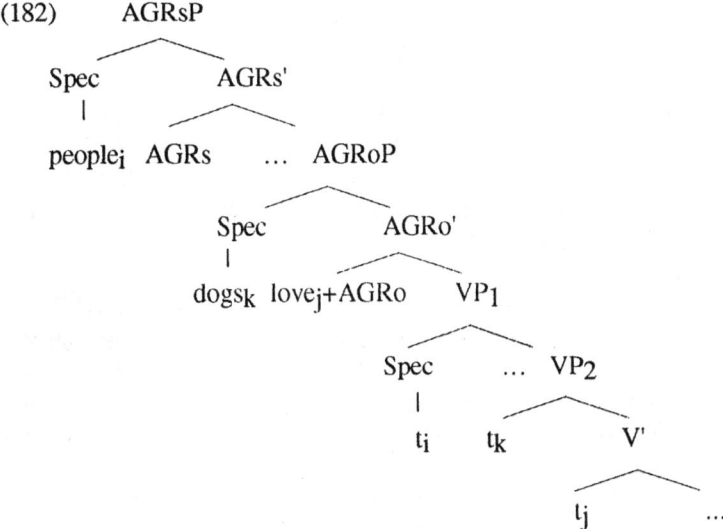

The object copy, as well as the subject copy, undergoes obligatory deletion, as dictated by the stative predicate *love*. As a result, both *people* and *dogs* are interpreted as generic by virtue of their positions.

To sum up, by integrating the notion of individual variable into the copy theory, we have achieved two things. First, the VP-internal subject hypothesis is maintained for both stage-level and individual-level predicates. Second, the copying mechanism is generalized to capture the stage-individual distinction, which gives us an edge to solve the seeming reconstruction effects on A-chains. With this fairly explicit theory in mind, we will proceed to examine Chinese indefinites.

3.4. Disagree Chinese Agreement

As mentioned in section 3.1, the most peculiar property of Chinese subject indefinites is probably that they never reconstruct to benefit from ∃-closure. This topic-like quality might be attributed to the conjecture that there is no genuine subject in Chinese-type languages, and all the subject-like items are topics (see, for example, Tsao 1979).

The following parameter proposed by Kim (1991) may also provide some partial answer to our problem:

(183) Every matrix clause in Chinese-type languages has a topic position that must be filled overtly at S-structure.

Nevertheless, evidence from VP-reconstruction effects strongly suggests that subjects originate from the VP Spec in both Chinese and English (cf. Huang 1993a). Moreover, as we have demonstrated earlier (cf. (16)), embedded subjects do not behave differently from their matrix counterparts. And hence the irrelevance of (183) as a way to derive the specificity in question.

The solution, in our opinion, still lies in the EMH. While our discussion mainly focuses on secondary predication, it is instructive to note that, for primary predication, the nuclear scope is also a relative term. For instance, by moving V to I, the nuclear scope may well extend to I' for a subject in the IP Spec. To derive the facts along this line, it would be necessary that Chinese primary predicates never move beyond the VP Spec, since only in this way can LF deletion apply freely without changing the semantics of subject indefinites. In other words, Chinese subject chains as a whole must be always beyond the scope of $\exists$-closure, as illustrated in (184a). English, in contrast, requires V-to-I movement at LF, as illustrated in (184b), presumably due to feature-checking reasons (cf. Chomsky 1993):

(184) a. Chinese LF:

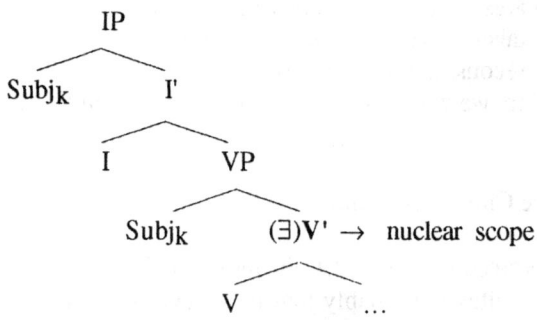

b. English LF:

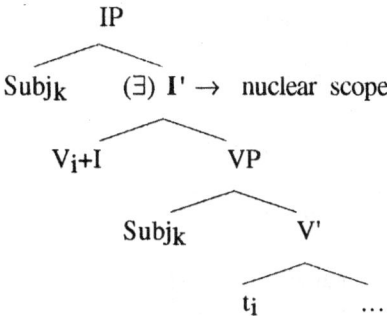

Since the English subject copy "submerges" under the nuclear scope, it is subject to ∃-closure when the head of chain deletes. On the other hand, since the head of the subject chain is above the nuclear scope, it has to be licensed in a marked way when its copy deletes. Chinese subject indefinites, in contrast, are never subject to ∃-closure, no matter which way LF deletion goes.[26]

Our task, therefore, is to show that Chinese lacks V-to-I movement, both in overt syntax and in the LF component. As observed by Huang (1993c), there is solid evidence indicating that Chinese verbs pattern with their English counterparts in not undergoing S-structure movement:

(185) a. Zhangsan bu xihuan Lisi.
Zhangsan not like Lisi
Zhangsan does not like Lisi.

b. *Zhangsan xihuan bu Lisi.
Zhangsan like not Lisi

(186) a. Zhangsan changchang ma Lisi.
Zhangsan often scold Lisi
Zhangsan often scolded Lisi.

b. *Zhangsan ma changchang Lisi.
Zhangsan scold often Lisi

As shown above, verbs can never locate higher than the negative morpheme *bu* and sentential adverbial such as *changchang* 'often' in Chinese. As a matter of fact, the same observation applies to auxiliary verbs like *you* 'have' and *shi* 'be' as well, as evidenced by the following contrasts:

(187) a. Zhangsan mei you kanjian Lisi.
Zhangsan not have see Lisi
Zhangsan has not seen Lisi.

b. * Zhangsan you mei kanjian Lisi.
Zhangsan have not seen Lisi

(188) a. Zhangsan bu shi zuotian lai de.
Zhangsan not be yesterday come DE
It wasn't yesterday that Zhangsan came.

b. * Zhangsan shi bu zuotian lai de.
Zhangsan be not yesterday come DE

From a cross-linguistic point of view, the fact that Chinese disallows gapping can also be correlated to the absence of V-to-I movement in overt syntax. First consider the following contrast:

(189) a. Southerners eat rice, and northerners noodles.

b. na-ren shi mi, bei-ren *(shi) mian.
south-people eat rice north-people eat noodles
Southerners eat rice, and northerners eat noodles.

While gapping is a common practice in English, as exemplified by (189a), the same construal is impossible in Chinese, as shown by (189b). As pointed out by Johnson (1994), gapping is unlikely to be an instance of ellipsis or deletion. Rather, he suggests that cases like (189a) involve across-the-aboard fronting of a verb in an coordinate construction, as illustrated below:

(190)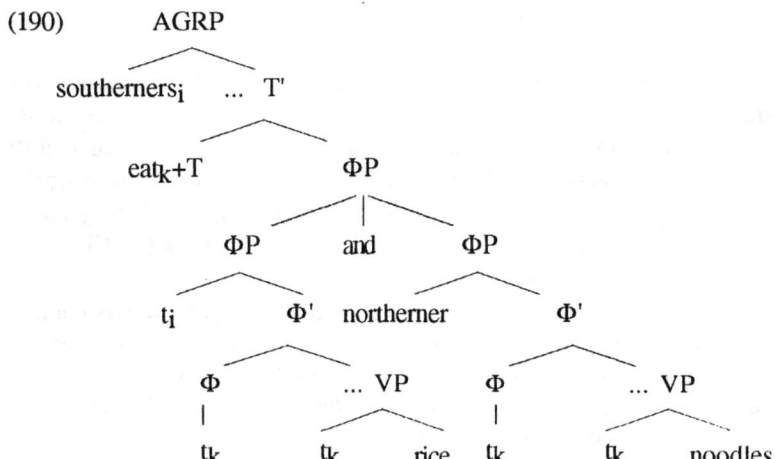

Consequently, the anti-gapping behavior of (189b) follows straightforwardly given the lack of V-to-I raising in Chinese, which in turn lends substantial support to Johnson's view.

Probably the only fact which can be taken to suggest otherwise is the position of Chinese aspects. Namely, they appear to be "inflected" on verbs as some sort of suffixes. Under some early head movement analysis, this would mean that verbs have been overtly moved to INFL, given that the projection of, say, AspP is higher than VP. On the other hand, this won't be the necessary conclusion if we follow Chomsky's (1993) view that verbs are inserted with inflection, and arguments Case-marking.

Furthermore, if we take a step back and look at the historical development of Chinese verbal elements, we will realize that the majority of so-called aspect markers actually come from the second half of compound verbs, which in turn derive from serial verb constructions. For example, compounds like *chi-wan* 'eat-finish' and *chi-dao* 'eat-reach' also have perfective or experiential flavor, in parallel to *chi-le* 'eat-Prf' and *chi-guo* 'eat-Exp'. In fact, *-le* and *-guo* still have contemporary verb counterparts, which literally mean 'finish' and 'pass' respectively (e.g., *liao-duan* 'finish-cut' and *guo nian* 'pass (New) Year'). The same observation applies to the durative aspect *-zhe*, as in *zhuo/zhao di* 'touch ground'. This indicates that modern Chinese aspects used to be and still are "secondary" verbs. As pointed out by Alec Marantz (p.c.), if there is an AspP projection in Chinese, it should locate under VP, rather than above VP.

Our observation, of course, does not guarantee that Chinese verbs do not raise in LF. To prove our case, we have to look at its consequences in a wider context. First let's assume a more articulated IP structure (cf. Emonds 1978, Pollock 1989). Saying that there is no V-to-I movement thus roughly means that there is no AGRP projection, which hosts LF Case-checking when V features are weak (cf. Chomsky 1993).

Evidence against the existence of AGRsP in Chinese has come a long way. As shown by (191a), *ta-ziji* 'him-self' differs from the genuine long-distance anaphor *ziji* 'self' in that it is clause-bound in object position, behaving exactly the same way as English *himself* (cf. Tang 1989, Huang & Tang 1989):

(191) a. Akiu$_i$ renwei [CP Lisi$_j$ hui xuan ta-ziji*$_{i/j}$].
Akiu think   Lisi will elect him-self
Akiu$_i$ thinks that Lisi$_j$ will elect himself*$_{i/j}$.

b. Akiu renwei [CP ta-ziji hui dang-xuan].
Akiu think   him-self will get-elected
*Akiu thinks that himself will get elected.

Nevertheless, the parallel does not hold in subject position: the binding domain of *ta-ziji* 'himself' in (181b) is the matrix clause despite the fact that the embedded clause is tensed. A natural account of this subject/object asymmetry is that Chinese does not have Agr in IP-related projections, which may serve as an accessible SUBJECT in defining binding domains (cf. Chomsky 1981, Huang 1983, Aoun 1985,1986). In addition, Huang(1984,1989b) argues for a typological distinction between Chinese and Romance pro-drop, based on the lack of AGR on the part of Chinese: Subject pro is licensed through identification from discourse, rather than agreement with INFL.

Another desirable consequence along this line comes from another significant distinction between Chinese-type and English-type languages, that is, the rigidity of scope interaction (i.e., the Syntax-LF isomorphism in Huang's (1982) sense). As is well-known, the following Chinese sentence does not have the ambiguity which its

English counterpart has, as illustrated by the contrast between (192b) and (193b):

(192) mei-ge nüren dou taoyan mou-ge nanren.
every-CL woman all hate some-CL man
a. For every x, x a woman, for some y, y a man, x hates y.
b. #For some y, y a man, for every x, x a woman, x hates y.

(193) Every woman hates some man.
a. For every x, x a woman, for some y, y a man, x hates y.
b. For some y, y a man, for every x, x a woman, x hates y.

Now consider the following LF representation of (192), where the object adjoins to V to check its Case feature in absence of the Spec of Agr_O:

(194) [$_{TP}$ meige nüren$_i$ [T^0 [... [$_{VP}$ t$_i$ [$_{V'}$ [$_V$ mouge nanren$_j$
every woman some man
[$_V$ taoyan]] .. t$_j$ ..]]]]]]
hate

Since the head of the object chain does not c-command any member of the subject chain, the (b) clause reading is impossible in violation of the Scope Principle (195) proposed by Aoun & Li (1989):

(195) A quantifier A has scope over a quantifier B in case A c-commands a member of chain containing B.

Analyses in the same vein can also be sketched by adopting the notion of "chain scope" advocated in Kim (1991).
    Consequently, it seems safe to assume the LF representation (184a) for Chinese subject indefinites, and thereby provide a mapping-theoretic account of the specificity in question.

4. Concluding Remarks

To justify the extension of the Mapping Hypothesis (1) and its correlation to $\exists$-closure, We have shown that there is a parallel between subject-predicate and topic-comment constructions with respect to the range of interpretations associated with indefinites. We also examined constructions involving non-restrictive relativization and secondary predication. The conclusion is quite clear. All these cases bear the hallmark of predication, i.e., specificity/definiteness effects on relevant subjects, just as the EMH (11) predicts in the spirit of the original IP-VP split (cf. Diesing 1992a,b). Furthermore, the asymmetry between non-restrictive relatives and secondary clausal predicates also lends support to our claim that the EMH is in work. The interaction between the (in)definiteness restriction and the predication requirement (82), on the other hand, suggests that the issue of specificity is more complicated than previously conceived, and should be treated accordingly with even greater scrutiny.

Despite of the fact that there are still some technical problems lingering around, the general approach taken in this thesis seems to point to the right direction, not only on conceptual grounds but also on empirical grounds.

Notes

CHAPTER ONE

1. Our regard for Economy here is more in line with the notion "local economy" as developed in Collins (1997) than the original "global" formulation by Chomsky (1993, 1995). Global economy requires derivations to converge with fewest operations as possible (cf. Kitahara 1995), while local economy enforces economy conditions locally and derivationally, and does not concern itself with whether a particular derivation eventually converges or not.

2. Here the term "barrier" is construed in the traditional sense, i.e., as "bounding node". According to Chomsky's (1986b) formulation of Subjacency, even one barrier suffices to induce marginality, since the two members of a chain link have to be 0-subjacent (namely, without any barrier inbetween). This point is illustrated by the contrast between (ia,b):
(i) a. ??What$_i$ did you remember [$_{CP}$ where$_k$ she bought t$_i$ t$_k$]?
     b. *?What$_i$ did you remember [$_{DP}$ the girl [$_{CP}$ who bought t$_i$]]?
One barrier (i.e., CP) is crossed in (ia), and hence the marginality. In contrast, two barriers (i.e., DP and CP) are crossed in (ib), and hence the ungrammaticality. This formulation certainly fits into the general scheme of the minimalist approach, that is, to "minimize chain links" (Chomsky & Lasnik 1991). Nevertheless, as Howard Lasnik (p.c.) points out, there is still substantial work to be done before we can implement the intuitive idea presented above, particularly before we can resolve the tension between Subjacency and Relativized Minimality.

3. Similar intuitions have been pursued as early as Chomksy (1964), Katz & Postal (1964), and Klima (1964), where *who* and *what* are analyzed as [WH+someone] and [WH+something] respectively. See also Kuroda (1965).

4. As Howard Lasnik (p.c.) observes, free relative constructions like (i) do not fall under the category discussed here:
(i)   I'll eat what you cook.
The usage of the free relative *what* in (i) is considered to be definite by C. L. Baker (1989), in contrast to the indefinite usage exemplified by (13a). The distinction is illustrated by the following paraphrase of (i):
(ii) I'll eat the food that you cook.
It follows that there may well be a (non-overt) definite counterpart of *ever* associated with the relative *wh* in question. As noted again by Howard Lasnik, our treatment here bears close resemblance to that of

Chomsky (1975:434), where *who* is taken to be [WH+(s)he], *what* [WH+it], and so forth. Consequently, there seem to be empirical bases for both the [WH+pronominals] and [WH+indefinites] analyses. If our proposal presented below is correct (cf. (14a) and (19)), the difference between the definite and indefinite usages then lies in the different operators involved in the internal structures of *wh*-words.

5. Another possibility, as entertained by Noam Chomsky (p.c.) is to assume that English does not allow Q-operators at all. This proposal, though stipulative in nature, is not further complicated by the tension between morphology and syntax. For a similar view, see Tsai (to appear), where the presence of Q-operators in Chinese in correlated to the positive setting of the null topic parameter in Huang's (1984) sense.

6. An apparent counterexample to the above observation comes from cases where NPs under quantification take singular determiners such as *(yi-)zheng-ge* '(one)-whole-CL', as evidenced below:
(i) a. (yi-)zheng-ge   fangzi   dou   shao-diao-le.
       one-whole-CL   house   all   burn-down-Prf
       The whole house has burnt down.
    b. Akiu   ba   (yi-)zheng-ge   fangzi   dou shao-diao-le.
       Akiu   BA   one-whole-CL   house   all burn-down-Prf
       Akiu has burnt down the whole house.
As suggested by Cheng (p.c.), the anomaly may result from some kind of partitive construals. The definite readings reflected by the English translations also support her conjecture. If this is indeed the case, then (ia) should be read as 'all parts of the house have burnt down", and (ib) as 'Akiu has burnt down all parts of the house'.

See also Lee (1986), Chiu (1990), and Cheng (1991,1993) for discussions and debates over the origin of *dou* and its S-structure position.

7. As Lisa Cheng (p.c.) points out, there is still a problem concerning why *dou* is ambiguous in regard to quantification over time segments. One way to look at it is to appeal to scope interaction and the aspectual distinction between (21) and (22). That is, we may assume that the generic tense tends to trigger the wide-scope construal of *dou* over *nali* 'where' in (21), while the perfective aspect of (22) suppresses the same reading in favor of the narrow-scope construal. We may also take the ambiguity to be a lexical one. Under this view, there is no scope interaction even in the following example (cf. May 1985):
(i)   What did everyone buy for Max?
    a. What is x, x a thing, such that for every y, y a person,
       y bought x for Max?
    b. For every y, y a person, what is x, x a thing, such that
       y bought x for Max?

Everyone in (i) is simply ambiguous between collective and distributive, i.e., between the *all*-type reading and the *each*-type reading (also cf. Lasnik & Saito 1992). The same observation applies to *dou* in (21) and (22).

8. As noted by Ken Hale (p.c.), Dutch *al* is also ambiguous between 'all' and 'already'. In addition, it can form compounds with nominal stems, e.g., *al-tijd* 'anytime', *al-ler-zijds* 'anywhere', *al-ler-wegen* 'always'.

9. For a non-movement analysis of the long-distance construals of *wh*-arguments and the postulation of an abstract Q-operator in sentential projections, see Li (1992), Aoun & Li (1993a,b), Tsai (1992), and to a considerable extent, Cheng (1991).

10. The PCOB is formulated as follows:
(i) If O is an operator and x is a variable bound by O, then for any y, y a variable of O, x and y are [a lexical].

11. One might notice that the readings given in (34) and (35) do not exhaust all the logical possibilities. For some reason, it is difficult to get the (ia,b) from (34) and (35) respectively:
(i) a. Who are the persons x,y such that if x defeats y, then x/y must pay for the treat?
    b. Who are the persons x,y such that if x/y wins, then x must treat y?
The absence of the two readings may result from pairing two uneven dependencies, i.e., one with a tripartite structure and the other without.

12. The *j*-indexed readings of matrix *shei* in (58a,b) result from marginal interrogative construals, as illustrated below:
(i)   ? Who is the person x such that whoever comes to visit, x will flush?

13. See Cheng (1991) for a cross-linguistic survey of the architectures of *wh*-phrases and *wh*-particles (i.e., $C^0_{[+wh]}$), which seems to be consistent with our conjecture. Particularly of our interest here is the descriptive generalization that if a language has a *wh*-particle, the language always uses it (cf. Cheng 1991:28). We will return to this issue later.

14. The possibility of distinguishing nominal *wh*-phrases from non-nominal ones in regard to their extraction behavior has actually been entertained by Huang (1982) along with the argument-adjunct distinction. He argues that *where* and *when* are actually nouns (vs. adverbs such as *how* and *why*), and hence their patterning with arguments in regard to LF locality effects. Based on Huang's initiative,

Tsai (1994) further explores the distinction in terms of the generalized binding theory (Aoun 1985, 1986, WAHL 1987), though still within the tradition of "all-out" movement analyses.

15. The notion of "absorption" is first defined by Higginbotham & May (1981) to explain the "paired" reading of multiple wh-questions. The intuitive idea is that (assuming the S-S' system,) a number of *wh*-phrases can be packed together into an *n*-ary operator at a Comp site, as illustrated below:
(i) $[_{S'} [_{Comp} Wh_1, Wh_2, \ldots, Wh_n] [_S \ldots]]$
   $\rightarrow$ $[_{S'} [_{Comp} Wh_{\{1, 2, \ldots, n\}}] [_S \ldots]]$

Although it has been suggested by Chomsky (1993) that this analysis can be adopted in a rather loose form to account for (83a), in that *what* is absorbed (or "attracted" in Chomsky's (1986b:53) terms) by another wh-phrase in a scope position, it is not entirely clear how this generalization can be properly formulated, and whether there is a genuine connection between the two operations. For instance, the absorption rule (i) may be independently needed in multiple *wh*-fronting languages (cf. Rudin 1988), while "scope absorption" from an abstract Q-operator (or a lexical Q-marker, if any) is a standard practice in Chinese-type languages.

16. Here we systematically leave out compounds such as *how-ever* and *some-how*, which do not fall into the same category as *why*. We will defer the relevant discussion to chapter two, where the peculiar properties of *how* and its Chinese counterpart *zenmeyang* will be re-examined.

17. For some reason, Japanese does allow *naze-ka* 'for some reason'. We will take it to be an isolated case for the time being. On the other hand, *however* and *somehow* do have counterparts in Japanese, i.e., *doo-mo* 'by any/every means' and *doo-ka* 'by some means'. See chapter 2 for further discussion.

18. Note that multiple *wh's-in-situ* are possible in conditionals, as exemplified by (ia):
(i) a. ruguo   shei   gei-le   shei   shenme,
       if   who   give-Prf   who   what
       ni   jiu   lai   gaosu wo.
       you   then   come   tell   me
       If someone gives someone something, then you come to tell me.
    b. $[_{CP}$ ruguo $\exists_{x,y,z} [_{IP}$ shei(x)   gei-le   shei(y)   shenme(z)]]], ...
              if   who   give-Prf   who   what

There are altogether three *wh*-phrases in the conditional clause, and all of them are construed as indefinites. It is therefore natural to assume that they are bound by an unselective binder (i.e., ∃-closure on the IP node), as in (ib).

19. Mahajan (1993) provides further evidence to his conclusion here. He points out that it is possible to replace the CP trace in (97b) with an expletive *yah* 'it', as exemplified by (i), in which case no extraposition is involved:
(i) ??? kis-ko$_j$ raam-ne yah$_i$ socaa [$_{CP}$ ki mohan-ne t$_j$ dekhaa]$_i$
 who Ram-erg IT thought that Mohan-erg saw
 Who did Ram think Mohan saw?
Consequently, there is no way for *kis-ko* 'who' to escape from the CED/Subjacency in terms of overt fronting, and hence the deviance of (i).

20. The same problem is independently noted by Mahajan (1993), who rejects the pure *wh*-operator analysis from quite a different angle.

21. See also Mahajan (1993) for arguments against extending the pure *wh*-operator analysis to kyaa-questions.

CHAPTER TWO

1. See also Cresti (1994) for a more elaborated view along the line of individual-variable accounts.

2. Here we may treat stative *weigh* as a middle verb in that its subject appears to originate from a small clause, as in (i), or derive from a logical object predicated by an infinitive, as in (ii):
(i) John$_i$ weighs [$_{SC}$ t$_i$ how many pounds/how much].
(ii) John$_i$ weighs t$_i$ [PRO how many pounds/how much].
In either case, *how many pounds* count as a predicative nominal, and *how much* a predicative adjectival.

3. Also note that the distinction between Q-operators and Q-Comps is a technical necessity if we take the view that selectional restrictions can be satisfied only through Spec-head agreement. If we assume instead that the presence of Q-Comps in itself fulfills the selectional restrictions, then the above issue does not arise, since no feature checking is involved in licensing question formation (also cf. Cheng 1991). As a result, there is no need for postulating Q-operators in Chinese.

4. Note that (25) is relatively acceptable without *you* 'have', as exemplified below:
(i) ? [[duo zhong] de zhu] dou keyi canjia bisai.
 how heavy PNM pig all can join competition.

For every degree x, pigs which are x heavy can join the
competition.

This is because *dou zhong* alone can be analyzed as a attributive adjective, which is subject to both long-distance question construals and *dou*-quantification:

(ii) [[Akiu yang-le [(*you) duo zhong de zhu]] de shuofa] bijiao
 Akiu breed-Prf have how heavy PNM pig PNM story more
 kexin (ne)?
 believable Q_{wh}
 What is the degree x such that [the story [that Akiu has bred x heavy a pig]] is not believable?

(iii) Akiu [(*you) duo pianyi de chezi] dou bu mai.
 Akiu have how cheap PNM car all not buy
 For every degree x, Akiu do not buy x cheap a car.

The presence of *you* in (25) thus guarantees that *duo zhong* is a predicative adjective rather than a attributive one. As for the cause of this asymmetry, we do not have a comprehensive answer except the hunch that attributive adjectivals tend to be nominal, while predicative adjectivals tend to be verbal.

5. For some speakers, marginal interrogative construals are allowed in *ruguo*-conditionals. Namely, (33b) can be read as a matrix question for them:

(i) What is the number/amount x such that if Akiu has gained x pounds, then ...

CHAPTER THREE

1. Based on Lewis's (1975), Kamp (1981) and Heim (1982) propose that indefinite NPs are not intrinsic quantifiers. Rather, they introduce variables, which, in absence of other potential binders, are licensed by a default existential operator. Diesing (1992), on the other hand, contends that there are two types of indefinites: quantificational vs. non-quantificational. Quantificational indefinites undergo Quantifier Raising (QR), resulting in presuppositions, while non-quantificational ones stay in situ, licensed by ∃-Closure.

2. Heim's (1982) original proposal is to associate ∃-Closure with the nuclear scope, roughly corresponding to the syntactic category IP. ∃-Closure, in this sense, is strictly a matter of semantics. As for the claim to confine ∃-Closure to VP, a similar proposal has been made by Higginbotham (1985:561) on a quite different ground to define the domain of existential generalization over event arguments (cf. Davidson 1967).

3. A pointed out by Orin Percus (p.c.), (4b) is acceptable when *a man* is construed as "a certain man", a specific interpretation unavailable for its Chinese counterpart in (5b). We will see in the later discussion that it is this asymmetry which allows us to single out the factors behind specificity effects, and to seek out a more accurate characterization of specific indefinites.

4. In (6a), *firemen* is adjoined to IP at LF under QR (quantifier raising), and accordingly mapped into the restrictive clause. For detailed discussions of indefinite objects and problems caused by obligatory QR in generic context, see Diesing (1992).

5. Carlson (1977) distinguishes stage-level predicates like *available* from individual predicates like *admirable*: Only the former allows a bare plural subject ambiguous between the generic reading, as in (ia), and the cardinal reading, as in (ib,c):
(i) Firemen are available.
    a. $Gen_{x,t}$[x is a fireman $\wedge$ t is a time] x is available at t
    b. Gen_t [t is a time] $\exists_x$ x is a fireman $\wedge$ x is available at t
    c. $\exists_x$ x is a fireman $\wedge$ x is available

In contrast, a bare plural subject can only be generic in the presence of an individual-level predicate, as shown by (ii):
(ii) Firemen are admirable.
    a. Gen_x [x is a fireman] x is admirable
    b. $^{\#}\exists_x$ x is a fireman $\wedge$ x is admirable

For detailed discussions of how individual-level predicates can be distinguished from stage-level predicates in syntactic terms, see Kratzer (1989) and Diesing (1992).

6. Following Huang (1987,1989a), Cheng (1991:131) treats *you* 'have' as an auxiliary, and further spells out its status as a modal heading a functional projection higher than AspP. This move allows *yi-ge ren* 'a person' to be accommodated by the AspP Spec in (15a). *Yi-ge ren* is thus existentially quantified due to the assertion by *you*, yielding the cardinal reading. On the other hand, there is also some evidence suggesting that *you* may serve as a (strong) determiner, as shown by (i):
(i) you-de   ren   zou-le.
    have-PNM person   leave-Prf
    'Some of the people left.'
The interpretation of *you-de ren* in (i) is clearly presuppositional. And the presence of *-de*, a prenominal modifier marker (PNM), indicates that *you* is a specifier rather than a higher predicate.

7. Here we do not necessarily commit ourselves to any particular theory of the stage/individual asymmetry, such as Diesing's (1992a,b)

proposal that an individual-level predicate takes PRO as its VP-internal subject, while an external lexical subject is independently q-marked by its INFL. In section 3, I will explore an alternative in terms of Chomsky's (1992) copy theory. At this stage, it suffices to assume that the subjects of individual-level predicates, just like Chinese subjects, never take scope positions under the local VP node.

8. It is also suggested by Culicover (1991) that, in English, there is an alternative PolP projection similar to FP in (33). One of its major functions is to host *wh-* or negative subjects in matrix clauses, which is supposed to account for the lack of subject-aux inversion in the same environment.

9. A more up-to-date version of our view can also be built upon Koizumi's (1994) layered specifiers analysis, as illustrated below:

(i) PolP

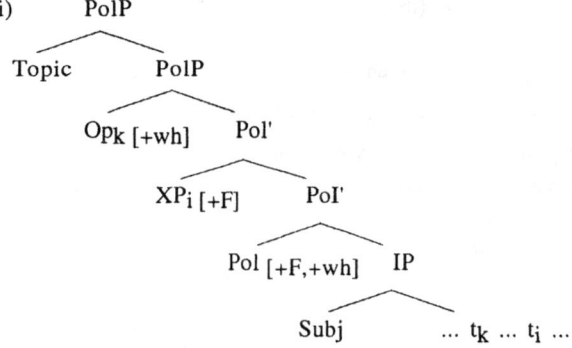

10. Cheng (1991) did not exactly talk about cases like (37c). However, there are some suggestive clues in her treatment of free choice *any* (cf. Ladusaw 1979). According to Cheng, free choice *any* is treated exactly like its polarity counterpart, with modality operators like *will* in (i) serving as both a trigger and a binder (contributing the universal reading of *any*):
(i) Any Chinese semanticist will tell you that white horses are not horses.
Dagai 'probably' and *keneng* 'possibly' in (37c) may well behave similarly to the English modal, except that they perform a single role as triggers.

11. The exact syntactic position of *dou* is still under debate, due to its clitic nature and various interpretations (at least including 'all', 'also', 'already', and 'always'). In the case of quantification over *wh's-in-situ*, *dou* takes scope over the immediate constituent to its left, serving as an universal unselective binder. As a matter of fact, if a *wh-in-situ* is not in the scope of *dou*, the interrogative construal is possible. This point can be made clear by comparing (i) with (42):

(i) Akiu (pingchang) dou chi shenme (ne)?
    Akiu usually   all eat what   Q
    What does Akiu eat all (the time)?

As shown by (i), when *shenme* is not fronted to the left of *dou*, the question reading emerges, with *dou* quantifying over time rather than individuals. For further discussions, see Huang (1982), Lee (1986), Chiu (1990), Cheng (1991), Li (1992b), Tsai (1993), Gao (1994), S. Huang (1994), and R. Hsieh (1994).

12. Our discussion here is inspired by comments from Lisa Cheng, Jim Huang, Toru Ishii, and Yuji Takano.

13. This issue, as Noam Chomsky (p.c.) observes, would not arise if we treat existential closure as some sort of interpretation procedure in the conceptual-intentional system. Under this view, existential closure has neither syntactic nor semantic status, and therefore is not subject to Economy considerations.

14. I owe the discussion here to Danny Fox, Martha McGinnis, and Colin Phillips. See also Lasnik & Stowell (1991) for some discussion.

15. As pointed by Uli Sauerland (p.c.), the following example appears to allow a distributive reading:
(i) *A Tale of Two Cities*, which everyone bought for Max on
    his birthday ...

But note that here *A Tale of Two Cities* really refers to a collection of copies rather than a single copy. In other words, it is construed as a kind in Carlson's sense. A similar construal in restrictive relativization will be like (ii):
(ii) The kind of books which everyone bought for Max on his
     birthday ...

16. But note that this restrictive/non-restrictive distinction is somewhat controversial. See Chao (1968) and Huang (1982) for a completely different view. We will return to resolve the difference in section 2.4.

17. See Hou and Kitagawa (1987) for an interesting ECP account of the above asymmetry. Based on Tang (1975), they observe that there is a subject-object asymmetry between (ia,b):
(i) a. [[e_i dai yanjing] de   neixie/*henduo xuesheng$_i$]
           wearglasses PNM those/many   student
        dou yonggong.
        all hard-working
        [Those/*Many students [who wear glasses]] are hard working.
    b. [[wo renshi e_i] de neixie/henduo xuesheng$_i$]dou
        I   know   PNM those/many   student   all

>   dai   yanjing.
>   wear   glasses

[Those/Many students [who I know]] wear glasses.

They contend that the deviance only occurs when a subject is relativized in the "outer" relative, as in (ia), due to standard ECP effects. And hence the grammaticality of (ib). However, we find that their observation applies only in the presence of factual verbs like *renshi* 'know', which presuppose the existence of their complements. The problem posed by (62b), therefore, does not go away even if we assume that Chinese INFL does not count as a lexical governor, as Hou and Kitagawa suggest. See section 2.3.1 for related discussion. Also thanks to Akira Watanabe for bringing the above issue to my attention.

18. A precaution here concerns that nominals allowing so-called "copy" readings do not fall under the definiteness effects induced by *you* 'have', as exemplified below:
(i) fangjian-li   you   na-ben/mei(-yi)-ben/da-duo-shu-de shu.
     room-inside   have   that-CL/every(-one)-CL/most   book
     In the room, there is (a copy of) the/every/most book(s).

As noted by Huang (1987), DPs like *na-ben shu* 'that book' in (i) are syntactically definite, but semantically indefinite. Huang further points out that when the subject position is not filled by a lexical NP, even the copy reading is ruled out.
(ii)*e you na-ben/mei(-yi)-ben/da-duo-shu-de shu zai fangjian-li.
        have that-CL/every(-one)-CL/most   book at   room-inside
     There is (a copy of) the/every/most book in the room.

The conclusion thus appears to be that, on the top of the semantic constraint associated with *you*-sentences, as evidenced by (b)-clauses of (67-69), there is a stronger syntactic constraint against an expletive subject linked to a definite NP, which constitutes an unbalanced q-chain in Safir's (1985,87) sense (also cf. Safir 1982, Heim 1987, and Higginbotham 1987).

19. At this stage, it is instructive to note that we largely follow Huang's (1987) descriptive generalization except one point: While Huang distinguishes *you*-sentences with empty expletive subjects like (69a) from the other two types of *you*-sentences like (67a) and (69a) based on the contrast between (i) and (ii) of footnote 10, we do not make the distinction and treat the contrast as a special case (due to the "copy" reading), in view of the parallel between (67b) and (68b) on the one hand, and (69b) on the other. As a matter of fact, this move can be seen as a projection of Huang's general approach towards the definiteness effects induced by Chinese existential predicates.

20. Here we use the term "secondary predication" in a rather loose sense. In fact, every instance of predication that we discuss so far counts as primary in Rothstein's (1983) sense if we add CP to the

inventory of primary predicates in the spirit of the EMH, as stated below:
(i) *Primary Predication:*

    A VP/CP bears a primary predication to an XP if
    a. XP and VP/CP mutually m-command each other, and
    b. XP binds an empty argument position in the VP/CP.

21. Note that ∃-closure actually closes off the V' node of the lower VP shell, since the domain of the predication CP should be extended to the verb trace to spell out the existential entailment of *-guo*, as illustrated by (92).

22. As Ken Hale (p.c.) points out, the definite-indefinite alternation in question can be attributed to the type-shifting effects observed in Warlpiri nominals (cf. Bittner & Hale 1994). Also note that bare indefinites generally do not construe as generic in the object position.

23. Depending on the choice of verbs, the contrast between bare plurals and singular indefinites could be very sharp. Take the achievement verb *kill* for example:
(i) a.   John killed rabbits twice/for two years.
      b. ??John killed a rabbit twice/for two years.
This is the so-called "differentiated scope" effect. Traditionally, the solution is based on the scope interaction between indefinites and temporal adverbials, and holds that *rabbits* allows a narrow scope existential reading which is unavailable for *a rabbit*.

In the light of Carlson (1977a), we will take the stand that the reading in question actually refers to a kind, and *rabbits* takes the wide scope just as a proper name does. Narrow scope existential readings contributed by ∃-Closure are ruled out equally for the bare plural in (ia) and the singular indefinite in (ib). The oddness of (ib), as pointed out by Noam Chomsky (p.c.), should be attributed to our world knowledge that a rabbit cannot be killed twice (also cf. Carlson 1977a), and the sentence should be fine if a rabbit can be resurrected from death.

24. As a matter of fact, there is evidence suggesting that A-chains reconstruct in psych-verb constructions, as far as Principle A is concerned (cf. Belletti and Rizzi 1988). But see also Pesetsky (1987b) and Mahajan (1990) for alternative views.

25. See also Kayne (1993) for interesting discussion as to how temporal sequence may restrict the possibiltiy of word orders in UG.

26. For recent discussions on more substantial support for this typology, see Tsai (1998).

Bibliography

If a name cannot be justified, it cannot be rightfully said.
—*Confucius*

Abe, J. (1993) *Binding, Conditions and Scrambling without A/A' Distinction*, PhD Dissertation, University of Connecticut.
——— (1994) "The Proper Characterization of Minimality," Paper presented at the Workshop on East Asia Linguistics, UC Irvine, January 1994.
Aoun, J. (1985) *A Grammar of Anaphora*, MIT Press, Cambridge, MA.
——— (1986) *Generalized Binding*, Foris Publications, Dordrecht.
Aoun, J., Hornstein, N., Lightfoot, D. and A. Weinberg (1987) "Two Types of Locality", *Linguistic Inquiry* 18: 537-577.
Aoun, J. and Y.-H. A. Li (1989) "Scope and Constituency," *Linguistic Inquiry* 20, 141-172.
——— (1993a) "*Wh*-elements in Situ: Syntax or LF?," *Linguistic Inquiry* 24, 199-238.
——— (1993b) "On some Differences between Chinese and Japanese *Wh*--Elements," *Linguistic Inquiry* 20, 265-272.
——— (1993c) *Syntax of Scope*, MIT Press, Cambridge, MA.
Arhens, K. (1994) "Specificity and *Wh-in-situ*," to appear in the proceedings of the Chicago Linguistic Society.
Baltin, M. R. (1982) "A Landing Site Theory of Movement Rules," *Linguistic Inquiry* 13, 1-38.
Baker, C. L. (1970) "Notes on the Description of English Questions: the Role of an Abstract Question Morpheme," *Foundations of Language* 6.2.
Baker, C. L. (1989) *English Syntax*, MIT Press, Cambridge, MA.
Barwise, J., and R. Cooper (1981) "Generalized Quantifiers and Natural Language," *Linguistics and Philosophy* 4, 159-219.
Bittner, M. and K. Hale (1994) "Remarks on Definiteness in Warlpiri," ms., Rutgers and MIT.
Bobaljik, J. (1994) "Phrase Structure and Predicates: May Day Musings from Kamchatka," ms., MIT and Kamchatka Institute of Ecology and Natural Resources.
Bresnan, J. and J. Grimshaw (1978) "The Syntax of Free Relatives in English," *Linguistic Inquiry* 9, 331-191.
Browning, M. (1987) *Null Operator Constructions*, PhD Dissertation, MIT.

Chao, Y.-R. (1968) *A Grammar of Spoken Chinese*, University of California Press, Berkeley and Los Angeles.
Carlson, G. (1977a) *Reference to Kinds in English*, PhD Dissertation, University of Massachussets, Amherst.
────── (1977b) "Amount Relatives," *Language* 53, 520-542.
Chierchia, G. and S. McConnell-Ginet (1990) *Meaning and Grammar*, MIT Press, Cambridge, MA.
Chierchia, G. (1992a) "Anaphora and Dynamic Binding," *Linguisitcs and Philosophy* 15, 111-183. Kluwer Academic Publishers.
────── (1992b) "Individual Level Predicates as Inherent Generics," ms., Cornell University.
Cheng, L. L.-S. (1991) *On the Typology of Wh-questions*, PhD Dissertation, MIT.
────── (1993) "On *Dou*-quantification," ms., UC Irvine.
Cheng, L. L.-S. and C.-T. J. Huang (1993) "Two Types of Donkey Sentence," Paper presented at the Fifth North American Conference on Chinese Linguistics, University of Delaware, and at *NELS* 24.
Chiu, B. (1990) "A Case of Quantifier Floating in Mandarin Chinese," paper presented at the Second Northeast Conference on Chinese Linguistics, University of Pennsylvania.
────── (1991) "*Suo* : an Object-Agreement in Mandarin Chinese," in S. Barbiers et al. (eds.) *LCJL3 Proceedings*, Leiden, 77-95.
Chomsky, N. (1964) *Current Issues in Linguistic Theory*, Mouton, The Hague, Paris.
────── (1965) *Aspects of the Theory of Syntax*, MIT Press, Cambridge, MA.
────── (1975) *The Logical Structure of Linguistic Theory*, Plenum.
────── (1977) "On Wh-Movement," in P. Culicover, T. Wasow, and A. Akmajan (eds.) *Formal Syntax*, Academic Press, New York, 71-132.
────── (1980) *Rules and Representations*, New York, Columbia University Press.
────── (1981) *Lectures on Government and Binding*, Foris Publications, Dordrecht.
────── (1986a) *Knowledge of Language: Its nature, origin, and use*, Praeger, New York.
────── (1986b) *Barriers*, MIT Press, Cambridge, MA.
────── (1991) "Some Notes on Economy of Derivation and Representation," in R. Freidin (ed.)*Principles and Parameters in Comparative Grammar*, 417-454, MIT Press, Cambridge, MA.
────── (1993) "A Minimalist Program for Linguistic Theory," in K. Hale and S. J. Keyser (eds.) *The View from Building 20:*

Essays in Linguistics in Honor of Sylvain Bromberger, 1-52, MIT Press, Cambridge, MA.
—— (1995) *The Minimalist Program,* MIT Press, Cambridge, MA.
Chomsky, N. and H. Lasnik (1991) "Principle and Parameters Theory," to appear in J. Jacobs, A. van Stechow, W. Sternefeld, and T. Vennemann (eds.), *Syntax: An International Handbook of Contermporary Research,* de Gruyter.
Cinque, G. (1989) "On the Scope of Long and Successive Cyclic Movement," Paper presented at Second Princeton Workshop on Comparative Grammar.
—— (1990) *Types of A'-Dependencies,* MIT Press, Cambridge, MA.
—— (1993) "A Null Theory of Phrase and Compound Stress," *Linguistic Inquiry,* 24, 239-297.
Cole, P. (1987) "The Structure of Internally Headed Relative Clauses," *Natural Language and Linguistic Theory* 5, 277-302.
Collins, C. (1997) *Local Economy,* MIT Press, Cambridge, MA.
Cresti, D. (1994) "Extraction and Reconstruction," to appear in *Natural Language Semantics.*
Cooper, R. (1983) *Quantification and Syntactic Theory,* Reidel, Dordrecht.
Culicover, P. (1991) "Polarity, Inversion, and Focus in English," in *Proceedings of ESCOL 1991,* 46-68, Department of Linguistics, The Ohio State University.
Davidson, D. (1967) "The Logical Form of Action Sentences," in N. Rescher (ed.) *The Logic of Decision and Action,* 81-95, University of Pittsburgh Press, Pittsburgh, PA.
Diesing, M. (1992a) *Indefinites,* MIT Press, Cambridge, MA.
—— (1992b) "Bare Plural Subjects and the Derivation of Logical Representations," *Linguistic Inquiry* 23, 353-380.
Dowty, D. (1972) Studies in the Logic of Verb Aspect and Time Reference in English, PhD Dissertation, University of Texas at Austin.
Emonds, J. (1976) *A Transformational Approach to English Syntax,* Academic Press, New York.
—— (1978) "The Verbal Complex V'-V in French," *Linguistic Inquiry* 9, 151-175.
Fiengo, R. and J. Higginbotham (1981) "Opacity in NP," *Linguistic Analysis* 7, 395-422.
Frampton, J. (1990) "The Fine Structure of *Wh*-Movement and the Proper Formulation of the ECP," ms., Northeastern University.
Fujita, K. (1994) "Middle, Ergative & Passive in English - A

Minimalist Perspective," ms., Osaka Univesity.
Fukui, N. and M. Speas (1986) "Specifiers and Projection," in N. Fukui, T. Rappoport, and E. Sagey (eds.) *MITWPL* 8, 128-172.
Fukui, N. (1993) "Parameters and Optionality," *Linguistic Inquiry* 24, 399-420.
Gao, Q. (1994) "Focus Criterion: Evidence from Chinese," paper presented at the Sixth North American Conference on Chinese Linguistics, USC.
Grimshaw, J. (1979) "Complement Selection and the Lexicon", *Linguistic Inquiry* 10, 279-326.
——— (1990) *Argument Structure*, MIT Press, Cambridge, MA.
——— (1993) "Minimal Projection, Heads, and Optimality," ms., Rutgers University.
Gundel, J. (1974) *The Role of Topic and Comment in Linguistic Theory*, PhD Dissertation, Indiana University Linguistics Club, Bloomington, IN.
Hale K. and S. J. Keyser (1991) "On Argument Structure and the Lexical Expression of Syntactic Relation," ms., MIT.
Heim, I. (1982) *The Semantics of Definite and Indefinite Noun Phrases*, PhD Dissertation, Umass.
——— (1987) "Where does the Definiteness Restriction Apply? Evidence from the Definiteness of Variables," in E, Reuland & A. ter Meulen (eds.) *The Representation of (In)definiteness*, 21-42, MIT Press, Cambridge, MA.
——— (1991) "Articles and Definiteness," in A. von Stechow & D. Wunderlich (eds.) *Semantics. An International Handbook of Contemporary Research*, de Gruyter, Berlin.
Higginbotham, J. (1983) "Logical Form, Binding, and Nominals," *Linguistic Inquiry* 14, 395-420.
——— (1985) "On Semantics," *Linguistic Inquiry* 16, 547-593.
——— (1987) "Indefiniteness and Predication," in E, Reuland & A. ter Meulen (eds.)*The Representation of (In)definiteness*, 43-70, MIT Press, Cambridge, MA.
Higginbotham, J. and R. May (1981) "Questions, Quantifiers, and Crossing," *The Linguistic Review* 1, 41-79.
Hoji, H. (1985) *Logical Form Constraints and Configurational Structures in Japanese*, PhD Dissertation, University of Washington, WA.
Horn, L. (1988) "A Presuppositional Analysis of *Only* and *Even*," ms., UCLA.
Hou, J. and C. Kitagawa (1987) "Null Operators and the Status of Empty Categories in Chinese," *Linguistic Inquiry* 18, 518-523.

Hsieh, M.-L. (1994) "On NPI Licensing in Chinese," ms., USC.
Hsieh, R. (1994) "*Dou* and Universal Quantification in Chinese," paper presented at the Sixth North American Conference on Chinese Linguistics, USC.
Huang, C.-T. J. (1982) *Logical Relations in Chinese and the Theory of Grammar*, PhD Dissertation, MIT.
────── (1984) "On the Distribution and Reference of Empty Pronouns," *Linguistic Inquiry* 15, 531-574.
────── (1987) "Existential Sentences in Chinese and (In)definiteness," in E, Reuland & A. ter Meulen (eds.) *The Representation of (In)definiteness*, 226-253, MIT Press, Cambridge, MA.
──────. (1988) "*wo pao de kuai* and Chinese Phrase Structure," *Language* 64, 274-311.
────── (1989a) "Shuo *shi* he *you* : jianta zhongwen de dongci fenlei [A Discussion of 'be' and 'have': with verb classification in Chinese]," ms., Cornell University.
────── (1989b) "Pro-Drop in Chinese: A Generalized Control Theory," in O. Jaeggli and K. Safir (eds.) *The Null Subject Parameter*, 185-214.
────── (1991) "More on Chinese Word Order and Parametric Theory," ms., UC Irvine.
────── (1992) "Complex Predicates in Generalized Control," in Larson, R. K., S. Iatridou, U. Lahiri and J. Higginbotham (eds.) *Control and Grammar*, Kluwer Academic Publishers.
────── (1993a) "Reconstruction and the Structure of VP: Some Theoretical Consequences," *Linguistic Inquiry* 24, 103-138.
────── (1993b) "On Lexical Structure and Syntactic Projection," ms., UC Irvine.
────── (1993c) "Verb Movement and Some Syntax-Semantics Mismatches in Chinese," ms., UC Irvine.
Huang, S. (1994) "*Dou* as an Existential Quantifier," paper presented at the Sixth North American Conference on Chinese Linguistics, USC.
Ioup, G. (1975) *The Treatment of Quantifier Scope in a Transformational Grammar*, PhD Dissertation, CUNY Graduate Center.
Iatridou S. and D. Embick (1994) "Conditional Inversion," to appear in the proceedings of *NELS* 24.
Jackendoff, Ray (1977) *X' Syntax: A Study of Phrase Structure*, MIT Press, Cambridge, MA.
Johnson, K. (1994) "Bridging Gaps," paper presented at MIT

Linguistics Colloquium.
Jonas, D. and J. Bobaljik (1993) "The Role of TP in Icelandic," in Bobaljik, Jonathan and Colin Phillips (eds.), *Papers on Case and Agreement I, MITWPL* 18, MIT, Cambridge.
Jong, F. de and H. Verkuyl (1985) "Generalized Quantifiers: The Properness of Their Strength," in J. van Benthem and A. ter Meulen (eds.) *Generalized Quantifiers in Natural Languages*, 21-43, Foris Publications, Dordrecht.
Kamp, J. A. W. (1981) "A Theory of Truth and Semantic Representation," In J. Groenendijk, T. Janssen, and M. Stokhof (eds.) *Formal Methods in the Study of Language*, 277-321, Mathematical Centre, Amsterdam.
Katz, J. and P. Postal (1964) *An Intergrated Thoery of Linguistic Descriptions*, MIT Press.
Kayne, R. (1981) "ECP Extensions," *Linguistic Inquiry* 12, 93-133.
────── (1993) "The Antisymmetry of Syntax," ms., Graduate Center, CUNY.
Kim, S. (1991) *Chain Scope and Quantification Structure*, PhD Dissertation, Brandeis University.
Klima, E. (1964) "Negation in English," in Jerry A. Fodor and Herrold Katz (eds.) *The Structure of Language*, Prentice Hall, Englewood, NJ.
Kitagawa, C. (1982) "Topic Constructions in Japanese," *Lingua* 57, 175-214.
Kitahara, H. (1995) "Target a: Deducing Strict Cyclicity from Derivational Economy," *Linguistic Inquiry* 26, 47-77.
Koizumi, M. (1994a) "Layered Specifiers," to appear in the proceedings of *NELS* 24.
Koopman, H. and D. Sportiche (1989) "Subjects," ms., UCLA.
Kratzer, A. (1989) "Stage and Individual Level Predicates," in *Papers on Quantification*, NSF Grant Report, Department of Linguistics, University of Massachussets, Amherst.
Kroch, A. (1989) "Amount Quantification, Referentiality, and Long *Wh*-movement," ms., University of Pennsylvania.
Kuroda, S.-Y. (1965) *Generative Grammatical Studies in the Japanese Language*, PhD dissertation, MIT.
────── (1988) "Whether We Agree or not," *Linguisticae Investigationes* 12, 1-47.
Larson, R. (1988) "On the Double Object Construction," *Linguistic Inquiry* 19.3, 335-392.
Lasnik, H. (1993) "Lectures on Minimalist Syntax," *UCWPL Occasional Papers #1*.

Lasnik, H. and R. Fiengo (1974) "Complement Object Deletion," *Linguistic Inquiry* 15, 235-289.
Lasnik, H. and M. Saito (1984) "On the Nature of Proper Government," *Linguistic Inquiry* 15: 235-289.
Lasnik, H. and M. Saito (1992) *Move a*, MIT Press, Cambridge, MA.
Lasnik, H. and T. Stowell (1991) "Weakest Crossover," *Linguistic Inquiry* 22, 687-720.
Lewis, D. (1975) "Adverbs of Quantification," in E. Keenan (ed.) *Formal Semantics of Natural Language*, 3-15, Cambridge University Press, Cambridge.
Lee, T. (1986) *Studies on Quantification in Chinese*, PhD Dissertation, UCLA.
Li, Y.-H. A. (1990) *Order and Constituency in Manadarin Chinese*, Kluwer, Dordrecht.
—— (1992a) "Indefinite *Wh* in Mandarin Chinese," *Journal of East Asian Linguistics* 1, 125-155.
—— (1992b) "*Dou:* Syntax or LF?," Paper presented at the Fourth North American Conference on Chinese Linguistics, University of Michigan, Ann Arber.
Li, C. and S. Thompson (1981) *Mandarin Chinese: A Functional Reference Grammar*, University of California Press, Berkeley.
Lin, J.-W. (1992) "The Syntax of *Zenmeyang* 'How' and *Weishenme* 'Why' in Mandarin Chinese," *Journal of East Asian Linguistics* 1, 293-331.
Liu, F.-H. (1994) "*Wh*-words in Chinese and *in particular*," ms., University of Arizona.
Napoli, D. J. (1989) *Predication Theory*, Cambridge University Press, Cambridge.
Mahajan, A. (1990) *The A/A'-Distinction and Movement Theory*, PhD Dissertation, MIT.
—— (1993) "On Certain Differences between Hindi and Japanese *Wh*-movement," talk given at the Department of Linguistics, Harvard University.
May, R. (1985) *Logical Form*, MIT Press, Cambridge.
Mei, K. (1972) *Studies in the Transformational Grammar of Modern Standard Chinese*, PhD Dissertation, Harvard University.
—— (1978) "Guoyu Yufa zhong de Dongcizu Buyu [On Verb-Phrase Complements in Chinese]," in *A Festschrift for Professor Chu Wan-Li*, 511-536, Lianjing Publisher, Taipei.
Milsark, G. (1974) *Existential Sentences in English*, PhD Dissertation, MIT.
Miyagawa, S. (1994) "Nonconfigurationality within a Configurational

Structure," ms., MIT.

Nishigauchi, T. (1986) *Quantification in Syntax*, PhD Dissertation, University of Massachusetts, Amherst.

―――― (1990) *Quantification in the Theory of Grammar*, Kluwer Academic Publishers, Dordrecht.

Oishi, M. (1993) "LF Legitimacy and Chain Formation," ms., Tohoku Gakuin University, Sendai, Japan.

Parsons, T. (1990) *Events in the Semantics of English: A Study in Subatomic Semantics*, MIT Press, Cambridge, MA.

Percus, Orin (1995) "A Predication-Based Analysis of Semantic Partition," to appear in *Proceedings of WCCFL 14*.

Pesetsky, D. (1982) *Path and Categories*, PhD Dissertation, MIT.

―――― (1987a) "*Wh in situ*: Movement and Unselective Binding," in E. Reuland and A. Ter Meulen (eds.) *Representation of (In)definiteness*, MIT Press, Cambridge, MA.

―――― (1987b) "Binding Problems with Experiencer Verbs," *Linguistic Inquiry* 18, 126-140.

Partee, B. H. (1988) "Many Quantifiers," in *Proceedings of ESCOL 1988*, Department of Linguistics, The Ohio State University.

Pollock, J.-Y. (1989) "Verb Movement, Universal Grammar, and the Structure of IP," *Linguistic Inquiry* 20, 365-424.

Reuland, E. (1983) "The Extended Projection Principle and the Definiteness Effect," in M. Barlow, D. Flickinger, and M. Wescoat (eds.) *Proceedings of the West Coast Conference on Formal Linguistics* 2, Stanford Linguistics Association, Department of Linguistics, Stanford University.

Reinhart, T. (1983) *Anaphora and Semantic Interpretation*, Croom Helm, London.

―――― (1987) "Specifier and Operator Binding," in E, Reuland & A. ter Meulen (eds.) *The Representation of (In)definiteness*, 130-167, MIT Press, Cambridge, MA.

―――― (1992) "Interpreting *Wh-in-situ*," to appear in the Proceedings of the Amsterdam Colloquim.

―――― (1993) "*wh-in-situ* in the Framework of the Minimalist Program," lecture given at Utrecht Linguistics Colloquium.

Rizzi, L. (1986) "On Chain Formation," in H. Borer (eds.) *Syntax and Semantics 19: the Syntax of Pronominal Clitics*, Academic Press, New York.

―――― (1990) *Relativized Minimality*, MIT Press, Cambridge, MA.

―――― (1991) "Residual Verb Second and the *Wh*-Criterion," ms., Universite de Geneve.

Rooth, M. (1985) *Association with Focus*, PhD Dissertation,

University of Massachussets, Amherst.
Ross, J. (1967) *Constraints on Variables in Syntax,* PhD Dissertation, MIT.
Rothstein, S. (1983) *The Syntactic Form of Predication,* PhD Dissertation, MIT.
Rudin, C. (1988) "On Multiple Questions and Multiple WH Fronting," *Natural Language & Linguistic Theory* 6, 445-502.
Safir, K. (1982) *Syntactic Chains and the Definiteness Effect,* PhD Dissertation, MIT.
———— (1985) *Syntactic Chains,* Cambridge University Press, Cambridge.
———— (1987) "What Explains the Definiteness Effect?" in E, Reuland & A. ter Meulen (eds.) *The Representation of (In)definiteness,* 71-97, MIT Press, Cambridge, MA.
Saito, M. (1989) "Scrambling as Semantically Vacuous A'-movement," in M. R. Baltin and A. S. Kroch (eds.) *Alternative Conceptions of Phrase Structure,* The University of Chicago Press, 182-200.
Stowell, T. (1981) *Origins of Phrase Structures,* PhD Dissertation, MIT.
———— (1989) "Subjects, Specifiers, and X-bar Theory," in M. R. Baltin and A. S. Kroch (eds.) *Alternative Conceptions of Phrase Structure,* The University of Chicago Press, 232-262.
———— (1993) "Syntax of Tense," ms., UCLA.
Srivastav, V. (1991) *WH Dependencies in Hindi and the Theory of Grammar,* PhD Dissertation, Cornell University.
Srivastav Dayal, V. (1993) "Scope Marking: Its Syntax and Semantics," paper presented at MIT Linguistics Colloquium.
Tai, H.-Y. J. (1973) "A Derivational Constraint on Adverbial Placement in Mandarin Chinese," *Journal of Chinese Linguistics* 1, 397-413.
Tai, H.-Y. J. (1981) "Temporal Sequence of Chinese Word Order," ms.,   Southern Illinois University, Carbondale.
Takano, Y. (1994a) "Scrambling, Relativized Minimlaity, and Economy of Derivation," Paper presented at *WCCFL* XIII.
Takano, Y. (1994b) "Predicate Fronting and Internal Subject," ms., UC   Irvine.
Tang, C.-C. J. (1990) Chinese Phrase Structure and the Extended X'-Theory, PhD Dissertation, Cornell University.
———— (1991) "Conditions on the Distribution of Postverbal Duration and Frequency Phrases in Chinese Revisited," paper presented at the Third InternationalSymposium on Chinese Languages and Linguistics.

——— (1993) "Adjunct Licensing, *Wh-in-situ* and the Checking Theory in Chinese," paper presented at ICCL2, Paris.

Tang, T.-C. (1975) "Contrastive Studies of Chinese and English Relativization," *The Concentric* 1975, 38-66.

Tang, T.-C. (1989) Studies on Chinese Morphology and Syntax: 2, Student Book Co., Taipei.

Tsai, W.-T. D. (1992) "On Parametrizing Unselective Binding Effects,"   paper presented at the Workshop on East Asia Linguistics, UC Irvine, June 1992.

——— (1994) "On Nominal Islands and LF Extraction in Chinese," *Natural Language and Linguistic Theory* 12, 121-175.

——— (1995) "Visibility, Complement Selection and the Case Requirement of CP," *Journal of East Asian Linguistics* 4, 281-312.

——— (1997) "A Note on *Wh*-adjunct Asymmetries," in *Chinese Languages and Linguistics III: Morphology and Lexicon*, 469-493.

——— (1998) "Subject Specificity, Copy Theory and Extended Mapping Hypothesis," in Sauerland, Uli and Orin Percus (eds.) *The Interpretive Tract, MIT Working Papers in Linguistics* 25, 1-28, MITWPL, Cambridge, MA.

——— (to appear) "On the Absence of Island Effects," in *Tsing Hua Journal of Chinese Studies*.

Tsao, F. (1979) *A Functional Study of Topic in Chinese: The First Step Towards Discourse Analysis*, Student Book Co., Taipei, Taiwan.

Wang, W. (1965) "Two Aspect Markers in Mandarin," *Language* 41.3.

Ura, H. (1994) "Super-raising and the Features-based X-bar Theory," ms., MIT.

Watanabe, A. (1991) "*Wh-in-situ,* Subjacency, and Chain Formation," ms., MIT.

——— (1993) *AGR-Based Case Theory and Its Interation with the A-bar System*, PhD Dissertation, MIT.

Williams, E. (1980) "Predication," *Linguistic Inquiry* 11, 203-238.

Yü, X.-L. (1965) "Yiwen Daici de Renzhi Yongfa," *Zhongguo Yuwen* 1, 30-35.

Index

Aoun, J.   7-8, 34, 81, 90-91, 110, 178-179

argument-adjunct asymmetry   5, 40

Baker, C. L.   41

Baltin, M. R.   102

bare conditionals   15-16, 18, 20, 24, 26, 29, 33, 54, 63-65, 67-68

Barwise, J.   116, 124

Bobaljik, J.   119

Carlson, G.   138-139, 146, 150-151, 170

CED   5, 19, 49-53, 79-81, 85, 91

Chain formation   3-5, 7-8, 34, 43-44, 53-54, 57, 78, 82, 97

Chao, Y.-R.   144, 149

Cheng, L.   7, 16, 20-21, 26, 33, 43, 45, 98, 108-110, 133, 136, 138, 165

Chierchia, G.   18, 136

Chomsky, N.   3-4, 7, 9, 12, 43, 47-50, 58-60, 83, 95, 97, 103-104, 106, 111, 114, 117-118, 144, 165-166, 168, 172, 174, 177-178

Cinque, G.   42, 53-54, 73, 75-76, 78, 81, 90-91, 168, 171

Complex NP islands   56, 78

Cooper, R.   116, 124, 168

Cresti, D.   168

Culicover, P.   103-104

Diesing, M.   42, 45, 93-94, 97, 99, 103, 107, 116-117, 119, 122, 131, 133-134, 163, 180

donkey sentences   17

dou-quantification   25, 33, 37, 54, 63-64, 67, 91

Dowty, D.   151

D-Structure   3, 5

Economy 3-4, 7-8, 34, 39, 42, 83, 108

ECP 6-7, 19, 37, 45, 47, 53-54, 58, 67, 72, 78-81, 91, 168

Emonds, J. 116, 178

existential closure 45, 65, 94, 96, 108, 112

Extended Standard Theory 5

Fiengo, R. 25

Frampton, J. 53, 165, 168-169

Gundel, J. 103

Hale, K. 117, 162

Heim, I. 7, 16-18, 26, 42, 53, 93, 97, 99, 108, 117, 136, 146, 150, 152, 165, 168, 171

Higginbotham, J. 25, 40, 90, 113-116, 152, 162

Hindi 5, 48-53, 55, 73

Horn, L. 14

Hornstein, N. 28

Hou, J. 119

Hsieh, R. 109

Huang, J. 5-7, 14, 16, 20-21, 26, 30, 37, 43-45, 49, 117, 123-127, 130-133, 145, 147, 153, 155-156, 158-159, 163, 174-175, 178, 54, 58-59, 63, 73-74, 81, 86, 88, 90-91

indefinite construals 43, 54-55, 97, 61, 64-66

Ioup, G. 116

Jackendoff, R. 115

Johnson, K. 176-177

Jonas, D. 119

Jong, F. 116

Kamp, J. A. W. 93, 114

Katz, J. 41

Kayne, R. 75, 78

Keyser, J. 117

Kim, S. 48, 174, 179

Kitagawa, C. 103, 119

Klima, E. 43

Koizumi, M. 30, 50-51, 69-70, 77, 121

Koopman, H. 54

Kratzer, A. 152

Index

Kroch, A. 42

Kuroda, S.-Y. 25, 51

Lasnik, H. 7, 35, 51, 55, 57, 83, 86, 95, 102-104, 117, 159

last resort 4, 8, 96, 107-108, 111-112

Lee, T. 33, 98

Lewis, D. 26

Lexical Courtesy Hypothesis 34, 55, 73

LF 3-9, 15, 30, 34, 41-45, 48-51, 53, 55

Li 7, 34, 43, 45, 91, 98, 108, 110, 161, 179

Lin, J. 81

Liu, F.-H. 109

Mahajan, A. 48-49, 51

Mapping Hypothesis 93-94, 96-98, 107, 112, 118, 180

Marantz, A. 15, 177

May, R. 8, 48, 113

McCawley, J. 116

Merger 3-5, 7, 11-12, 16, 34, 44, 53

McConnell-Ginet, S. 136

Milsark, G. 116

minimalist 3-5, 8-9, 39, 49, 111

minimality 19, 43, 47, 53, 67, 72, 74, 91, 108, 110

mo-quantification 25, 36, 67

Napoli, D. J. 111, 116

Nishigauchi, T. 7, 26-28, 31, 35, 48, 51, 67, 77-78

nominality 42, 59, 81, 90-91

nuclear scope 93-94, 96-97, 100-102, 107-108, 111-112, 115, 118, 121, 137, 150, 174-175

operator features 5, 9, 47, 49, 53, 55, 70, 72

operator-variable pair 4, 12, 16, 39-40, 55, 167

Partee, B. 116

Percus, O. 102, 118

Pesetsky, D. 7-8, 35, 40-42

Pollock, J.-Y. 106, 178

presuppositionality 133, 138

Q-operator 11-12, 20, 22, 24-25, 36, 47, 55, 59-60

quantifier 11, 48, 93, 96, 100, 108, 110, 179

question formation 6, 13, 43, 53-54

referentiality 42, 58-59, 66, 81, 90

Reinhart, T. 11, 40-42, 60, 90, 116, 168

Relativized Minimality 19, 43, 47, 53, 67, 91, 108, 110

restrictive clause 42, 93, 96, 99-101, 115, 118

Reuland, E. 116

Rooth, M. 14, 104

Ross, J. 168

Rothstein, S. 117, 155

Safir, K. 18, 116

Saito, M. 7, 35, 51, 95, 102-103

secondary predicate 97, 117, 129, 133, 150-151

singulary substitution 4

SPELL-OUT 5, 12, 70

Sportiche, D. 54

Srivastav Dayal, V. 53

S-Structure 5, 8-9, 16, 48, 94-95, 168, 174

Stowell, T. 78, 104, 152, 162

strict cyclicity 50-52

Subjacency 5-8, 16, 37, 42-43, 47-49, 53-54, 58, 72-73, 78, 85, 91

subject chain 60, 96, 112, 175, 179

topicalization 85, 95, 102, 106, 112-114, 116, 126

Tai, J. 105

Tang, J. 119, 126, 147, 153, 156, 178

Truckenbrodt, H. 102

Tsai, W.-T. D. 34, 40, 81, 83, 90, 159

Tsao, F.-F. 173

unselective binding 5, 7, 11, 16-17, 24-25, 30, 34-36, 41, 43-44, 46, 53-54, 59, 66-67, 70, 73, 77-

Index

78, 82, 88, 91

Ura, H. 30, 120-121

vacuous quantification 12, 44, 70, 91, 96, 112, 166, 172

Watanabe, A. 25, 34-36, 50-52, 70, 78

Wh-Criterion 8, 48

wh-dependencies 5, 8, 53

wh-fronting 82-83, 85, 90

wh-in-situ 4, 17, 19-21, 26, 29-30, 32, 36, 45-46, 60, 68, 70-71

wh-islands 35, 37, 55, 82

wh-movement 5, 9, 12, 34, 41, 48-51, 53, 55, 58, 70, 76, 78, 163, 169, 171

For Product Safety Concerns and Information please contact our EU
representative GPSR@taylorandfrancis.com
Taylor & Francis Verlag GmbH, Kaufingerstraße 24, 80331 München, Germany

www.ingramcontent.com/pod-product-compliance
Lightning Source LLC
Chambersburg PA
CBHW050557170426
43201CB00011B/1731